The Parent and Child Group Handbook

A Steiner/Waldorf approach

Dot Male

Hawthorn Press

Published by Hawthorn Press, Hawthorn House, 1 Lansdown Lane, Stroud, Gloucestershire, GL5 1BJ, UK

Tel: (01453) 757040 Fax: (01453) 751138

info@hawthornpress.com

www.hawthornpress.com

Cover illustration *Mère et Enfant, 1951* by Pablo Picasso © Succession Picasso / DACS 2005

Illustrations © Dot Male

Photographs by Kim Billington, Sheila Clarkson, Dot Male, Janni Nicol, Mary Triulzi and Susan Weber

Raffael: *Die Sixtinische Madonna*, Gemäldegalerie Alte Meister, Staatliche Kunstsammlungen Dresden

Cover design by Hawthorn Press

Design and typesetting by Lynda Smith at Hawthorn Press, Stroud, Gloucestershire

Printed in the UK by The Bath Press, Bath

Printed on paper sourced from sustained managed forests and elemental chlorine-free

British Library Cataloguing in Publication Data applied for

ISBN 1 903 458 46 3

978-1-903458-46-4

Contents

List of Illustrations and Photographs

Chapter 6

Chapter 7

Chapter 8

Chapter 9

List of Text Boxes

List of Songs

Dedication

This book is lovingly dedicated to my husband Barry and son Antony.
We are all on this journey together.

Acknowledgements

The gentle beginnings of this book may have been conceived 13 years ago when a couple from the Netherlands – Marianne de Nooif and Ernst Tempstra – introduced a group of parents, including myself, to Steiner education, and helped us to set up a Steiner Parent and Child group in Lancaster. My deep thanks to them for changing my life, and to the fellow pioneer mums and kindred spirits with whom I shared those early years, especially Dorothea Williamson, Rachel Theobold and Fiona Scrase. I learnt then what parent power can achieve!

I am very grateful to Martin Large at Hawthorn Press for entrusting me with the adventure of writing this book, and to those many people who have helped and supported me along the way. I would like to give my heart-felt thanks to all the local and global folk who offered their work and wisdom for inclusion in the book – Lourdes Callen, Letitia Costain, Bonnie Romanow, Mary Triulzi, Sheila Clarkson, Bella Tan, Julie Lam, Eva Libalova, Dorien Versluis, Stefan Krauch, Patricia Rubano, Cynthia Aldinger, Susan Weber, Janet Parsons, Kim Billington, Suzanne Down, Joy de Berker, Richard House, Marjorie Theyer, Brenda Watson, Sibylle van der Schilden, Miranda Armstrong, Rena Osmer, Vivienne Morpeth, Patsy Collinson, Deirdre Pyzer, Sylvie Hétu, Janet Klaar, Janni Nicol, Kathy McQuillen, Ann Strauss, Jane Gerhard, Carole Cole, Emma Tyer, Kate Pigeon-Owen, Lynne Oldfield, and Erika Grantham. A huge warm thanks too to all those who have read and given invaluable feedback on various draft chapters, particularly Lynne Oldfield , Erika Grantham, Keith Bramall, Letitia Costain, Anna Semelyn, Sonia Perry, Vivienne Morpeth, Glenda Shearer, and my husband Barry (who I know has read every word!). Many thanks to all the parents who filled out questionnaires and offered photographs, and my special gratitude to the Nursery children, the Parent and Child group, and staff at York Steiner School, all of whom are the rich ground for my learning. Finally, I would like to thank my editor Richard House for his deft insight, skill, and ever-available help.

Foreword

'I love coming here, I feel I can relax at last, and both I and my children are able to be in an environment where we don't have to perform, compete, or achieve. This is my weekly haven', said a parent one day, in a Steiner (Waldorf) Parent and Child group. To provide this 'haven' for parents is something I still work with as a parent and child group leader; and after many, many years of doing so, I find it more important and rewarding than ever before.

We, as parents, are the child's first teachers, but where is our school? How do we learn to be parents? We no longer live in close-knit communities supported by our own parents and grandparents, and sometimes move huge distances away from our families. We often have to work, and occasionally employ nannies or child-minders to take care of our children. This means that we sometimes spend little but precious time with our children, and making the most of this special time often becomes 'a battle' within ourselves which we deal with on a daily basis. Guilt and anxiety can also accompany our parenting…are we doing the right things for our children? Is it enough? Should we do more?

We are inundated by information today, telling us 'everything we need to know' from birth onwards – the terrible two's, sleep problems, toilet training, and more, more, more! It certainly made my head spin as a new parent, and led me to mistrust my own instincts!

Living with babies and toddlers can be wonderful, but we can also find it lonely, isolating, challenging, and very tiring; so just what is available today that nurtures not only us as individuals, but our children and families too? It is *contact with others* – talking, sharing, belonging, meeting together in a space which is both caring and inspiring.

Within Steiner Waldorf Parent and Child groups, support is given to parents in the first years of creating a family. There are opportunities for parents to gain new understanding and security of their own abilities and the abilities of their children; to build friendships with others who are like minded, to inspire their parenting, explore questions, and develop the confidence to find answers in discussion with others. Babies and toddlers begin to explore their world and each other in an environment which is specially created to provide nourishment for their senses.

Entering the room where a Waldorf Parent and Child group is held is, in itself, an inspiration. We are struck by the quiet and calm where so many are gathered together. Beautiful gentle pastel colours surround us, provided by hanging muslins, cosy corners, and comfortable cushions. A table display brings the seasons into the room, spring flowers and butterflies hanging from the 'tree' or autumn leaves with a squirrel jumping amongst the branches, or 'spider webs' woven by the parents during a craft session decorate the walls. The toys provided are made from natural materials such as wooden animals, pine cones, wool and silk cloths, soft dolls, home corners and gentle floor play with push-and-pull equipment, soft balls, wooden blocks for building and climbing, and more. This enables us to support the unfolding of our children's interests, develop their physical bodies, and encourage healthy development of their social interaction. Seasonal and other crafts that are provided allow adults to develop new skills, providing a space for us to communicate with others. The fact that we are busy with an activity while observing our children gives them the freedom to interact with others while secure in the knowledge that we are still 'with' them.

Familiar and seasonal games, nursery rhymes, songs, and stories are a part of each session, and bring an intimate moment for parent and child. Snack-time provides an opportunity to eat together, listen to, and communicate with each other, and is also nourishing for the physical body.

When part of a Steiner Waldorf community, we begin to open doors to a different way of seeing, we come to a new understanding of child development, the importance of imitation and being role models, and child-initiated play as integral to learning about the world. We celebrate festivals together and become more aware of nature's bounty and seasonal changes. We find a new way of living with rhythm which helps us find space and time in our daily routine to breathe; repetition which aids the development of memory in the child, and helps us find a new relationship to creative discipline; and reverence – for the child, for each other, and for the environment.

This long overdue and inspiring book will provide answers for parents and educators alike, showing us how to create an environment where we can experience this way of being which leads to a new outlook on parenting. Where we can learn new skills, make new friends. Where we can be nourished (both parents and children),

and find new gifts within ourselves. Where we can find our way in a new social community.

The twelve easy-to-read chapters in this book cover everything from the care of the senses and child development from a Steiner Waldorf perspective, to singing and practical activities for you and your children. The reference sections are comprehensive, and the information is clearly written and easy to access. Dot Male has provided the ultimate handbook, which I wish had been available when I began my own group. It will inspire you either to start your own Parent and Child group, or to bring some ideas or ideals into your own home and parenting.

My work (as an educational consultant, trainer, and representative) for the Steiner Waldorf Schools Fellowship is underpinned by continuing, hands-on, practical work as a Parent and Child group leader in Cambridge. Keeping in touch with the needs of parents and children in today's frenetic world, and seeing the continuing benefits of attending and leading a Steiner Waldorf Parent and Child group, is what underpins and inspires my work. It is eternally rewarding.

Whether you are a parent looking for inspiration, or a potential Parent and Child group leader, this book is essential reading.

Janni Nicol
Early Childhood Consultant and Representative
for the Steiner Waldorf Schools Fellowship

An introductory note for parents

FOR PARENTS – a toddler-sized book within a book!

This book – The Parent and Child Group Handbook – was conceived as a resource book for anyone who wishes to understand, and perhaps become involved with, Parent and Child group work from a Steiner perspective.

Many parents do not have time to read...

It became apparent on completion of the main text that something else was also required... In meeting the need for comprehensiveness and detail in this rapidly growing field, there was a danger that the book's contents might never reach the hearts and laps of many parents with very young children – those, perhaps, who currently have neither the time nor the inclination to read a lengthy book packed with detail and explanation...

but want to know...

- what, succinctly, the Steiner perspective has to offer;
- more about the approach, as you are already attending a Steiner Parent and Child group;
- a bit more about it, as you are thinking about joining a group;

- more about the approach for use and adaptation in the home.

Hence the birth of this toddler-sized 'book-within-a-book'!

The 'mini' chapters follow the thread of the main book but are biased toward information that may be useful for mums and dads who have little knowledge of the Waldorf way, but are curious and have time for page-sized chunks at a time! You will also then be able to make informed choices as to which parts of the main text you might especially wish to pursue further, without necessarily needing to read the whole book.

The 'mini chapter' sections are called 'FOR PARENTS...'

These sections appear at the beginning of each chapter; and for the more general or specialist reader, they also serve the dual function of being a brief summary-introduction to what is to follow in each chapter. More detailed explanations and examples can be found within the main chapters if you would like to know more. The 'Main Points' sections at the end of every chapter also provide a succinct summary of chapter contents.

To begin, an imagination ...

FOR PARENTS – a toddler-sized book within a book!

This book – The Parent and Child Group Handbook – was conceived as a resource book for anyone who wishes to understand, and perhaps become involved with, Parent and Child group work from a Steiner perspective.

Many parents do not have time to read...

It became apparent on completion of the main text that something else was also required... In meeting the need for comprehensiveness and detail in this rapidly growing field, there was a danger that the book's contents might never reach the hearts and laps of many parents with very young children – those, perhaps, who currently have neither the time nor the inclination to read a lengthy book packed with detail and explanation...

but want to know...

what, succinctly, the Steiner perspective has to offer;
more about the approach, as you are already attending a Steiner Parent and Child group;
a bit more about it, as you are thinking about joining a group;
more about the approach for use and adaptation in the home.
Hence the birth of this toddler-sized 'book-within-a-book'!

The 'mini' chapters follow the thread of the main book but are biased toward information that may be useful for mums and dads who have little knowledge of the Waldorf way, but are curious and have time for page-sized chunks at a time! You will also then be able to make informed choices as to which parts of the main text you might especially wish to pursue further, without necessarily needing to read the whole book.

The 'mini chapter' sections are called 'FOR PARENTS...'

These sections appear at the beginning of each chapter; and for the more general or specialist reader, they also serve the dual function of being a brief summary-introduction to what is to follow in each chapter. More detailed explanations and examples can be found within the main chapters if you would like to know more. The 'Main Points' sections at the end of every chapter also provide a succinct summary of chapter contents.

Introduction

It is early March. Imagine walking into a room in a home where six parents and young children, from babes-in-arms to three year olds, have gathered for a regular get-together. The room is uncluttered; all breakables and everyday children's toys have been put away. One of the parents has brought a big bunch of spring flowers that now sweetly scent the room. In the corner stands a table decorated to reflect the new busyness of spring outside. There is a pot of crocuses on the table and some little animals. A teasel hedgehog pokes his nose out from under the shelter of a log. A tiny bird made from coloured wool has alighted on the log and there is a twig and moss nest nearby. Pussy willow stands in a tall jar of water at the back of the table, and beneath it a family of coloured wool dolls are ready to go for a walk. A few children have just arrived and the older ones immediately rush over to the table to see what has changed from last week, with each adding their own found treasures – little stones, a daisy, a broken blackbird's egg shell...

Boots and shoes have been taken off and replaced with slippers, and the older children busy themselves with the toys laid out for them. There are simple wooden toys such as blocks, and logs sawn into different shapes and sizes. There are baskets of pine cones, conkers, and shells. There is a pile of coloured muslin sheets – or 'veils', as the parents call them – fabrics of different textures, and ropes of plaited wool. The children use them to represent an infinite variety of everyday objects in their imaginative play. A 'house' has been erected in the corner – a wooden clothes-horse frame providing the wall, with a blanket across the top for a roof. Inside, there is a family of soft dolls made by the parents during a series of parents' evenings, and some wooden furniture. There is a little stove with pots and pans. The older children quickly move into the house, and an extension is soon built with an upturned chair, and the veils and ropes providing materials for the walls. It first serves as a shop selling conkers and pine cones; soon it has become a bus going to the seaside.

The younger children are happily exploring the basket of logs and wooden animals. One child is trying his newly discovered climbing and balancing skills on a simple structure of wooden boxes and planks. Another sits quietly on his mother's lap as she, along with the other parents and older children, decorate eggs for an Easter tree using coloured dyes and wax crayons. The adults are discussing plans for an Easter Egg hunt and a shared meal to be held on Easter Day...

There is an atmosphere of calm and harmonious busyness...
In these challenging times for parents, this book seeks to offer an inspiring and practical vision of Parent and Child group work based on a spiritual understanding of the needs of the young child and family given to us by Rudolf Steiner.

What do I mean by 'spiritual'? Perhaps it is

here that I need to state my personal position and understanding, as the book is in all its many respects based on this! I am a mother who came to Steiner (Waldorf) education when my son was 9 months old. For me it was truly a profound gift, one that provided, at last, a holding ground for all my personal interests and strivings: ecological aspirations, natural medicine, artistic interests, personal searching, a questioning of my religious background, the realization of the difficulties and personal limits I was experiencing as a mother – an awful sense that I had few inner resources to call upon to guide and support me as a parent. I needed something that would help me, and in the Waldorf approach I was fully and finally 'met'. It was as if the small child in me recognized the soul warmth, the beauty, the nourishment, and wholesomeness of what the Waldorf approach offered. And the parent in me recognized a deep wisdom and 'a way'.

Out of a single public talk, held in Lancaster in the north of England, a group of parents came together, and gradually we gave birth to a Steiner early years project, first as a Parent and Child group and later as a Steiner Kindergarten. A few years afterwards, other parents then founded a Steiner school. Through the struggles and triumphs of the birth and growth of our little Waldorf initiative and in our own parenting journeys, we and our children grew…. In my early years as a mother, a mantra began to inhabit my quiet moments; it went, 'Hark parents, look after your children; they are the hope of the world'.

Although our son is now a teenager and has moved on from Steiner education into the mainstream world, I have stayed in the realm of early childhood, wanting to learn and understand all I can about these crucial early years of life. I organize introductory courses on various aspects of early childhood for parents and those wishing to set up Parent and Child groups, I help to organize conferences, and I do Parent and Child work.

Through my work with very young children, I continually experience the noble spirit and self-determination they bring into life. How do we 'meet', care for, protect, and honour the children who come to us? and how can we more fully embrace our awesome responsibilities as parents? How can we better understand and embrace our own deeper inner journeys in life?

We live in complex times, and there are many conflicting factors that we, as parents, need to contend with. We are becoming more aware of the crucial importance of the first few years in influencing the later health, well-being, and self-determination of an individual. But there are many new pressures on our children and families – like the effects of technology, too early intellectual education, and stress-filled life-styles that we are only just beginning to question and understand. On top of all that, parents, like myself, can feel that we walk into parenthood empty-handed, needing to learn everything afresh. We can feel uncertain in our parental roles; and in this questioning we are met by 'the experts' in the form of numerous books, websites, and groups. Just whom do we trust and where do we go?

This is where I feel the Parent and Child group has such a crucial role to play in helping parents with very young children. The traditional Parent and Child group (or 'Parent and Toddler group', as it is more commonly called) is often the first and most important place where parents with very young children go to be with others and to share experiences of parenting. This place of meeting, in all that it offers at the grass-roots level, in all that it brings both to us as parents and also to our children in terms of activities, materials, advice, and support, needs to be wholly rooted in an understanding of what is truly healthy for the child and the family. As parents, we need Parent and Child groups that we can trust to show us what is appropriate for our young children and families. In its depth, comprehensiveness, warmth, and delight, the Waldorf approach has offered a strong and steady light to many, many families – my own included.

The decision to write this book has arisen out of my personal journey as a parent, and my continuing creative and deeply healing encounter with the Waldorf approach to child development and parenting. I am neither an expert nor an academic – more an informed amateur researcher and spiritual 'quester'. There are others who have more experience and skill than I in research and in the practice of Parent and Child work, and I have tried to give at least some of them a voice in the various chapters that follow.

I hope this book can be used either as a comprehensive guide to setting up a Parent and Child group or dipped into for occasional inspiration and for resource ideas. Reference is made to a wide variety of groups and projects in an attempt to do some justice to the richness and diversity of Waldorf Parent and Child group work both in Britain and abroad. Most chapters are full of detailed information and, therefore, lengthy. For those who wish for – or only have time for – a more simple overview, there is a summary-introduction at the beginning of each chapter. In addition, listed at the end of each chapter are 'key points' covered within the chapter, useful books, and contacts. Some important references are repeated at the end of several different chapters.

Following this introduction, there are twelve chapters in all – here is a brief summary of their contents:

Chapter 1: The importance of Parent and Child groups, the principles underlying Waldorf Parent and Child work, and why these groups are largely unique. Examples from around the world.

Chapter 2: The spiritual perspective of child development underlying the Waldorf approach to Parent and Child work, including the importance of free uninhibited movement for healthy physical, emotional, and intellectual development. Why parents need to know about the phases in child development and the inherent sensory sensitivity of the very young child.

Chapter 3: Creating a healthy, nourishing Parent and Child group setting, including the physical space, what to put in it, the significance of simplicity, care, and the nature table. Health and safety questions.

Chapter 4: The essential play needs of young children from a Steiner (Waldorf) perspective. Appropriate toys for different ages. Inside and outside play.

Chapter 5: Shaping the Parent and Child group session, including the natural ordering of activities to suit the young child, timing, transitions, and creating a harmonious 'hum'.

Chapter 6: Practical activities in the Parent and Child group session – who they are for and why they are important. Ideas and different approaches.

Chapter 7: The importance of the shared meal in creating community. An example from York.

Chapter 8: The circle time – an exploration of appropriate movement games, songs, rhymes, stories, and puppetry from a Steiner (Waldorf) perspective. Ideas and resources.

Chapter 9: The celebration of special occasions for parents with young children. The spiritual and community aspects of family festivals Examples of seasonal festivals from different Parent and Child groups, and a birthday story.

Chapter 10: Parenting as a spiritual path. Parent and Child groups as learning communities. Examples of ways in which parents are supported in the Waldorf movement.

Chapter 11: Parent and Child groups and the
birth of community. Aspects of starting a
Parent and Child group initiative, including
stages, practical and legal aspects, and
working/learning in groups.

Chapter 12: If you were given just one wish for
your child… My granted wish. The Steiner
perspective providing a real hope for the
world.

There are eight appendices, which cover: fund-
raising; the practical aspects of running a Parent
and Child group; marketing and publicity;
registering with the British Steiner Schools
Fellowship; foundation books for study groups
and libraries; working with the twelve senses;
inner and outer qualities of a Parent and Child
group leader; and finally the Series Editor's essay
on the Hawthorn Press 'Early Years' series.

A note on terminology

One feature of the world-wide Steiner Waldorf
education movement is the variable – and
arguably confusing! – terminology which is used
to name the education. There are differing uses
of terminology both between and within
countries: in Britain, for example, some
authorities argue that 'Steiner (Waldorf)' is the
most appropriate usage, while others use just
'Steiner' – and a few use just 'Waldorf'. Between
countries, there is a broad tendency for 'Steiner'
(education) to be used in the UK, while on the
continent and in the USA, 'Waldorf' (education)
is more commonly used. This book will be
widely distributed within both Britain and North
America, as well as on the continent; and
accordingly, I have opted for a mixed
terminology usage – sometimes using 'Steiner'
…, and sometimes 'Waldorf' …, so that readers
from any and every country will find Parent and

Child groups referred to in a way they will
recognize.

Also, when referring to the young child, both
genders are used at different times – sometimes I
use 'he', 'him', or 'his'; and sometimes 'she' or
'her'.

Finally, if, when you have finished reading
the book, you feel inspired either to start a
Parent and Child group of your own, reappraise
an existing one, or bring some of the ideas into
your own home, then this book will have served
its purpose.

CHAPTER 1

The importance of Parent and Child groups

'One feels that childhood is no longer a safe or healthy world for children... Just as we have learned how to clean up the physical environment, we need to learn to clean up the unhealthy lifestyle that is polluting the lives of children. There is no one single cause of the problems. The answers lie in the total environment which surrounds the child, the physical environment, the social environment and the cultural environment... Each has grown unhealthy, and the combination is proving lethal for many children.'

Joan Almon [1]
Co-ordinator of the US branch of the Alliance for Childhood

FOR PARENTS...

Part 1: Steiner Parent and Child groups

Who was Rudolf Steiner?

Rudolf Steiner (1861–1925) was an extraordinary educationalist, philosopher, artist, sociologist, and spiritual scientist. World-wide initiatives which have arisen out of his work and insights include *Steiner Waldorf education* (including university degrees, schools, Kindergartens, day nurseries, play groups – and Parent and Child groups), bio-dynamic agriculture (a form of organic agriculture), Weleda homeopathics, Anthroposophical medicine, Camphill Communities, Eurythmy (a form of movement used artistically and therapeutically), and many other diverse architectural, agricultural, educational, artistic, and spiritual enterprises. The first Steiner school (founded in 1919) was called the Waldorf Free School, as it was started by Emil Molt, the owner of the Waldorf-Astoria factory in Stuttgart, for his workers' families. The name 'Waldorf' stuck, and is now used by many Steiner educational initiatives around the world.

What are Steiner Parent and Child groups?

Steiner/Waldorf Parent and Child groups are meeting places for parents and carers with young children (usually babies up to $3^1/_2$ years of age), based on the spiritual perspective of child development given to us by Rudolf Steiner. They aim to demonstrate what is naturally holistic in the broadest, deepest sense for the young child and for family life, and they provide a safe place of support, friendship, learning, and community for parents.

Steiner Parent and Child groups are largely unique

Parents have said:

- The groups are more relaxed and relaxing, less chaotic than similar experiences elsewhere.

- The toys and general environment are wholesome and beautiful.
- There is more regularity and structure, yet more freedom at the same time.
- There is more parental involvement.
- Care and thought have been given to every aspect of what happens.
- The choice of seasonal songs and verses, together with the festivals, makes sense.
- Children are not over-stimulated or frenetic.
- There is a quiet, calm atmosphere.
- There is a reverence for nature, the child, and the parenting journey.
- A feeling of 'warmth'.

Steiner Parent and Child groups are an important resource for parents

Very young children today are faced with many challenging cultural influences – over-stimulation, inappropriate technology, unstable life-styles, the pressures of early intellectual learning, to name but a few... Because the Steiner approach is based on a profound understanding of child development, it can help parents experience and understand normal and healthy environmental influences on their young child. The Steiner approach empowers and ensouls.

Finding a Steiner Parent and Child group

There are over 60 in the UK, and many in other countries around the world. Visit the Steiner Parent and Child website: www.steinerparentandchild.co.uk for UK information, or phone the UK Steiner Waldorf Schools Fellowship on 01342 822115 for your nearest local contact.

Raising children in our times

All is not well with our children. Our fast, technological, and pressured Western way of life is taking its toll on the fundamental health of our youngsters. The pressures are coming from many different directions, and the causes are complex and inter-related. Here are some quotations from a few of the writers who are focusing on the worrying symptoms appearing in young children today.

From educators:

'Compared with 25 years ago, today's children display a worrying rise in nervousness, stress and hyperactivity. The drug Ritalin is being administered like a behavioural aspirin to a whole generation of children, sweeping some of the troublesome symptoms under the carpet but doing nothing about the causes. There is an increase in eating and sleeping disorders, in eczema, asthma, and other allergies. There is also growing evidence of impaired speech development and various other characteristics typical of the "autistic spectrum". Dyslexia is on the increase. In general we are seeing ever more children in need of developmental and learning support.'

Martyn Rawson and Michael Rose [2]

'Today's sophisticated, technological toys leave today's children very little room to be creative and original, only endlessly to repeat what has been done before. Now children are absent as cars dominate our streets, outdoor play is risky; children's designated play areas, with notable exceptions, are sanitized, safe and devoid of imagination. Our children are housebound, waiting for childhood to be over in order to gain some sense of freedom. In cocooned safety they watch television, video, play computers and learn how to think, feel and react to the world as they experience it – as it has been designed for them to experience. Sometimes it seems that packaged and passive childhood is the only kind on offer.'

Sally Jenkinson [3]

From psychologists:

'For today's parents, childrearing may often be in conflict with career, with finding a new mate, with loyalties to children from previous marriages, and with retaining even a modest standard of living. Our new family styles make it next to impossible for the majority of parents to provide the kind of childrearing that goes along with the image of children as in need of parental nurture.'

David Elkind [4]

'We are at the beginnings of a new era, and like every time of transition from one way of thinking to another, ours is characterized by resistance, anxiety, and no small amount of nostalgia for those familiar landmarks that most contemporary adults still recall from their own "old-era" childhoods. And yet the change has occurred so swiftly that most adults are hardly aware that a true conceptual and behavioural revolution is under way, one that has yet to be clearly defined and understood. At the heart of the matter lies a profound alteration in society's attitude towards children. Once parents struggled to preserve children's innocence, to keep childhood a carefree golden age, and to shelter children from life's vicissitudes. The new era operates on the belief that children must be exposed early to adult experience in order to survive in an increasingly complex and uncontrollable world. The Age of Protection has ended. The Age of Preparation has set in.'

Marie Winn [5]

From scientists:

'A study conducted by scientists in America found that for every hour of television watched daily, toddlers face a 10% increased risk of having attention problems by the age of seven…. Dimitri Chrisakis, the report's author, said that findings had shown that children would become mesmerised by the television screen which appeared to affect the development of the brain…. The findings suggested that television might over-stimulate with its unrealistically fast-paced visual images and permanently rewire the developing brain… The latest findings come after a warning last year from David Bell, the Chief Inspector of Schools, that communication and behavioural skills among five-year olds were lower than they had ever been.'[6]

These quotations provide just a few of the many indicators of growing concern about what is happening to children and childhood. As parents we are faced with the problem of trying to find our own way through these very difficult issues. We may indeed be unsure about how to raise our children, given the complexity of pressures. What might be seen as *normal* (in our life-styles as adults) may not be *healthy* for children, but how do we know?

In the confusion of information we are given, in all the choices that our technological culture promises, in the pressures of our life-styles, we look first and foremost to respected peers and other parents for help. In the UK, the traditional Parent and Toddler group has for many thousands of parents fulfilled this need for information and support.

The tradition of the 'Parent and Toddler' group

The traditional Parent and Toddler group is a fundamental part of local community life in Britain. Every neighbourhood, whether rural or urban, will generally have at least one Parent and Toddler group, often several, each reflecting a particular religious persuasion or neighbourhood flavour.

Parent and Toddler groups meet in a great variety of locations, from church halls to front rooms, and they provide a place for parents/carers accompanied by young children under 4 to come together to play and to socialize. They are generally low key, unglamorous, non-profit making ventures, organized and run by dedicated souls who, more often than not, give their time and energy voluntarily. The group sessions generally follow a similar formula of play, with or without a craft activity, tea break, and songs. They last between one and two hours, and meet once or several times a week, morning and afternoon.

To run a traditional Parent and Toddler group, you do not need a qualification and there are no statutory requirements, as the parents stay with their children – though there are guidelines for health and safety regulations and insurance. Parent and Toddler groups thus fall outside formal government legislation, and groups arise very much to serve and respond to local needs. Anyone with energy and commitment can be a catalyst for a new group. Having said this, the Pre-school Learning Alliance (PSLA) supplies booklets on the practicalities of setting up and running Parent and Toddler Pre-school groups,[7] as they are called, and there are also very comprehensive training courses for Parent and Toddler group leaders offered by the Alliance and, more recently, by many local councils.

Although they are an essential part of British life, they are not so common in other countries. Many factors play into this, for example the relative expense of day care in the UK compared with other countries. In some European countries, up to 30 per cent of the cost of day care is borne by Government. In the UK it is expensive for parents with very young children to go back to work. Parent and Toddler groups may also be more common in the UK because there is, compared with other countries, a greater fragmentation of traditional extended family structures and community networks. New parents are often faced with the problem of not knowing other families with young children. The networks of friendships, which will give support and company during the crucial early years of parenting, often need to be made from scratch.

There seems to be a lack of information about the origins of Parent and Toddler groups – just when they first began serving our local communities, and where the concept was birthed. Perhaps this in turn reflects the lack of value and attention that has been given, until very recently, to the needs and concerns of parents with very young children.

This is all now changing, however – certainly in Britain. Government initiatives such as Sure Start, set up in the last few years to tackle child poverty and social exclusion in disadvantaged communities, are at the forefront, pioneering comprehensive packages aimed at supporting parents and young children. The traditional Parent and Toddler session does still exist in these ventures, but it is increasingly being supplemented by a whole range of classes and activities aimed at high quality early years care, parental support, and community building. These richly diverse schemes are very exciting in their scope.

In addition to these central government initiatives, there is a growing interest in Parent and Toddler group work at local government level. Most councils now have an Early Years Development and Childcare Department offering a register of local Parent and Toddler groups and a variety of courses and trainings for

people working with young children and parents. There is also a variety of new grants available from local government and other agencies available to help set up and run new Parent and Toddler groups. Certainly they are becoming more and more popular: in the relatively small city of York, for example, there are over 60 Parent and Toddler groups. Group leaders report growing numbers, sometimes as many as 30 parents (each with one or two children), in an individual session. Child minders and au-pairs can, in some groups, outnumber the parents. Many parents and carers will visit several groups in a week.

In its leaflet titled 'Running a Parent and Toddler Pre-school',[8] the Pre-school Learning Alliance lists a group's many functions (see Box 1).

Box 1: The functions of the Parent and Toddler group

- A place to go, where both adults and children are welcome
- Company, for both children and adults
- An opportunity for parents to be with their children without being distracted by household responsibilities
- Time and space for children to learn through satisfying play, perhaps with more equipment than can be provided at home
- The chance for parents to compare notes with others doing the same job
- Opportunities for both adults and children to learn by observing and absorbing new practices and ideas
- Access to community resources
- The beginning of friendships which may last long beyond Parent and Toddler pre-school days

Informed by this overview of the most important functions of Parent and Toddler groups, and the essential role they play in the lives of new parents with young children, is there anything more that can be added? Don't Parent and Toddler groups already amply cater for the needs of parents with young children?

The potential blind spot

For all the important functions that Parent and Toddler groups fulfil in the life of young families, there can be a 'blind spot'. Because Parent and Toddler groups grow out of, and are therefore embedded in, our cultural norms, they tend to reflect collective fashions and concerns. A resultant danger is that Parent and Toddler groups may only be able to offer what we know already, or else simply reinforce popular cultural norms; and as argued earlier, it is difficult for today's parents to know on what basis to judge what is 'normal' and what is 'healthy' for our young children.

Although Parent and Toddler groups provide a place where parents can share concerns, they often cannot help parents to find a way through the maze of contradictory consumer pressure which can come from the realms of entertainment, education, and even medicine. Over the last few years there has been an explosion of books, magazines, and websites dedicated to parenting issues. As parents, we can feel that there are no right or wrong answers and that, in a sense, anything goes, if it seems to work some of the time. We can feel overloaded by the sheer volume of often contradictory information on parenting matters. What the Parent and Toddler group offers to parents in terms of help and advice will naturally also reflect all these contradictions and dilemmas.

Some of the practical aspects of Parent and Toddler groups can also be quite confusing to many parents with young children, but are accepted because they are normal practice – for example, large noisy halls with a bewildering choice of toys; a chaotic atmosphere, particularly at transition times between one part of the session and the next; sugary snacks, and even television. The pressure to introduce formal early learning activities may also be quite strong. But unless we can see more clearly what would be more nourishing both for the young child and for ourselves as parents, we can feel at a loss to improve the situation. These are difficult waters to navigate because, as parents and group leaders, we want the best for our children, and of course we hope we're offering it. Even though we know that these groups provide an essential life-line to parents with young children, there are assumptions and conventions embedded in what they offer that need to be questioned. Not least, we need a broader perspective from which to recognize the difference between 'normal' and 'healthy'.

The Steiner (Waldorf) Parent and Child group

The vision for Parent and Child groups informing this book, drawn as it is from the Steiner educational movement,[9] provides a different perspective from which to view these dilemmas, taking as its starting point a spiritual understanding of child development and the role of parenthood.

This wider vision for Parent and Child groups encompasses the many strengths that already exist in traditional Parent and Toddler groups. In addition, however, it provides a profound perspective on child development, out of which a broader understanding of the challenges facing parenting today can emerge, as well as new creative means of support. This wider vision takes us beyond the limited view that a Parent and Child group essentially offers a social escape *from* the home environment, with its responsibilities and loneliness, to the concept of a 'total environment' where healthy, nourishing approaches and attitudes, once experienced, can be directly transferred back *into* family life.

Although the order of activities in a session is broadly similar to traditional Parent and Toddler groups there are some very essential and fundamental differences. In a questionnaire carried out amongst parents attending a Steiner Parent and Child group, and quoted in Lynne Oldfield's book *Free to Learn*,[10] parents were asked what they thought the distinguishing features of a Waldorf Parent and Child group are. Box 2 summarizes their replies.

There are other distinguishing factors, like the importance given to natural organic food, the attention given to the natural cycle of the year, and community events like the celebration of seasonal festivals.

Box 2: Distinguishing features of the Steiner Parent and Child group

- More relaxed and relaxing, less chaotic than similar experiences elsewhere
- The toys and general environment
- More regularity and structure, yet more freedom at the same time
- More parental involvement
- The care and thought which goes into every aspect of what happens
- The choice of songs and verses make sense
- The children are not over-stimulated or frenetic
- The quiet calm atmosphere
- A feeling of warmth

Group setting with parents and children

The main principles underlying Steiner (Waldorf) Parent and Child groups

We can specify these basic elements and qualities that characterize these groups, but it is important that there is an understanding of the 'why' of things. In this book, through the different chapters I will attempt to explain the 'whys' in a way that is accessible. However, what is shared in this book can only be an introduction to the riches and depth of understanding about the young child found in Rudolf Steiner's many books and lectures.

As a foretaste of what will be covered, Box 3 sets out some important principles which underlie the Steiner approach to Parent and Child groups.

Box 3: Principles underlying Steiner Parent and Child groups

- Children are spiritual beings, and incarnating is a gradual process. The first three years are crucial for healthy development, not only physically, but emotionally, intellectually, and spiritually.
- During the first seven years, children are in the process of growing healthy bodies and learning the skills of everyday living. Formal learning comes later.
- Young children need the freedom to develop at their own pace in their own time. This is especially true of the huge task of learning to gain control and agility in the physical body. Physical movement needs to be free and unhindered. There is no need to rush development: young children need the freedom to make mistakes, to learn through trial and error.
- Children need to have time to play. Play is essential and vital for healthy development in all respects, and there are identifiable toys and materials that encourage strong healthy play.
- During the first few years young children are very open to all sensory impressions: they soak in everything. Over-stimulation, which affects healthy development at all levels, is a real danger in our times. Children need to be protected 'under their carer's wings', particularly in the first three years.
- Rhythm and repetition are fundamentally important qualities in a young child's life. They bring security and containment, and help to build a strong physical body.

- Young children are totally trusting and learn everything through imitation and 'doing'. Most of all they need to be able to imitate the everyday tasks of life.
- The young child needs to experience the world as beautiful, true, and good, and to know that we care for our everyday surroundings, for nature, and for each other.
- Young children need the warmth and security of a few committed known adults. More than this, they need us to 'meet' them, to be willing to recognize their essential spiritual individuality.
- Parents and carers of young children need respect and an acknowledgement of their crucial and often difficult task. They need to be reminded of their own innate spiritual wholeness and innate wisdom. Experiencing the qualities of openness, warmth, acceptance, authenticity, and joy in a group nourishes both parents and children.
- Celebrating the cycle of the year through songs, rhymes, festivals, and seasonal crafts all helps to create a sense of wonder and reverence for nature and the Divine.
- Caretakers of young children benefit enormously from having artistic or craft hobbies, which can help replenish and refresh them, and enrich family life.
- The human speaking and singing voice, simple instruments, told stories, and puppetry nourish the young child deeply in ways that tapes, videos, and even books cannot reach.

With these principles in mind, it becomes possible for us, as parents and group leaders, to take a fresh look at almost every aspect of a Parent and Child work. For example:

- How can we as parents be more awake to the deeper needs of our children?
- How can we encourage play?
- What are appropriate toys and play for different ages?
- What activities and experiences can be taken back into the home to nourish family life?
- What can we do which is worthy of imitation by the young child?
- How do we respect the sensory sensitivity of the young child? What can we bring to a child that is authentic, natural, and true?
- How can we empower parents so that they feel more confident to deal with the challenges of our times?
- How can we work with music, singing, puppetry, and stories in beautiful natural ways which are appropriate to the developmental stage of the young child? And how can these activities be encouraged into family life?
- How can we encourage domestic, artistic, and craft work?
- How can we honour the gifts and seasons of our earth?
- How can we be environmentally conscious?
- What quality of food and nutrition do we want to offer?
- How can we nurture a spirit of caring and community?
- How can we help and support parents?

These questions are continuously addressed by those who work with parents in Waldorf Parent and Child groups.

The qualities of a Steiner Parent and Child group

Kim Billington, a Waldorf early years teacher in Victoria, Australia, describes the Parent and Child group (or Steiner playgroups, as they are called in Australia), in an article available on the internet,[11] as a place of 'heightened adult consciousness'. She explains:

'The adult is fully awake; the child is in "dream consciousness". The adult's nature is to experience the world through the intellect with such ponderings as "How can I improve life?" and "What does this child need to grow into a healthy older child?". The young child's nature is to experience, explore and come to know the world through the senses and by physically "doing". To grasp this premise and use it as a guide in our work is essential to the practical application of Steiner's philosophy.'

In the Parent and Child group session there is no intentional teaching; the experience is offered without formal explanation. Parents come to understand, through direct experience, what the benefits of the approach are both to themselves and to their children. Explanations are only given in response to questions, through the offering of reading material and in special discussion times. Everything is offered in freedom, not as dogma which has to be accepted, but as information that can be tested out and worked with. In the heightened adult awareness that the group can foster, parents can find it easier to be more 'present' for their children.

At their best, the sessions have a very special quality which embraces the participants like a loving mantle – a quality that can be described as timeless, full, and nourishing. It comes into being through a conscious awareness of the parents, as well as the leader, for the well-being and care of the children, and through acceptance and respect for each other. The balance between the social needs of the adults and the needs of the children is very carefully and gently managed so that a 'container' is created where both child and adult can feel inwardly free and safe. Rudolf Steiner explained that in this deeper encounter, we help to awake each other's soul and spiritual depths; and out of this the spirit of community arises.[12]

In comparison with modern cultural norms, Steiner Parent and Child groups can seem to come out of another age, or even 'out of time'. The décor, equipment, and toys can look old-fashioned and rather quaint to our technologically jaded eyes. Yet these groups can function like oases in our increasingly synthetic deserts. What they quietly demonstrate is a positive affirmation of the natural, simple, and fundamental things of life. They can remind us that there are still simple activities and pleasures that cost very little, and that these things can magically bring 'soul' streaming back into everyday life. The Waldorf Parent and Child group model, standing aside as it does from 'normal' convention and cultural fashions, is able, at its best, to show us simply and clearly a model which deeply nourishes children and parents. The spiritual understanding of the young child translates into practical guidelines which have the 'ring' of wisdom.

Parents say what they value about Steiner Parent and Child group sessions

Recently parents attending various Steiner Parent and Child groups around the UK were asked about why they attended the sessions. The following are some of their comments about what they value about the group:

- 'Friendships made with other parents. Opportunities to find out more about Steiner education, by experience rather than just reading. Meeting new people.'

- 'I value the sense of support and community that the group offers and the friendships we have made through the group. We particularly appreciate that fathers are welcomed and encouraged at the sessions. We also love the emphasis on nature: the rhymes of the seasons, the toys made from natural materials, the "blessing on the fruit".'

- 'The possibility to turn to the children, without being distracted by housework. Meeting like-minded mothers.'

- 'An unknown journey into self development.'

- 'Parenting can be isolating. Adults meet other adults like themselves. Parenting journeys are shared.'

- 'It is so nourishing, it sets me up for the week – it reminds me of what is important.'

- 'A haven of calm in a hectic world. I'm not sure who gets more out of it – me or Cameron. I always come home feeling grounded and capable of being the type of mum I want to be.'

- 'I value the community spirit of like minds.'

- 'I value the way that the children learn to play together; the parents learn skills that can be taken home. Also, it is good that the parents can come and have coffee and a chat. Relationships are built and it is safe.'

Parents write about how the group benefits their children

- 'The playgroup rhythm, especially the snack and song time. Even at 20 months my son has anticipation for what is coming next, and especially likes sitting around the table for fruit salad.'

- 'Charlie, I think, likes the fact that the room isn't too big – he feels very safe and secure here. He has always loved sitting at the table for fruit and the lighting of the candle. He often asks us to do "hands everybody" at mealtimes at home. He enjoys the craft activities very much.'

- 'The calmness of the environment. The

mutual respect shown for all children. Play, singing, and snack time.'

- 'The group is more organized, purposeful, and focused. There is a real sense of thought going into the sessions.'
- 'The peaceful atmosphere. The gentle guidance children receive through the established rhythm.'
- 'My child benefits from the routine, the songs, rhymes with actions, the freedom of choice – free play or crafts, the quiet stilling times.'
- 'The small group size, the routine of free play – activities – fruit – story with songs. The awareness of the seasons.'
- 'My daughter learns a lot from the older children, and over time she has made relationships with the other children. There is a routine, so she knows what to expect. She is learning skills that I would find hard to teach her, and her walking and singing have really been helped.'

Parent and Child group leaders reflect on their work

Sheila Clarkson, who helped to start the Lancaster Steiner Educational Initiative, now runs a Parent and Child group from premises at her home in Clitheroe:

'For some of the children attending Acorn, I think they benefit from having their mother's or carer's undivided attention for a good part of the morning. There is no electrical gadgetry or motors. Nothing to bombard the child's senses. The child comes to learn about the social sharing of food around the table at elevenses. There is a preparation for the young child to learn about sharing.

Parent and Child groups are a wonderful support for parents. It is an excellent 'taster' for Kindergarten and its Steiner early years education. The toys and playthings – i.e. cut off branch pieces, fir cones, shells, feathers,

pebbles, fleece – simple toys show parents they don't have to go to toy shops. A barn can be constructed with small logs. Parenting can be so isolated. Adults meet other adults like themselves. Parenting journeys are shared. Parenting is challenging, often with little to show after a very busy day. I like to think that I can help parents redeem this often unrecognized work when they come to the group. Many parents are unequipped for the multiple challenges. I hope I can help parents when they meet these difficulties.'

Richard House, publishing editor, psychotherapist, Waldorf teacher, and Parent and Child group leader in Norwich, writes:[13]

'In my experience, Waldorf early childhood settings are distinctive and largely unique in their provision of an environment in which children learn the nourishing benefits of both unimpinged-upon freedom and individual creativity, and a clear, child-sensitive structure that invites co-operation and sociality. It is easy to create either formless chaos and mayhem, or, at the other extreme, authoritarian over-regimentation – but far more subtle to create that most nourishing of spaces that lies "between form and freedom". It is the latter which the Waldorf Parent and Child group at its best provides.'

Letitia Costain is the national UK Parent and Child group leader representative for the Steiner Schools Fellowship. She has worked in Parent and Child group settings for many years, and currently runs a group at Rudolf Steiner House in London:

'I feel it is so important for parents and carers to have support and understanding in a very underrated task these days. I try to help them understand what wonderful work they are doing. (I feel) the benefits are realizing you are not alone, and that other people find it difficult too. It is about sharing the joys of childcare, enabling the children to meet and play/share/learn together.'

Lourdes Callen, who has much experience in counselling and group facilitation as well as in Waldorf Kindergarten and Parent and Child group work, writes about one of her groups:

'What is this particular group offering apart from a rhythmical and social time with quality toys, good food, and seasonal craft work? This group focuses on the work with adults. Children are very busy building themselves and taking very fine steps in their process of growing. How can this group support these developments? The less expectation and pressure children experience from their surroundings, the better they can orientate their efforts to this very important endeavour. I believe that to support the parent means to support the child, especially so in the case of the very young, and I see that my task is to empower and trust the work that the parents do or can do.

There are plenty of occasions where parents can be engaged to make them feel that the group is their own and we are in a continuous learning process: writing an article, planning an outing, bringing a song. They have shaped the sessions in a natural way with suggested themes, contributions, and questions: exchange of books on one occasion, understanding tantrums on another; travelling with a child, sharing discoveries and insights into what works. All these themes can be explored further in talks and discussions offered in the evenings.'

Examples of Steiner Parent and Child groups from around the world

Although the same broad principles underlie all Waldorf Parent and Child groups, each one is unique, reflecting not only the location – whether inner city or rural, in hired premises or in the home – but also the strengths and interests of the groups' leaders and parents. Here are some brief descriptions and reflections from people involved in a number of very diverse Parent and Child group settings.

Brenda Watson has run Parent and Child groups at Wynstones Steiner School, Stroud, UK for 15 years. Brenda has four groups which meet on different mornings, with ten families in each. Her sessions last for two hours and combine play, a shared meal, finger games and songs, a walk, and a little story. She likes a large range of ages, and often has infants up to 4–5 year olds. Over the years she has developed an approach which is now used as a blueprint for many Waldorf Parent and Child groups in the UK. She has shared her insights and wisdom on the London Steiner Kindergarten training course and in Ireland, and has been a major influence on and inspiration for a whole generation of Parent and Child group leaders. Brenda's way will be referred to often in this book.

Kim Billington, in Victoria, Australia, has 20 years' experience of helping parents to set up and run Waldorf Parent and Child groups. Kim told me that she sets up Parent and Child groups wherever she lives in Australia. She will start a group by finding premises, advertising, and then running the group for 2–3 terms. Gradually over this time, a core of parents will take over the running of the group, and she will gradually withdraw, while maintaining a mentoring role. Often these groups will later develop Kindergartens for older children. There

Kim Billington and group in Australia

is no formal training in Parent and Child group leadership as such, as Kim feels that the parents come to the approach initially through their hearts and through fully experiencing the approach. The experiencing comes first, the explanations later. After the sessions, for example, parents may phone to ask for explanations and then Kim explains why things are done in a certain way. She has written a general booklet giving guidelines for setting up and running groups, which is available on the web from www.steiner-australia.org, and has also produced a book and video on songs and stories.

Bella Tan, one of the early pioneers of Waldorf education in the Philippines in the 1990s, runs a Parent and Toddler programme at Manila Waldorf School:

'I began a Parent-Toddler programme in 1997 for parents with young children who are almost 2–3 years of age. The parents make toys and engage in crafts while the toddlers have indoor and outdoor free play, drawing, crayoning, and play in the sand pit. We have a simple ring time or morning circle where we sing songs and recite rhymes and verses, accompanied with movement and gestures. We share a healthy morning snack, and we end the morning with a short story/table puppetry, farewell verse, and farewell song. The parents and I meet periodically to discuss various themes, like child development, play, and appropriate toys, rhythm and repetition, movement, and the will. We also have regular conferences to address parents' concerns about their respective toddlers, and other relevant parenting questions.'

Bella told me that the Philippines is a predominantly Christian society and so the main festivals that are celebrated in Waldorf settings are also celebrated in her Parent-Toddler group. She also celebrates the 'Rice Festival', which is a major annual occasion in the country, and other local festivals.

Eva Libalova works in a Waldorf Kindergarten in Prague, Czech Republic. Eva told me that the Kindergarten was founded in 1992, and now there are 105 children between 3 and 6 years of age. The Parent and Child group was started later for 2–3 year olds and their siblings. The group meets once a week for two hours, and has between 6 and 12 children. She said:

'The program is very similar to a Waldorf Kindergarten. After the children come with their mothers, they make a circle to greet themselves all together. Then the finger games follow. During playing the teacher is explaining to the mothers all the activities they are going to play and the mothers are usually sewing. The children are doing children's plays, fairy tales, songs, craft activities, and festivals. After the snack/fruits and tea, the games continue. If the weather is nice they spend some time in the garden playing there. Twice a year there are weekend courses for the teachers from all around the Czech Republic. The courses are about bringing up children from birth, and also we do craft activities, making toys, instruments…. For example, last time everyone made a cantela instrument.'

Dorien Versluis started one of the very first Waldorf Parent and Child groups in the Netherlands. Dorien emailed me to share her experience in the Netherlands. She told me that the first Parent and Child group in the Netherlands was started in 1979 for two-and-a-half year olds by a lady called Mars Hempel, in the university town of Gottingen. This was in response to a request by parents who wanted to get involved in Waldorf education before their children went to the Waldorf Kindergarten there. Dorien was so excited by Mrs Hempel's experiences that she started one in her home town that same year. The intention was to run the group for 6–7 couples for 6 weeks at a time. However, the parents were so enthusiastic for more that they stayed until their children went to playgroup. She realized that parents did not know how to be with their children in the home; they did not know songs to sing to them and had not learnt domestic crafts. By using the name 'playgroup', the parents thought the group was for their children. However, they only understood much later that it was for them as well! Dorien shared her experiences of the group at the Dutch Waldorf pedagogy course covering 0–7 years, and from this 22 similar groups were formed across Holland.

She explained that there is no special training in the Netherlands, just the Kindergarten training which covers the period from birth to 7. So many mothers came to the training that a special course was set up for them, which was not training as such, but covered similar material.

Julie Lam, who runs a Steiner Kindergarten in Hong Kong, has also set up a number of Parent and Child groups there. Julie moved out to Hong Kong from England in 1985. She then returned to the UK in 1996 and discovered Steiner education for her fourth child. She read avidly and learned all she could from visiting various Steiner Parent and Child groups. When she returned to Hong Kong in 2001, she met a Waldorf teacher with whom she studied for nine months, and then she set up her own group, which her young son could attend. She has since trained some other women to be leaders, and now there are six groups, two that meet on Tuesday and Thursday mornings and one on each of the afternoons. The sessions are one-and-a-half hours long.

Each group has up to twelve families who come from a wide range of ethnic backgrounds – Chinese, Japanese, and Indonesian, Euro-Asian as will as British. Many children in Hong Kong are cared for by 'maids', and the Parent and Child groups tend to have a 50:50 mix of children with their parents and children with helpers. There is a strong ethos of mutual respect and acceptance.

Julie says that these groups are unique in Hong Kong. There are many groups for parents and young children that are early-learning orientated, but the Waldorf groups are the only ones which provide a homely atmosphere, craft and free play, and the celebration of seasonal festivals. The parents make simple objects for their children, or to decorate their homes; and all the food, which is wholesome, is prepared in the group. The Waldorf festivals are celebrated alongside the local ones, and with the groups being so multi-cultural it makes for a rich and full year. Some are celebrated during the Parent and Child group sessions where the focus is the making of little crafts, singing, telling a short seasonal story, and the sharing and enjoyment of food. Others are celebrated with the larger Kindergarten community.

It can be seen from this very brief survey that Waldorf Parent and Child groups, which exist worldwide, are rich and varied in their expression. People ideally come together out of need and a shared vision, and the new impulse, fired by the enthusiasm and will of those involved, forms in a way that is 'living' and directly relevant. Every initiative will be an intimate expression of the particular needs of the situation and the personalities involved, and that is how it should be. It is the shared spiritual understanding of the young child which unites all these endeavours, and gives the Waldorf work its special characteristics.

Although it would be wrong to dismiss or diminish the wonderful work that more conventional groups carry out, it is true to say that Steiner Parent and Child group settings *are* distinctive and largely unique, and do show a way

that has been successfully serving parents and very young children for many years. If Parent and Child groups have a crucial role in supporting young families in these complex times, then there are some very important treasures to be found inside the doors of Waldorf settings. In the chapters that follow, these are presented, hopefully in a way that is inspiring, accessible, and useful.

Main points again

- There is growing evidence that the healthy development of our very young is being compromised by a constellation of many factors, including complex and rushed life-styles, inappropriate technology, and the drive toward intellectual-cognitive early learning.

- Parents with small children can feel not only isolated in their task but overwhelmed by the amount of contradictory information about 'what your child needs'.

- Parent and Toddler groups traditionally offer an essential place for parents to make friends, support each other, share difficulties, and learn new skills. But they may potentially reinforce popular cultural norms which may not necessarily be the healthiest ones for the young child.

- Steiner (Waldorf) Parent and Child groups are based on a spiritual understanding of the young child. This perspective helps us to see more clearly what is naturally healthy for young children. What specifically these Parent and Child groups offer is largely unique.

- There are very strong principles that underlie the Waldorf approach to Parent and Child work. These principles infuse every aspect of the work, from how the setting is arranged, to the order of group sessions and the various activities undertaken.

Many families testify to the benefits of attending Waldorf Parent and Child groups.

- There are many examples of Waldorf Parent and Child groups from around the world, which have arisen through local need and individual enterprise.

Useful books

Johann Christoph Arnold, *Endangered – Your Child in a Hostile World*, Plough Publishing House, Farmington, Pa., 2000

Martyn Rawson and Michael Rose, *Ready To Learn*, Hawthorn Press, Stroud, 2002

Martin Large, *Set Free Childhood*, Hawthorn Press, Stroud, 2003

Neil Postman, *The Disappearance of Childhood*, Vintage Books (Random House), New York, 1994

David Elkind, *The Hurried Child: Growing up Too Fast Too Soon*, 3rd edn, Perseus Publishing, Cambridge Mass., 2001

Eugene Schwartz, *Millennial Child*, Anthroposophic Press, Hudson, New York, 1998

A model of a Waldorf Parent and Child program
Sarah Baldwin, *Nurturing Children and Families: One Model of a Parent/Child Program in a Waldorf School*, Waldorf Early Childhood Association of North America, New York, 2004

Books by and about Rudolf Steiner
The Child's Changing Consciousness and Waldorf Education, Anthroposophic Press, Hudson, New York, 1996.

The Education of the Child and Early Lectures on Education, Anthroposophic Press, Hudson, New York, 1996.

The Roots of Education, Rudolf Steiner Press, London, 1968.

Rudolf Steiner: An Autobiography, Steiner Books, Blauvelt, New York, 1980.

Rudi Lissau, *Rudolf Steiner*, Hawthorn Press, Stroud, 1987.

Useful organisations

Steiner Parent and Child Groups UK – website
www.steinerparentandchild.co.uk
email: info@steinerparentandchild.co.uk

Steiner Schools Fellowship
Kidbrooke Park, Forest Row, Sussex RH18 5JB, UK; tel. 01342 822115; mail@swsf.org.uk Phone or email here to ask for the national Parent and Child group representative in the UK.

www.steinerwaldorf.org.uk – this site lists all Steiner Educational Initiatives in UK and Ireland, and you can use this site to find your nearest one.

www.anth.org.uk – this site has links to many anthroposophical websites.

Pre-school Learning Alliance
69 Kings Cross Road, London WC1X 9LL, UK; Tel.: 0207 833 0991 www.pre-school.org.uk
Publications include:
'Running a Parent and Toddler pre-school'
'Parent and Toddler groups – self assessment for good practice'

Scottish Pre-school Play Association
45 Finnieston Street, Glasgow G3 8JU, UK; tel. 0141 221 4148, www.sppa.org.uk
Publications include:
'Running a Toddler group – Code of Practice'
'Learning through play for the under threes in Parent and Toddler groups'

CHAPTER 2

Fresh perspectives on child development

'We need to begin to see the child in a new way, one which takes into account physical, emotional and mental development as well as the less tangible spiritual dimension of the human being. Once we begin to perceive the whole child and how he or she unfolds, then our choices will begin to have coherence. No longer wanting a cookbook of "how to's", we will trust our own decisions, based on our understanding of children.'

Rahima Baldwin[1]

FOR PARENTS...

Part 2: Fresh perspectives on child development

Why is it important to understand child development from a spiritual perspective?

Our child comes to us from the spiritual worlds, and the process of incarnating into the physical body is a gradual process which involves the emotional, mental, and spiritual aspects of the child. There are distinct progressive phases that naturally unfold, if undisturbed and protected. If we can begin to see our child in this holistic way and broadly understand these natural stages of unfolding, then it becomes much easier to decide for ourselves what is and what is not appropriate to bring to our young children at any age. In this way we can cut through much cultural confusion.

The natural developmental phases of the young child in a nutshell

This is a huge and multi-layered subject but, very simply put, there are three main phases a child passes through from birth to the coming-of-age at 21 years of age:

The first seven years

The physical foundations of the bodily constitution for life are being laid down, and the child's spiritual individuality, albeit unconsciously, is gradually moving into this growing, forming body. During this time the child is very open and impressionable on every level, and learns everything through imitation. Early intellectual learning, over-stimulation, and the unnatural forcing of any skills disturbs this delicate process. The first three years are critical in this respect, as during this time the child is learning to walk, talk, and think with memory.

7 to 14 years

The change of baby teeth to adult teeth signals the next phase, when the child becomes ready for formal learning. During this period it is the feeling life of the child which naturally wishes to unfold. All teaching needs to be given in an artistic way which feeds the imagination and soul. We have to take care to offer living bread rather than stones.

14 to 21 years

The rush of puberty marks the beginning of the last phase, during which intellectual abilities and critical thought naturally develop. At the end of this phase there is the possibility of recognizing one's self as a freely motivated individual, and to become aware of a life purpose.

How do Steiner Parent and Child groups use these understandings?

Everything – the physical setting, the activities, the order of activities, the mood in the Steiner Parent and Child group – is founded on the spiritual understanding of the young child. In particular, we:

- encourage free, unrestricted, and exploratory movement in the very young child;
- create a mantle of soul 'warmth' around the child and parent;
- provide activities that encourage positive imitation in the broadest sense;
- create an environment which is appropriate for, nourishes, and protects the sensory sensitivity of the young child;
- demonstrate by example how these considerations can be taken back into the home.

Parent and Child groups can show us in very simple and practical ways what is healthy and nourishing for both parents and children. The approach demonstrated in Waldorf Parent and Child groups is based on a perspective of child development which takes into account the spiritual dimension of the human being as well as the physical, emotional, and mental. Here we will look at three of the main understandings which underpin the work in Waldorf Parent and Child groups, which are:

- The natural developmental stages of the young child
- Imitation
- The young child as a sensory being

The spiritual perspective on childhood is concerned with 'a big picture'; and although this vision can be translated into practice, there is often quite a substantial gap between what is demonstrated in these settings and the realities of our everyday lives. I hope to offer some light to help us in our choices about what to include in environments for young children. In his compassionate understanding of parenthood, the famous child paediatrician, Donald Winnicott, gave us the phrase 'good enough mother (parent)'. Perhaps this 'good enough' notion applies to Parent and Child groups as well! We need a loving understanding of the continuous tension between the striving and the reality, and an acknowledgement of what we do achieve.

1. The natural developmental stages of the young child

In our consumer-driven society it is easy to assume that we have to buy or hire what young children need for their healthy development. For example, our society values intellectual development very highly, and as a result many early learning packages and toys are geared toward exclusively developing the mental abilities

of young children. How can we know whether what is being offered is truly age appropriate? On what basis can we judge?

There are many phases and stages through which a human being moves from birth to adulthood – emotional and spiritual as well as physical and mental. There is an intricate and immaculate order in the *unfolding* of a whole human being; and this unfolding takes place naturally with its own perfect timing, if allowed.

In a spiritual understanding of childhood,[2] there are three major phases of development that a child moves through from birth until adulthood, the latter taking place around 21 years.

First phase – birth to 6/7 years: The main tasks in these years are the building of a strong healthy body and learning to feel 'at home' in it, as well as in the world. It is the phase where crucial foundations for life are laid – fundamentally, a trust in one's own body, in the love of others, and in the goodness of the world and of life itself. In the first three years the child learns three essential abilities – walking, talking, and thinking. Over the next few years the basic skills of everyday living are mastered through the means of imitation and play. The emphasis is on 'doing' and 'being' rather than intellectual learning.

Second phase – 6/7 to 14 years: This is when the child is at home in the realms of feeling and imagination, and learns naturally through her feeling nature. Although it is appropriate that formal learning starts at this time, the child learns best when drawing, music, dancing, movement, and story telling infuse all subjects. She learns her place in a larger community – of the school and peer group.

Third phase – 14 to 21 years: This is the time when critical thought and the ability to work with abstraction naturally develop. There is a great delight in ideas and an opening up to personal love as well as spiritual ideals. By the age of 21 the young adolescent can become a self-motivated adult.

A baby's openness to her world

During the first 21 years the three major qualities found in a whole and free adult have been nurtured at their appropriate times – the ability to be effective in action in the first seven years, to feel widely, deeply, and imaginatively in the second seven years, and the ability to think creatively and clearly in the last seven years. At 21 years of age there is the possibility of being able finally to recognize oneself as a freely motivated individual and to become aware of a life purpose.

Even a brief insight into these three phases can help us to understand what is appropriate to bring to children at any particular age. In the first phase the child needs to *do* and to *be*; in the second phase, to have experiences which primarily enrich the feeling nature; and in the third phase, the adolescent needs fully to engage the intellectual mind.

It is helpful to look at what this 'unfolding' entails during the first seven years, and particularly in the first four – the period when a child may well be attending a Parent and Child group.

The first year

A new-born baby comes to us from the spiritual world. We are spiritual beings and the physical body will be our life-long home. However, as has been described in the above section, we don't move all in one go! Rahima Baldwin beautifully describes the process as 'growing down and waking up'.

Babies gradually gain control of their physical bodies from the head downwards, learning to move head and arms, then the torso, and finally claiming the lower half of the body through crawling and walking. This is the great work of the first year of life, and we can see how, during this time, the baby begins to 'wake up' in herself, moving from the undefined consciousness of a new born to the involved and assertive sense of self-hood of a toddler. What we see is the determined instinctive will of a spiritual being, wanting to move into her body and learn how to use it. It is this deep desire which finally brings the small child to her feet.

The second and third year

Once the ability to stand and walk is achieved, the intrepid adventurer turns to a new task – that of learning to talk – to name and therefore to welcome this new home and all who live here. This is the work of the second year. Gradually over the next year or so, the ability to distinguish and to separate everything in the world is developed. The young child begins to differentiate himself from his surroundings, and realizes he is a separate being. 'No!' is the salute of a proud divine being!

There is a particularly special moment when the 2-3 year old says 'I' instead of their name to tell you what he wants. Some children occasionally start to say 'I' as early as two years of age, although still mainly calling themselves by their own name. The use of 'I' comes more as the child's consciousness slowly dawns. The newly discovered 'I' heralds a new stage in the emerging sense of self, and is an important milestone in the spiritual task of coming into the world. The faculties of thinking and memory are now able to develop, gradually allowing a development of the imagination as well as the deepening of human relationships.

Mary Triulzi, Waldorf-trained teacher and Parent and Child leader in the United States, describes the 'terrible twos' thus:

'The toddler is now beginning to perceive her separateness as well as her lack of power and feelings of dependency on the parents. This budding feeling/perception can often lead the toddler to having "temper tantrums", which is an expressed panic of attempting, through the power of her independence and control, to find her way to a more powerful relationship to the world around her… It is an important stage which I feel can be wonderfully helped along,… through allowing her to experience mastery in all that is possible… The toddler who, throughout the day, is offered repeated opportunities to work toward independence in dressing herself, getting up to the changing table, climbing down from the meal table, and feeding herself, is a more confident as well as engaged child.'[3]

The fourth to seventh year

During this time the young child needs, above all, an environment which is secure, predictable, and loving, and which allows the freedom and challenge to hone and refine these basic skills of living in a physical body and in the earthly home. She needs to know that the world is good and safe. The child also needs to be able to play freely, both physically and imaginatively, because this is the way he orientates himself to life on many different levels.

Free movement and emotional and intellectual development

The quality of the first seven years, and particularly the first three, determines in many respects the health of our physical body throughout the rest of life. Our physical constitution for life is actually laid down in these early years.[4] This is a sobering thought, but there is also research indicating that emotional and intellectual development is also intrinsically linked to motor co-ordination in the first few years of life. Writers such as Sally Goddard Blythe have extensively investigated the intricate connection between sensory-motor development and learning difficulties in young children. She quotes a study carried out at the Institute for Neuro-Physiological Psychology in Chester in 1996,[5] where it was found that children who had reading and writing problems had experienced a cluster of difficulties with early motor co-ordination. These had included delay in walking and speaking, riding a bike, and fine motor tasks such as doing up shoe laces. Many of these children had not passed through the developmental stages of crawling or creeping. It was also found that delays or missed stages in motor development are not 'grown out' of, but continue to have an effect on cognitive development later on. Goddard Blythe offers a warning:

'The development of modern baby equipment has reduced the time young babies spend playing on the floor, from where the infant learned to hold its head up, to sit and develop the movements necessary for crawling. Contact with the floor provides tactile stimulation which is important for the development of a child's sense of body map, a precursor to spatial awareness. Younger siblings today can spend up to 2 hours of their day strapped into car seats ferrying brothers and sisters to school and after-school activities. Hours which might have been spent in physical play are too often replaced sitting in front of a television or a computer where there is a surfeit of stimulation but no physical interaction – arousal without integration.'

Sally Goddard Blythe[6]

The Pikler Institute and Resources of Infant Educarers

There are several other organisations at the forefront of promoting the importance of free un-inhibited physical movement in the young child. The Pikler Institute in Hungary carries on the work of Emmi Pikler who, in the last century, was instrumental in highlighting the need for babies and very young children to master their bodies unhindered, for their emotional and spiritual health as well as for their physical and cognitive development. However, not only is the individual timing of a young child's physical development honoured, but there is also an emphasis on how all care-giving to a young child can be seen as an opportunity for intimacy and tenderness. In all these activities the care-giver learns how to observe and respond to the child in a respectful and interactive way.

'While learning during motor development to turn onto the belly, to roll, to creep, to sit, stand and walk, he is not only learning how to learn those movements, but also how to learn. He learns to do something on his own, to be interested, try out, to experiment. He learns to overcome difficulties. He comes to know the joy and satisfaction that is derived from this success, the result of his patience and persistence. I am, of course, always speaking of children who have not been stimulated, let alone pushed by adults to try a new movement. Only then can you see the quietness, deep concentration which notices nothing else, the joy and satisfaction which characterizes the learning process... The child who is learning in that way... wants to learn independently, undisturbed, in her own way.'

Emmi Pikler[7]

Free movement in the very young child

The work of the Pikler Institute has been taken to other countries, most notably to Los Angeles in the USA where Magda Gerber, who worked with Emmi Pikler, has founded an organisation called Resources for Infant Educarers (RIE)[8] which trains people to help parents observe and care for their very young in this deeply respectful way. Mary Truilzi, experienced in RIE and Waldorf Parent and Child work, writes of the difficulties many parents face today:

'I have observed that already in the first months of life the cultural attack on the very young child is immense. This is first expressed through the anxiety of many mothers toward their infants. I myself experienced this; as a conscious and modern mother of an infant, I felt parenting to be a weighty deed, yet I had few tools to address the needs of my wide awake, arrhythmic baby. Any signs of distress from my newborn infant only increased my feelings of anxiety and inadequacy... Rather than feeling comfortable with allowing babies the opportunity for free, self-initiated learning through movement and life experience, mothers are anxiously protecting, distracting, and stimulating their babies. The infants are thereby free from any experience of struggle... Most babies have been inundated by baby swings, baby saucers and walkers, vibrating bassinets, noise-making toys, baby gyms that fit over them when they are lying in their crib, and various other movement-invasive and -inhibiting equipment. The parents are often unable to find a way to help the infants to sleep without using the vibrating bassinets, car rides, vacuum cleaner noise, or various other overwhelming sense experiences. Over-stimulation, sleep deprivation, and inhibited movement are the norm for most of our infants.'

Mary Triulzi[9]

In these confusing times, people like Mary are helping parents to appreciate the deeper needs of their babies and young children. Understanding the importance of the various natural stages in child development, learning observation skills so we see better our children's needs, learning to be fully present to our young child and facilitating our young children's noble struggle into their bodies and the world, can be part of the work in all Parent and Child groups. In the USA and Canada as well as on the continent of Europe, Waldorf early years projects have forged very successful partnerships with organisations such as RIE and the Pikler Institute.

Box 4: Characteristics of physical settings which respect the natural physical development of the young child

- Provide safe loving places where the young child can, in her own time, learn to gain control over her body and surrounding space
- Provide ample opportunities for safe free play and exploration, particularly in the natural world or with natural materials
- Avoid equipment which falsely speeds up developmental stages – e.g. baby walkers, bouncers, intellectual toys
- Avoid long periods where movement is restricted or where the young body is bent into unnatural postures – e.g. car seats and buggies
- Avoid activities which prevent the young child experiencing real everyday life – e.g. computers, TV, videos

2. Imitation

The developmental tasks of the first seven years, this 'coming into the world', are achieved because the child is totally open to all influences in his environment. The young child unconditionally imitates everything and everyone. As parents we are probably well aware of the ways in which our child wants to copy our actions and how quickly he learns new skills. However, we may not realize the depth and importance of this impulse. Rudolf Steiner writes:

'There are two magic words which indicate how the child enters into relationship with his environment. They are Imitation and Example... The child imitates what goes on in his physical environment, and in the process of imitation his physical organs are cast into forms which become permanent. Physical environment... includes not only what goes on around the child in the material sense, but everything that takes place in the child's environment... This includes all the moral or immoral actions, all the wise and foolish actions that the child sees... what the grown-up people visibly do before his eyes.'

Rudolf Steiner[10]

It is not just we parents and adults whom our children imitate; they also imitate what they see on TV and video. Professor Robert Wilson described a series of experiments carried out for a recent adult television series.[11] Four three-year-old children viewed on a TV screen events that were happening in an adjoining playroom. First of all, the children saw a grown man cuddling a life-size rubber doll. The children were then led into the same playroom. Without prompting they all stroked or kissed the doll, mimicking what they had seen. A little later the children saw on the TV screen the man come back and hit the doll vigorously over the head with a hammer.

When the children were taken back into the playroom each attacked the doll. The average 3-4 year old watches a screen for around five hours a day, and more than 50 per cent of three year olds have a TV set in their bedrooms. An estimated 10 per cent of children become actively violent themselves later in life because of their viewing of violent behaviour.

It is actually the 'real' and simple everyday work and jobs which the young child loves to imitate best – the brushing and cleaning, cooking, and putting away. But it is not just the physical tasks of everyday living that are copied, as we know. It is also the behaviour and the mannerisms, the feelings (and even our thoughts!) that our young children so deeply soak up, in total trust that what they receive will be good. In recognizing our young child's deep instinct to imitate, we begin to realize the enormous responsibilities that we carry.

Our response to this deep need to imitate in young children, however, is not simple. In reality, many of our everyday domestic tasks are often experienced as a burden and drudgery. And very young children can be exhausting and leave us feeling exasperated! We will, if we can afford to, invest in labour-saving devices and domestic help. Or the TV and video are the baby-minders while we get on with the necessary domestic work – even though our little ones would in fact *love* to help! Work outside the home may well be preferable to home-making. Alternatively we are often forced, for economic reasons, to juggle outside employment and home life. In our times, the role of the home-maker is still perceived to have very little value. What may be in the child's best interests may not feel life affirming for us!

The Parent and Child group is one of the few places where parents with young children can escape the confines of the home. Here we can relax away from domestic responsibilities and our children can play. But what if our children actually need those activities from which we so wish to escape?

The Living Arts

Cynthia Aldinger, a co-founder of an innovatory organisation called LifeWays North America[12] which promotes holistic, anthroposophically informed child care, uses a term which re-frames and transforms the dilemma. The skills involved in creating a healthy home life have been re-defined as the Living Arts:

> 'It refers to the domestic, nurturing, creative, and social arts. Examples of the domestic arts would be cooking, cleaning, and laundry, baking, gardening and such. Examples of the nurturing arts include diapering, bathing, clothing, feeding, putting children to sleep, singing, storytelling, etc. Creative arts… includes painting, crafting, drawing, etc. Examples of the social arts would be playing, conversation, sharing, and listening.'
>
> *Cynthia Aldinger*[13]

Re-envisioning these skills can help us to realize that creating a home life which provides positive experiences for imitation involves various skills. We are empowered by being able to name the sorts of skills and activities that deeply nourish our young child, knowing that we can learn them and get deep satisfaction from them.

Erika Grantham who has for many years run the Kindergarten training course at Emerson College, UK, also reminded me of a fundamental spiritual truth. At some level that is difficult to describe, we, as well as our families, are deeply supported and nourished by the caring that we give to our homes and everyday tasks of life. What we give out in love returns. As well as providing examples for imitation, the everyday tasks of life, carried out with enjoyment, produce a sort of safe 'life bubble', 'life field', or mantle which is filled with love and which young children thrive in. This can be a particularly difficult concept for us to take on board, however, when home-making has such a low value in our society.

Related to all this is the question of how we, as parents, need to reconnect with our own creativity for our own sake, and not just for that of our children. We know that young children call on our energy and that is a central reason why being a parent can be so exhausting. Rahima Baldwin reminds us that there are various things we can do for ourselves which replenish our energy – for example sleep, meditation, and artistic activity: 'Artistic activity involves the same vital or creative forces that your baby is using, but it replenishes rather than depletes them. Playing a musical instrument, drawing, sculpting, painting, all can help mothers to have more energy.'[14] Activities like taking a walk each day can have a similar effect, as can writing a journal or meditating. As our child gets older, little walks and artistic activities can become the basis for many shared interests in the family.

A Parent and Child group is an ideal place to experience these living arts in a friendly and supportive environment.

Box 5: Characteristics of settings which respect the forces of imitation

- Simple craft and artistic activities for adults and children
- Songs, stories, and rhymes which are presented in a way that a young child can easily follow and imitate
- Simple toys and materials which allow young children to re-enact the simple everyday tasks of home life
- An atmosphere that has an openness and warmth of heart
- Ways of introducing experiences and activities which allow children to learn by natural imitation, rather than through verbal instruction and explanation

3. The young child as a sensory being

'During the first seven years of a child's life, declared Steiner, its body, soul and spirit constitute a unity, and during this period more than any other, that which affects one member necessarily affects the other two'.

Gilbert Childs[15]

'Small children, unprotected, are at the mercy of their immediate environment. Their whole body acts as a single sensory organ unselfconsciously uniting external impressions with the child's internal world… This interaction… is revealed in the wonderful power of imitation with which every healthy child is born. Every perception is first deeply assimilated, then grasped with the will and reflected back to the outside in echo-like activity.'

Freya Jaffke[16]

'From birth to age seven a child's forces are primarily devoted to building up her physical body… The sense impressions she absorbs can so strongly influence these forces that they make the difference between a strong healthy body and a body that may be prone to chronic illness later in life.'

Barbara Patterson and Pamela Bradley[17]

A young child is an open sensory organ. The individual senses work as a whole and they cannot filter or prevent impressions entering from the external world. This is revelation enough! From a spiritual perspective, we actually have more than five sense organs and they are much more complex than is generally understood. Rudolf Steiner describes twelve senses which gradually develop to their full capacity over the first 21 years of life. These include the five we generally recognize – taste, smell, touch, sight, and hearing – together with seven other subtle sense organs, which are:

- Sense of warmth
- Sense of balance
- Sense of movement
- Sense of life
- Sense of thought
- Sense of speech
- Sense of each other's individuality (or sense of ego)

Some of our senses have definite physical organs, such as the eye or ear; others are located throughout the whole body, working in a much more subtle way. With practice it is possible, as an adult, to separate out and experience each sense individually. We can come to understand that a deficiency in the working of one sense – like sight – affects all the others, which are then called upon to compensate as best they can. The development of the full twelve senses starts from birth, and it is these very early years that are most crucial in their healthy development. This is particularly true for the senses that are called the lower or body senses – the senses of touch, life, balance, and self-movement. They provide the foundation for the unfolding and flowering of the others.

It is far beyond the scope of this book to take a detailed look at the twelve senses (see books listed in the bibliography). What I want to do here is summarize why we need to protect and care for these delicate and very open senses in our young child, and what we therefore need to be aware of in a physical setting.

Sense of touch

'After the baby is born, the mother communicates something to him in every way she touches him. This is the way babies get their information about the universe that determines to a very large extent what kind of personality they will have as grown-ups.'

May Gaskin[18]

Touch is our most direct experience of the 'other' and the world, and human touch is deeply experienced by a young child. Early experiences will affect later self-esteem and the ability to relate to others. As we know, for a young baby breast-feeding, cuddling, and holding are basic ways in which the sense of touch can be nourished.

'Through touching a child makes a loving connection to their environment. At the same time they feel the separations and boundaries between themselves and another person – gradually this awakens the child to the experience and value of relationships.'
Barbara Patterson and Pamela Bradley[19]

As the child grows, so the sense of touch is developed and sensitised by appropriate stimuli in her environment. The sense of touch in a young child is not just affected by the quality of the carer's touch but also by the quality of all physical objects – in a sensory way and at a soul level. For a child deeply to know what is authentic and true (to their nature) in her world, she needs to touch and experience these things. There is an important difference between

materials which are 'real' (close to their natural origins) and those that are synthetic. This includes clothing as well as toys and equipment.

Box 6: Ways to protect and nourish the sense of touch

- Careful, loving and respectful handling
- Sensitive choice of clothing
- Careful choice of toys and other equipment

Sense of life or health

This sense is one we are not normally aware of unless we are 'out of sorts', although when all is well in our bodies, we can experience a deep sense of joy and contentment. It is a body sense par excellence. A healthy diet of natural foods, a regular rhythmic life, enough sleep and play, love, and attention will all contribute to a deep sense of well-being which will in time develop a strong sense of life in a child. ('It is good to be alive!'). Then, as adults, we will know what is good for our health in the deepest sense – and what isn't.

Exploring the world

Box 7: Developing a healthy sense of life or health

- Close and sensitive observation of young babies to find out what their needs, likes, and dislikes are – e.g. what different cries mean
- Understanding of how warmth, right feeding, rhythm, regular sleep, and other daily activities build good body habits

---

Sense of movement

At a very fundamental level an inner experience of personal freedom comes from our sense of movement in our joints and muscles and is reflected in how comfortably we can move in our body. It is important that a young child is given the freedom to learn to gain control of his body in his own time.

The successful learning of speech and other abilities is directly related to harmonious bodily movement. There is a reason why a young child learns to walk before he learns to speak. All other processes like thought, memory, imagination, and future abilities like reading and writing arise out of our early experiences of learning to move and co-ordinate our bodies. The first three years are therefore fundamentally important in this respect.

Box 8: Encouraging the sense of movement

- Providing uninterrupted periods of free movement in a safe environment
- Allowing our children to learn to creep, crawl, and walk in their own time without intervention
- Trusting in our young child's ability to find their own way to competent and agile movement
- Providing a life-style with plenty of opportunities for play and free activity
- Avoiding as far as possible long periods in any body-restricting device – including slings, buggies, baby walkers, bouncers, and car seats

---

Sense of balance

This sense organ is located in the inner ear. The sense of balance must be allowed to develop in its own time, and is achieved through the young child's determined efforts to master body equilibrium in stillness and movement. In adulthood, a sense of balance is not only physically experienced as agility and grace but can also be sensed as an inner peace and strength. Forcing, manipulating, or restricting movement too early in life may make it harder to find this inner balance later in life.

Sense of warmth

A new-born baby cannot regulate her body temperature, hence the importance of natural clothing that can breathe, and the old fashioned habit of covering a baby's head for the first year to preserve body heat. It takes several years before a child can properly regulate her body temperature. A warm body relaxes, and it is easier for the work of building a strong body to take place. A chilled body stiffens and contracts. In these early years, it is imperative that carers are sensitive, on behalf of the child, to extremes of heat and cold in the environment. Overheating can be as much of a problem as cold or damp.

Babies and young children are also very sensitive to whether a person has a 'warmth' or not, and will be deeply affected by the soul qualities of their carers. Loving warmth is soul and bodily food for the young child. A young child will flourish in an environment which has qualities of warmth, joy, and acceptance, much like a tender plant will grow in the protection of a light, warm greenhouse.

Box 9: Protecting the young child's sense of warmth

- Appropriate clothing, especially to the head where most heat is lost
- Clothes made of natural fibres wherever possible
- 'Soul' warmth from carers

Sense of sight

It takes a while for a new-born baby to learn to focus on specific objects – to actively look. However, colour impressions will be taken in deeply even in a very young child and will, like the impressions from the other senses, affect both her growing body and feeling life. A real danger in our times is over-stimulation. Bright primary colours which are deemed suitable for the young child are very strong and harsh; pastel colours create a more soothing and restful environment

---

Box 10: Protecting the young child's sense of sight in physical settings

- Using pastel colours rather than primary colours
- Using true/natural colours – e.g. retaining the natural condition of wood
- Avoiding 'busy' wall coverings, curtains, and posters, and providing restful places for the eye such as uncluttered wall space
- Using natural light when possible and avoiding harsh strip lighting
- Carefully choosing the colours and textures of furniture, equipment, clothes, etc.

Senses of taste and smell

Tastes and smells make a very strong impact on a young child. We can see this by the strength of the bodily reaction a young child will have to tasting something very bitter or sweet. Bad tastes and smells cause a contracting and, over time, can at a soul level contribute to a mistrust in what comes from the outside world. On the other hand, a child's whole being responds instinctively and enthusiastically to pleasant smells and tastes.

Memories associated with smell are carried right into adulthood. How often have we remembered a long-buried event of childhood through a particular smell? Lifelong attitudes to food and, at a deeper level, openness to life's goodness are formed early. We can do a lot to lay healthy foundations by providing:

- natural wholesome food whenever possible;
- being mindful of the quality of smells in our environments – whether they are natural and pleasant, the effects of strong or synthetically created smells, and so on.

Sense of hearing

A young child's hearing is much more sensitive to sound than that of an adult, and she is easily startled by loud noises. Over-stimulation of the sense of hearing causes a young child to become irritable or, in more extreme cases, to close down and therefore become somewhat desensitized. Is there a possible link between ear problems and chronic disharmony or noise in a young child's environment? The most pleasing and soothing sound is a kind human voice, and the importance of talking and singing to your child cannot be overestimated There is a difference between the quality of a carer's voice and a tape or CD – it is to do with quality of soul in the living presence of the speaker.

Hearing depends on listening, and listening comes from being able to experience an inner quiet. A child's ability to listen will affect the development of speech and language. It is becoming increasingly evident that prolonged exposure to TV and videos are affecting young children's ability to learn language. We can be more mindful of our child's delicate sense of hearing in a number of ways (Box 11).

Box 11: Nurturing the young child's sense of hearing

- Be mindful of the quality and volume of sounds in the immediate vicinity of our young child
- Avoid environments where there is loud and confusing noise
- Value and encourage warm human interaction whether in talking, story telling, singing, and instrument playing rather than relying on tapes, videos, and TV to soothe and entertain

---

The thought, speech, and ego senses

Of the twelve senses that Steiner describes, these 'higher' senses are the most difficult to visualize. We need to imagine that our ability to understand another person's speech, to understand the thoughts behind the speech, and really to 'meet' another person in an authentic way depends on these subtle senses.

Simply put, the *sense of thought* allows us to picture the ideas and pictures behind someone's thoughts – an ability used, for example, by story tellers who fill their words with their own inner images. These enrich the visual pictures formed by the listeners. The *sense of speech* allows us to formulate words and to understand when language is being spoken, even in a language we do not know. The *ego sense* allows us to recognize the essential individuality of another human being. Young children use these senses in an unconscious way to learn to speak and to understand people in their environment. Mary Triulzi again:

'There is a great difference between mechanically taking a child out of their chair after lunch without any communication, and making a connection and softly saying now we will get down and play… In this way they are not treated like something to

manage but instead we are interacting with them out an understanding of the "I" of the child in front of us.'[20]

How much these 'higher' senses are formed and how much a child will trust these senses depends very much on the quality of human interaction in a child's environment. Many of us need help in developing these abilities. As adults we often need to learn how to be good listeners and to honour another's individuality.

Box 12: Encouraging healthy development of the higher senses

- Care of the other senses, particularly the inner senses
- Loving respect for the needs and individuality of our young child
- Authenticity in our conversations and actions with our child and others in our child's environment
- Careful observation of our children so we can begin to understand who they are

---

Protecting the senses of the young child

This subject is difficult to grasp because the implications for young children can seem very unrealistic, even over-protective. We will all have accounts of children growing up with seemingly no ill-effects from what might be considered rather excessive sensory stimulation. In reality, we really don't know the true effects on our children of some of the more extreme aspects of our modern life-styles, although there are writers, who are beginning to sound the alarm. It may only be possible to see the effects in adulthood, and then only if we give value to our more subtle soul and spiritual faculties.

The brief overview of each of the senses has been included so that we, as parents and carers of young children, can think through the implications ourselves. We may only begin to see the challenges if we accept that there are growing dangers in our life-styles.

'The invasion of the soul of our child by sensory "junk" calls for us to be awake and courageous. We may need to make independent decisions as to what influences our child. What can we do? We must look at the amount and pace of the sensory impressions that we offer the child.'

Lynne Oldfield[21]

'If all the 12 senses are not daily given the best stimuli in the first 18 months and above all in the first year, no foundation is laid for a healthy experience of self.'

Michaela Glöckler[22]

Parent and Child groups are places where awareness of these issues can be gently raised – primarily through example. They can be an oasis where what is 'healthy' for the young child, as opposed to what may be 'normal', can still be experienced.

Final thoughts

In this chapter we have explored three spiritual understandings about early childhood development – understandings which can help us in making our decisions about what is appropriate in a group setting. These understandings are not generally known, and can constitute a challenge to our more familiar views and assumptions!

What helps to bridge the gap between our commonly held assumptions and these perhaps more challenging views? The careful observing of our children in different environments is a first step. By being open, initially without judgement, to these new ways of perceiving the young child, we can first watch how children respond in different settings and then experiment with the various elements in a Parent and Child group. We can make our own decisions based on our deepening understanding, validated by our careful observations of young children.

In the next chapter we will see how these understandings can be put into practice in different Parent and Child group settings.

Main points again

- Waldorf Parent and Child work is based on an understanding of the young child which recognizes different phases of physical, emotional, mental, and spiritual development between the ages 0 to 7, 7 to 14, and 14 to 21 years of age.

- Coming into the body and into life is a gradual process. In the first seven years, the awakening spiritual individuality of the child is gradually taking control of, and making its home in, the physical body. Intellectual learning comes later.

- The first three years are critical: in these years, the child learns to walk, talk, and think – to become truly human. The work of Emmi Pikler and organisations such as Resources for Infant Educarers (RIE) show how we can respect a child's natural unfolding in these years with love and minimal interference. This work complements and enriches Steiner Parent and Child work.

- Young children learn everything by imitating those in their environment.

- What young children need to see is the work of everyday life – and the 'Living Arts' concept helps us to re-envisage the value of simple domestic and family life in the healthy development of the young child.

- There are twelve sense organs in the body, not five, and some of them are very subtle. The young child is like an open sense organ; how this sensitivity is met will affect physical and soul development.

- As adults we must be aware, and courageous in the protection and care of the sensory sensitivity of young children.

Useful books

General

Barbara Patterson & Pamela Bradley, *Beyond the Rainbow Bridge – Nurturing our Children from Birth to Seven*, Michaelmas Press, Amesbury, Mass., 2000

Rahima Baldwin, *You Are Your Child's First Teacher*, Celestial Arts, Berkeley, CA, USA, 1989

David Marshak, *The Common Vision Parenting and Educating for Wholeness*, Peter Lang Publishers, 1997 (reviewed on www.inspiredinside.com)

Freya Jaffke, *Work and Play in Early Childhood*, Floris Books, Edinburgh, 1996

Stephanie Petrie & Sue Owen (eds.), *Authentic Relationships in Group Care for Infants and Toddlers, Resources for Infant Educarers (RIE), Principles into Practice*, Jessica Kingsley Publishers, London, 2005

The senses

Albert Soesman, *Our Twelve Senses*, Hawthorn Press, Stroud, 1990

Willi Aeppli, *The Care and Development of the Human Senses*, Steiner Schools Fellowship Publications, Forest Row, Sussex, 1993

Child development – first three years

Karl König, *The First Three Years of the Child*, Anthroposophic Press, Hudson, New York, 1984

Magda Gerber & Alison Johnson, *Your Self Confident Baby*, John Wiley, New York, 1998

Sally Goddard, *Reflexes, Learning and Behaviour – A Window into the Child's Mind*, Fern Ridge Press, Oregon, 2002

Michaela Glöckler (ed.), *The Dignity of the Young Child – Care and Training for the First Three Years of Life*, Congress Proceedings, International Waldorf Kindergarten Association, Medical School of the Goetheanum, Dornach, Switzerland, School of Spiritual Science, 2000

Helmut von Kügelen (ed.), *Understanding Young Children* – Extracts from Lectures by Rudolf Steiner, compiled for the use of Kindergarten teachers, International Association, Stuttgart, 1975

Attachment and parenting

T. Berry Brazelton M.D. & Bertrand G. Cramer, *The Earliest Relationship – Parents, Infants and the Drama of Early Attachment*, Perseus Books, Mass., 1990

D. W. Winnicott, *Talking to Parents*, Perseus Publishing, Mass., 1993

Useful organisations

Pikler Institute

Loczy Lajos u. 3. H-1022 Budapest – Ungarn; Tel: 00 (36) 1 326 63 92; Email:pikler@matavnet.hu

and

Pikler/Loczy Fund USA, C/o Day School Inc, 321 S. Norwood Suite C, Tulsa, Oklahoma, 74135, USA; Tel: 00 (1) 918 665 0877; www.pikler.org

Resources for Infant Educarers (RIE), 1550 Murray Circel, Los Angeles, CA 90026, USA; Tel: 00 (1) 323 663 5330; Email: educarer@rie.org   www.rie.org

CHAPTER 3

The Setting:
The physical space and what to put in it

'The first time I entered a Steiner early years setting I was immediately struck by qualities of warmth, peacefulness, and timelessness which infused the room. It was not empty, in fact it was full of young children building and playing. But there was a very distinctive hum of harmonious activity which seemed to be held in what can only be described as "the warm embrace" of the room. The room had been decorated in a way which was simple and restful to the eye. The materials and toys were functional but beautiful. The walls were a soft pink colour which created a feeling of being enclosed and protected. Everything looked cared for. On entering I instinctively took in a long deep breath – "here I feel safe and welcome".'

Parent, York Steiner School

FOR PARENTS...

Part 3: The physical space and what to put in it

The Steiner Parent and Child group setting

It is possible to create environments which have a healing quality. Based on the spiritual perspective of child development and care, Steiner Parent and Child settings aim to incorporate the following:

- Beauty and simplicity – in the decoration, and the amount and quality of toys and equipment
- A preponderance of natural materials – wood instead of plastic, objects from nature for play and for display, home-made toys
- A nature table for observing and celebrating the cycle of the year
- Waste recycling and use of environmentally friendly products
- An ordered, cared-for environment – a place for everything
- Clean equipment in good repair
- A welcoming home-like environment – e.g. comfortable seats for nursing mums, fresh flowers, rugs for infants to crawl on, a pleasing picture on the wall....
- Safe, clean, and totally toddler-friendly
- Light, airy, and at the right temperature
- A large table with chairs for craft activities and the shared meal
- An outside space if possible
- A lending library and useful information

These conditions can be aimed for whether the group meets in a parent's home or in a public space.

All of these aspects of a Steiner Parent and Child group setting, once experienced by parents, can be taken back and experimented with in the home. Many parents, for example, discover the great delight of creating nature tables for themselves and their children, or making simple toys and play equipment.

We create our environments. They can be stimulating, relaxing, dull, or depressing. We can create environments which have a healing quality. There are writers on architecture like Christopher Alexander and Christopher Day[1] who are able to describe how different environments affect us, and how we can build in a way that honours our deeper spiritual needs. We breathe in our surroundings! It is not just our senses of seeing and hearing which register the quality of a place, but all our senses soak in our surroundings, mostly unconsciously. If this is so for adults, how much more so is it for young children who are much more sensitive?

We can argue that it is not the aesthetic appearance or practical layout of a physical setting which is important, but the quality of relating and activity fostered in the space which counts. Great things can happen anywhere! And aren't our tastes subjective, so that what works for one person might not work for another? Personal subjectivity does create differences in style and decoration, but isn't it also true that environments work for all those concerned when they meet, in an authentic way, the human purposes for which they have been created? For example, Waldorf Kindergarten rooms are laid out and decorated in a way that reflects the work which is being done with the young children. Some people may call it a style – but it is fundamentally a functional solution – 'spiritual functionalism', as Christopher Day has called it. Each Kindergarten teacher will bring his or her own personal taste into the room and so each setting will be uniquely individual, but all will reflect the values that underpin the common work in all the Kindergartens.

Taking some time and care to reflect on the purposes of a Parent and Child group will make it easier to create a space that works – for the space will then be working for the deeper purpose rather than against it.

Choosing and using a Parent and Child group setting

Many Parent and Child groups will often begin in someone's home. Others will rent a public room in a community hall or similar. In either of these cases, creating a setting for a Parent and Child group becomes the art of making the best of what you have been offered! Occasionally a group will be lucky enough have access to a dedicated room in a home, school, or family centre, and in such an environment a more ideal setting can be created. But as Richard House from the Norfolk Steiner Initiative wrote to me:

'Parent and Child groups can work very successfully in many different settings and circumstances. Although having a guiding vision of the ideal is important, whether the setting "works" will depend on the intentions of those running the group and what they can make of the environment they have been given. Beauty and care can be brought to the most seemingly unattractive of venues!'

Bearing all this in mind, there are several principles that are worth remembering when choosing and using a space – even if, in the end, some of them cannot be followed for practical reasons.

Safe space

Parent and Child groups take up a lot of space! Before the session has even started, each family will have arrived by car, by bike, or with a buggy. There needs to be adequate car parking, and safe and dry places for buggies and bikes. There also needs to be space for coats and boots, nappy bags, and – sometimes – shopping! Each venue will present its own unique space-related challenges.

The setting needs to be safe for small children – no unexpected steps or hidden exits;

safe access away from dangerous roads and traffic; potentially dangerous equipment or materials safely out of sight and reach. Although these considerations seem very obvious, many public venues which cater mainly for adults or older children may not be 'safety-proofed' for the very young child. Stair gates which can be put across doorways or other home-made barriers can quickly create helpful boundaries and create a safe manageable group space. It is important to consider disabled access and the advantages of having the group room and toilets on the ground floor. Other more detailed suggestions are discussed under 'Health and Safety' later in this chapter.

The proposed size of the group is a primary consideration. Waldorf Parent and Child groups tend to favour small group sizes – 10-12 families at the most – and therefore smaller venues. This is because a smaller group makes it is easier for everyone to get to know each other, and the atmosphere is more likely to remain calm and manageable. Having said this, many groups are dependant on larger numbers to survive financially, or are just extremely popular. Luckily, groups seem to have a natural limit: beyond a certain number of young children and adults in the same room, new parents can easily be put off by the impersonality factor, the noise, and the increasing difficulties of group management.

Less is more!

As discussed earlier, young children are more open and therefore easily over-stimulated by too many impressions. Go for simplicity if at all possible. Box 13 offers some suggestions.

Box 13: Suggestions for simplicity in the Parent and Child group

- Bare walls with a few carefully chosen pictures/posters rather than busy walls full of posters and a fussy colour scheme. Although it is often assumed that young children need to be surrounded by the bright bold colours, pastel colour schemes are much more restful and containing.
- Using plain material temporarily to cover unwanted images on walls during the sessions
- All unnecessary objects and furniture, e.g. other groups' or children's play equipment, moved to another room while you are using the group room.
- Stacking and covering those articles that can't be removed from the room but which serve no purpose for the group (e.g. TVs, hi fi sets in a home, or inappropriate equipment or furniture in a public space). They need to be safely out of reach of exploring toddlers.
- Cupboards to store materials and equipment safely between sessions.

Home from home

It is easier to create a meeting place which is welcoming if it has some of the qualities (see Box 14) which we would wish to have in our homes.

Parent and Child group setting, Clitheroe

Box 14: Home-like qualities of the Parent and Child group

- A comfortable sized room, not too barn-like or pokey. Some larger halls suffer from acoustics which badly amplify any sounds. In larger halls it is also harder for the children to feel contained.
- A light and airy room with windows that can open
- Heating that can be regulated
- A large table (or smaller tables which can be put together) and chairs, preferably child size, for craft use and the shared meal
- Easy access to a kitchen and toilets

- Easy access to an outdoor space – ideally an enclosed garden or park, but alternatively any space where the group can take a safe walk through nature (even if it is a quiet street with trees) that will change with the seasons
- A carpeted floor or a supply of your own rugs to break up the floor, muffle sound, and create specific play spaces in the room
- Some comfortable seats for nursing mothers in a quiet corner of the room
- A special area with seats, rugs, and cushions for nursing mothers and crawling babies

Groups can use a number of joined rooms which can serve different purposes (craft area, play area, story area) very successfully, as long as there is a sense of containment and safety, with parents and carers being able to keep a watchful eye on their children at all times. Alternatively, one room, even quite a small one, can work well with thoughtful organisation, i.e. careful stacking of toys and tables when not in use.

Close to nature

A particular quality of Waldorf early years settings is the absence of plastic. There are, as described in the previous chapter, good reasons for this:

• Wooden and fabric toys and equipment are closer to their natural origins, and the natural organic forms of such toys make a deep impression on children. The young child needs to be in contact with the strong life forces of the natural world and in natural objects, because these are the same forces that build a strong body. Highly finished plastic toys and equipment are 'dead' in this respect.[2]

• From a more practical point of view, in our increasingly technological world we are in danger of forgetting that everything comes from nature and we are totally dependant on her bounty. Our young children will learn to honour our planet only through our example – what we bring into their environment.

• Toys made from natural materials are generally less formed or less 'perfect' in their representation and therefore more adaptable for imaginative play. Just why this is important will be explained in the next chapter.

• Simple things made with care are also very beautiful.

Wooden toys and materials

Can we make this?

There are many good reasons for making some of the more simple equipment for your group yourselves. First, it is cheaper, especially at the start of an initiative when there might not be much money to spend, and it is also ecological.

The restoring or making together of simple toys, dolls, furniture, and other equipment is creative and brings heart warmth into the group. This is good 'glue' for the adults involved but also for the children as well. Even though they may be too young consciously to appreciate the care that is being taken on their behalf, they will nonetheless take in and be nourished by these efforts. Restoring and making things with care for the group setting will also add to the ambience of the venue in a very positive way.

Finally, promoting resourcefulness and creativity will also bring many opportunities for the members of the group to try out and learn new skills.

Vivienne Morpeth who co-founded the Mayflower Project in North Lincolnshire, UK, says this about making equipment for her group in its early days:

'Our Mayflower P & C group started with eight families meeting in the warm inviting kitchen of one of the group. When we went public and moved to a church hall we suddenly realized we needed low tables, chairs, screens, soft toys, and a home corner. We held a Sunday workshop, and we made a prioritised list of equipment we needed to make, so we could buy or source the materials prior to the workday. Whole families came, and whilst the children played in the garden and house and one or two parents kept an eye, the rest of us either worked on the kitchen table or in the open garage. That day we transformed some old trestle tables, made about ten stools, a couple of screens, and some lovely soft toys.

Home-made toys

My husband and I made a three-sided wooden "home corner" with windows and door. We had a terrific sense of achievement, and it has been wonderful and incredibly special to watch our own three children and many, many others play in it over the years.

Since the success of that first workday, we have gone on to have several more. It is a very productive, sociable, and bonding way of building up and maintaining our equipment, skill base, and group ethos. You can imagine our sense of fulfilment when we have visitors to the P & C group and we say "yes", in Mayflower we make much of our own furniture and play equipment for the children!'[3]

Only have those things with a reason to be there!

This is good feng shui! Remembering this principle makes it easier to prevent 'accumulation congestion', which can become more of a problem over time. Parent and Child groups, in particular, seem to attract toys and materials that other people have outgrown. It is important not to be seduced into becoming the dumping place for other people's cherished discards (the ones they can't quite let go of !). One way around this is to receive donations gratefully, with the proviso that articles that are not needed will be sold to raise funds for the group.

If you care for something, it glows

Many of the limitations of a less than perfect venue can be ameliorated by tender loving care, as illustrated in Box 15.

> ### Box 15: Improving the group venue
>
> - Having a nature table
> - Cleaning and tidying before your session starts
> - Bringing in fresh flowers or natural seasonal elements
> - Having a few special articles – like a seasonal picture or mobiles that 'lift' the room
> - Covering up those things you don't want to look at
> - Making sure that there are no pieces of equipment or toys that are dirty and broken
> - Getting rid of unwanted smells by opening windows or vaporizing essential oils
> - Keeping the space uncluttered
> - Having a sense of order, especially at the beginning and at the end of the session

If we see the Parent and Child group setting as providing a safe, harmonious, and healthy place for adults and their young children, then it is worth taking some time to create a setting which feels special. We feel personally cared for in an environment which is created with our needs in mind, and where simple beauty is given a place.

Room layout

It is obviously impossible to prescribe an ideal layout as every venue will present its own challenges and opportunities, but there are some general guidelines that can help when initially deciding on an arrangement (Box 16).

Box 16: Venue layout considerations

- Coat and buggy space near the entrance door
- Flexible play space in the centre of the room – used for free play and then cleared for story and song time
- Designated home corner for quieter play
- Craft and meal table near natural light
- Different rugs on the ground to designate different play areas – e.g. one for brio and farm animals, one for stacking blocks, etc.
- Craft and meal table near kitchen facilities
- Nature table at the heart of the room with space in front for stories and songs
- Designated area for comfy seats and rugs for nursing mothers and crawling babies - this could also have a range of simple books for quiet moments
- Baskets for all toys and materials so that everything has its home - particularly important if the room needs to be set up and cleared away every session

---

It takes a while to find the layout which works best. Once found though, it is worth keeping the arrangement consistent. Young children experience a deep security in knowing that things will be in the same place, week after week. It also makes it much easier to set up and clear away if everybody knows where different pieces of equipment live!

Indoor and outdoor play

Parent and Child groups cater for a wide range of play needs, from babes in arms to children as old as four or even five years of age. Because play is so important in the life of the young child, the whole issue of appropriate play equipment needs careful consideration. For this reason a separate chapter – Chapter 4 – has been set aside for a full discussion on play and play equipment.

Outdoor space

It is very fortunate if the Parent and Child group has access to safe enclosed outdoor space next to the group venue. It opens up all sorts of possibilities for play and for experiencing the cycle of the year. It is ideal if the outdoor space has natural elements like trees, grass, flowers, places to sit out, a space for a sandpit. But even hard surfaced spaces can be used creatively. In the next chapter, the many different possibilities for using outdoor space will be discussed.

The nature table

The nature table in a Parent and Child group setting is a place where the cycle of the natural year is quietly witnessed and celebrated indoors. The nature display changes through the weeks to reflect the seasonal changes outside. In Waldorf early childhood settings the nature table has a special importance, demonstrating in a very clear way an underlying ethos of honouring and caring for the natural world. Even in the most unpromising of environments, it is a little shrine offering beauty and peace, and both adults and children are nourished by its changing beauty. Young children experience nature's beauty and rhythms unconsciously. By bringing nature indoors, they experience how we as adults value the natural world. Children love the security of the rhythmical progression of the year, enjoying the predictability of each change, savouring the

Nature table, winter scene

return and repetition of each season in each New Year. The nature table provides a focus for all of these feelings and experiences.

Once adults have experienced the nature table in a Parent and Child setting, they are often inspired to create their own, back in the family home. It can become a 'beautiful necessity',[4] much like the altars and shrines which, for millennia, home-makers have created for quiet contemplation, remembrance, and celebration. It is often only when we have young children that our lives slow down enough to notice the particular qualities of each month. Marking seasonal changes in the form of a nature display can become an inner meditative journey through the year; and we may discover, perhaps for the first time, the year's many moods, especially when combined with seasonal festivals.

Nature table in a Community Hall, temporary setting

Creating a nature table can be altogether a delightful endeavour, and it is often the place where the imaginative and creative skills in the group are expressed to their fullest. In the Parent and Child group, however, the display needs to be kept simple if it is to be in reach of the smaller children.

In the remainder of this section I set out some ideas for creating your own nature table.

• Use a table, shelf, sideboard, or even an upturned round of wood for the surface for the nature table. It is nice if it has a central position in the room, but not too near doors or thorough-ways where objects can get knocked over. It is best placed beside a wall. Many groups use the nature table as a focal point for seasonal songs, stories, and festivals.

Nature table, early spring

- Use coloured cloths to drape the surface to be used for the nature table and the wall behind, to reflect the moods of the seasons.

Spring – pastel colours such as pale greens and yellows, pinks, and violets

Summer – bright colours such as golden yellow, turquoise blue, grass green, purples, or reds

Autumn – warm colours such as reds, oranges, browns, and yellows

Winter – cool colours such as pale blue and green, white, and brown

Some Waldorf Parent and Child groups use Goethe's colour cycle. Lynne Oldfield describes how she worked with this colour cycle in her Stroud Kindergarten nature table:[5]

Autumn to Advent: Lilac, deepening to purple arriving at a 'mood of blues' for Advent

Early spring to Easter: Green, turning to yellow-green and finally a 'song of yellow'

Early summer to Midsummer: Peach/pale orange, burst of red at St John's

These seasonal colours can also be used consciously when decorating the meal table and in preparations for seasonal festivals.

The coloured drapes can be used as accents on a plain coloured under-cloth. Muslin cloths are particularly suitable for using as drapes as they are cheap and lightweight, and can be dyed easily and cheaply, and to any colour. A special box can be used to store the cloths so that they can be used year after year.

- *Use a vase or pot as a focal point* and fill with bulbs, branches and flowers as the weeks and months outside dictate:
  * Spring – leaf buds, pussy willow, catkins, snowdrops, crocuses, daffodils
  * Summer – blossoms, herbaceous and annual flowers
  * Autumn – sunflowers, berried branches, branches with coloured leaves
  * Winter – bare branches, evergreen branches, holly, Christmas roses

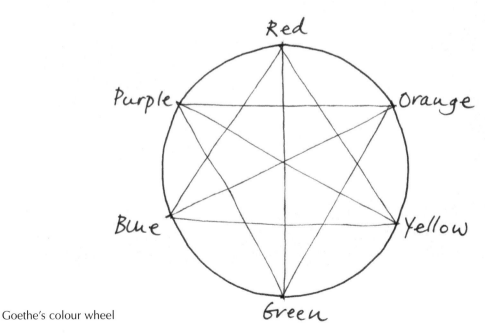

Goethe's colour wheel

Natural objects

- *Display natural objects* which reflect the mood and bounty of the season if the table is out of the reach of small children, e.g.
  * Spring – old bird's nests,
  * Summer – shells, beach rocks
  * Autumn – conkers, acorns, pumpkins, autumn leaves, seed pods
  * Winter – pine cones, stones, crystals

Children and adults can be encouraged to add their own found treasures to the display.

- *Make animals out of felt, wool, and natural objects.* An interestingly shaped branch or root with nooks and corners can provide little homes for felt hedgehogs, mice, robins, spiders, snails, and other wild creatures. There are several books that are good for ideas, and these are listed at the end of the chapter.

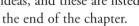

Felt animals

Gnomes and fairies

- *Make a family of simple hand puppets* – Mum, dad and children, who can be used in the song and story time. The nature display can be the stage for their adventures. This idea will be discussed in Chapter 8 on Circle Time.

- *Make and display 'elemental' creatures* such as fairies and gnomes whose homes are in the natural world. Finding these little beings hidden amongst the flowers and natural objects on the nature table can bring such joy and wonder to children and adults alike. Books with ideas for making them are listed at the end of this chapter.

- *Display postcards, poems, or home-produced paintings* that reflect the time of the year.

- *Make a seasonal picture to hang behind the nature table* – this can be made in felt, wool, or painted, for example.

In some Waldorf Parent and Child groups the nature table is low enough for children to be able to see the display clearly; in others, the surface is safely out of the reach of little hands.

Brenda Watson in Stroud, UK uses a half log with an intricately formed branch on top. Veils for the different seasons are draped behind, and a vase of seasonal flowers stands in front. At story time the display is used as the setting. A puppet family 'live' in a log at the back of the display and little animals inhabit the holes and crevices of the tree branch. After each story, about the family and the various animals, the children in the group are welcome to play with the puppets.

The Sistine Madonna and Child

Some Waldorf Parent and Child groups, like most Waldorf Kindergartens, have a copy of the Sistine Madonna and Child by Raphael (1483-1520) hanging in the room. Why is this? The Madonna and Child in the painting seem to stand at the threshold of the physical and spiritual worlds, and they both look steadily and with great peace towards the viewer. Letitia Costain, Steiner Parent and Child national representative in the UK, explains in an article on the Sistine Madonna:[6] 'The painting of the Madonna with the child is the symbol of the eternal spirituality in people which comes certainly to the earth from beyond.' The whole painting represents the divine feminine, even the two figures looking up at the Madonna and child. They are representations of Sixtus (257-258), a Pope who renounced his position for the sake of peace, and St Barbara (235-313), who, although renowned for her beauty, spent her life caring for the poor and ailing: 'Power transformed into peace and beauty transformed into spiritual love... they are both inspired by the eternal feminine archetype that had borne the child. [It is] an archetype that can appeal strongly to men and women of any religious persuasion.'[7]

Rudolf Steiner suggested that this painting, like the other Madonnas in a series painted by Raphael, have a very real healing presence. He suggested that the painting works in a similar way to a mantra or verse, and helps to awaken and strengthen spiritual faculties. The original painting, which is eight or nine feet (nearly three metres) high, is housed in a gallery in Dresden, Germany.

In her notes on Australian Steiner playgroups,[8] *Kim Billington* suggests that, unfortunately, the picture can sometimes be misinterpreted as some kind of sectarian religious statement. She suggests that in these circumstances the picture can be brought out on a child's birthday or during Advent without adults feeling uncomfortable.

The craft and meal table

Craft activities and the shared meal are both important aspects of Parent and Child groups. The practical aspects of both these activities will be discussed in the next chapter. Here, it is enough to say why it is important that they take place around a single table, large enough to seat the whole group.

Sistine Madonna

A craft activity period serves many functions. It brings adults together in an unselfconscious way, learning and enjoying making things, and creating a sociable atmosphere – a space where adults and children can enjoy time together. The meal time is likewise a time when the warm community of the group can be experienced.

The nourishment that these two activities bring to parents and children is not possible if there are scattered tables, or if there is only room for the children, and not the adults, around the table. It is ideal if the table (or several joined tables) are child-sized, with child-sized chairs. These can often be bought quite cheaply from sales of old school stock. However, young children very successfully negotiate large tables with the help of cushions or parents' laps.

The Parent and Child group as an information resource centre

The Parent and Child group has an important function as an information resource for parents and carers. Box 17 sets out some ideas.

Box 17: Group 'information resource' possibilities

- A small library with a selection of parenting and craft books and parenting magazines (Book suggestions are given at the end of Chapter 10 on Supporting Parents.)
- Directory of local businesses offering useful products and services for young families, e.g. organic foods, natural clothing and toys, health practitioner listings, child-friendly cafes, etc. that are recommended by members of the group
- Directory of useful mail order companies and web sites
- Information on useful local council services for families - social services, welfare rights
- Notice board for local places and events of interest
- Baby-sitting circle information
- Parenting classes and support group information

It is ideal if there can be a table or surface somewhere in the room which is designated as 'the information place'. It may be that between sessions all this information will need to be put away somewhere safe in a box. It is the sort of task that one parent can take charge of.

Health, safety and ecological soundness

There are some practical safety considerations which need to be taken into account, whether the Parent and Child group meets in a hired hall or in someone's home. Because groups are voluntary, they do not need to be checked by Social Services, so it is especially important that Parent and Child group organizers are aware of possible dangers. It is advisable to contact your local Health and Safety officer and also the local Fire Station inspector, and arrange for them to look over any new premises with you. Here (Box 18) is a basic checklist of safety 'musts'.

Box 18: Essential safety requirements

- Easy access to fire exits
- Access to fire extinguishers and fire blanket
- Child locks on kitchen and toilet cupboards
- Lockable storage cupboards
- Clean, smooth floors and surfaces
- No sharp corners on tables and furniture at child height
- Watch out for and remove broken toys, anything with sharp edge
- No toys or toy materials which could be choked on. When offering natural objects for play, make sure they are larger than 1 inch (2.5 cm) in diameter. Watch out for small beads etc. on cushion covers, dolls, and other materials
- Windows that can be opened but also properly shut and locked
- Smoke alarm
- Safety plugs on unused sockets
- Protection around open heat sources, e.g. fires, bar heaters, etc.
- Stair gates where access is to be restricted or prevented
- Electrical leads to kettles and other equipment out of sight and reach
- First Aid Box
- Recycling system for glass, paper, plastics, and food waste
- Ecologically sound cleaning materials

The group should have its own First Aid kit, available from chemists/pharmacies, or made up with the necessary basics like antiseptic wipes, antiseptic cream, plasters, cotton buds, eye wash, cotton wool, pincers for splinters, scissors, various sizes of dressing, and tape. A simple illustrated booklet on First Aid needs to be with the First Aid kit at all times.

Waldorf Parent and Child groups tend also to include some of the common homoeopathic remedies for the treatment of everyday bumps and bruises, tummy aches, and other simple ailments. There is also usually a bottle of the Bach Rescue Remedy or similar, which is invaluable for those moments of shock when a young body collides with something solid.

As a matter of principle, Parent and Child groups need to choose environmentally safe cleaning materials. Ecologically sound soaps, washing up liquids, floor cleaners, cream cleaners, and toilet cleaner can be bought from whole food shops and also many supermarkets.

It is likewise worth considering ecological paints for walls and woodwork, and resin or oil-based finishes for wood equipment and furniture. Materials such as plaster or wood left bare have their own beauty. Natural products can still be quite a lot more expensive than the synthetic high street versions, although grant funding and inspired fund-raising can help to make these healthier choices possible.

Finally, consider recycling. Have separate boxes or bins for plastic, paper, and glass and, if possible, a compost heap somewhere close outside for raw food waste. A parent can take charge of this area. There can even be a rota for taking waste home for recycling. Try and encourage the use of washable nappies rather than disposables. In many areas there are nappy-washing services that will collect dirty and deliver clean nappies to your door step.

Main points again

- Think about the deeper purposes of the Parent and Child group and how the physical setting can support them.

- Wherever possible, use objects of quality and beauty.

- When choosing a venue consider:

  * How the space can be divided up and made safe
  * 'Less is more' – in terms of decoration and equipment
  * Making the space homely
  * Introducing natural elements
  * Making rather than buying
  * Avoiding 'accumulation congestion'
  * How 'tender loving care' can improve an environment

- The quiet significance of a nature table

- The craft and meal table – a large single table creates community

- The Parent and Child group as an information resource

- The nuts and bolts of health and safety

- Homeopathic remedies for your First Aid kit.

- Recycling

- Natural and healthy choices in cleaning materials, paints, and varnishes

Useful books

General reference books on creating healing environments

Christopher Day, *Places of the Soul: Architecture and Environmental Design as a Healing Art*, Aquarian Press, place, Northamptonshire, 1990

Christopher Alexander, *The Timeless Way of Building*, Oxford University Press, Oxford, 1979

Christopher Alexander, *A Pattern Language*, Oxford University Press, Oxford, 1977

Daniel D. Chiras, *The Healthy House: A Complete Guide to Healthy, Energy Efficient, Environmental Homes*, Chelsea Green Publishers, Vt., 2000

Ideas for nature tables

Mv Leeuwen and J Moeskops, *The Nature Corner: Celebrating the Year's Cycle with a Seasonal Tableau*, Floris Books, Edinburgh, 1990

Thomas and Petra Berger, *The Gnome Craft Book*, Floris Books, Edinburgh, 1990

Thomas and Petra Berger, *Feltcraft: Making Dolls, Gifts and Toys*, Floris Books, Edinburgh, 1994

Carol Petrash, *Earthwise: Environmental Crafts and Activities for Young Children*, Floris Books, Edinburgh, 1992

Dagmar Schmidt and Freya Jaffke, *Magic Wool: Creative Activities with Natural Sheep's Wool*, Floris Books, Edinburgh, 1993

Christel Dhom, *Making Magical Fairy-Tale Puppets*, Rudolf Steiner College Press, Calif., 2001

Angelika Wolk Gerche, *Making Fairy-tale Wool Animals*, Rudolf Steiner College Press, Calif, 2000

Homoeopathic medicine

Miranda Castro's Homeopathic Guides – Mother and Baby, Pan Books, London, 1996

Miranda Castro, *The Complete Homeopathy Handbook*, Saint Martin's Press, New York, 1991

Weleda homeopathic preparations: Heanor Road, Ilkeston, Derbyshire, UK; Tel.: 0115 944 8200; www.weleda.co.uk

Homeopathic First Aid Kits – Helios pharmacy, 89-97 Camden Road, Tunbridge Wells, Kent, UK; Tel.: 01892 537254; www.helios.co.uk

Parenting Magazines

Juno – A Natural Approach to Family Life, The Quarry House, Woodshill Lane, Ashurst Wood, West Sussex RH19 3RF, UK; Tel.: 01444 891 460

The Mother magazine, www.themothermagazine.co.uk The Cottage, Glassonby, Penrith, Cumbria CA10 1DU, UK; tel. +44 (0) 1768 897 121

Mothering Magazine – The Natural Family Living Magazine, P.O. Box 1690, Santa Fe, NM 87504, USA (Physical Address: 1611-A Paseo de Peralta, Santa Fe, NM 87501, USA); tel. 1-800-984-8116, www.mothering.com

Practical Parenting, IPC Publishing.

Useful organisations

Pre-school Learning Alliance

69 Kings Cross Road, London WC1X 9LL, UK; Tel.: 0207 833 0991 www.pre-school.org.uk
Publications include:
'Running a Parent and Toddler pre-school'
'Parent and Toddler groups – self assessment for good practice'

Scottish Pre-school Play Association

45 Finnieston Street, Glasgow G3 8JU, UK; tel. 0141 221 4148, www.sppa.org.uk
Publications include:
'Running a Toddler group – Code of Practice'
'Learning through play for the under threes in Parent and Toddler groups'

CHAPTER 4

Providing the essential play needs of the young child

'Although play is a steady part of healthy children's lives, it is not easy to define what play is. I prefer to think of it as a bubbling spring of health and creativity within each child – and, for that matter, within every human being.'

Joan Almon[1]

'Research and experience show strong relationships between a child's capacity to play and his or her overall development – physical, social, emotional and intellectual. There is reason to be deeply concerned that as play disappears from childhood children will suffer in all these areas. In many countries, play is diminishing and the first indications of such suffering are becoming apparent. Yet nation after nation is rushing towards removing play from young children's lives in the misguided belief that three to six-year-olds are ripe and ready for direct instruction in early literacy and other academic subjects. For the sake of the children, and for the sake of the society they are part of, this direction needs to be reversed now and play needs to be restored as a healthy essential of childhood.'

Joan Almon[2]

FOR PARENTS...

Part 4: Essential play needs of the young child

Why is creative play important, and how can we encourage it?

Research shows that there are strong relationships between a child's capacity for imaginative play and his or her overall development. A truly healthy child is able to play freely and creatively without the distraction of adult assistance or direction. A child who can play will grow into a creative adult.

The 'golden years' of imaginative play are arguably between around 3 and 6-7 years of age. Simply made and open-ended toys give far more scope for creative play than perfectly representative ones. Basic objects like smoothed timber lengths, pinecones, and blankets can be creatively transformed into many different play scenarios. A 'perfect' plastic piece of pizza is more difficult! Objects from nature, wooden toys, and hand-made dolls have a special quality that plastic toys don't have.

The foundations for creative play are laid in the earliest months and years of life.

The very young child and play

Before the age of 3, the very young child does not play imaginatively, as this requires the development of memory. Memory, and therefore the capacity for creative imagination and image-linking, arises as a consequence of the learning of language, and this normally happens in the second to third year.

However, up to the age of 3 the child naturally imitates everything in her environment. (Even a very young baby uses imitation creatively in dialogue with its carer.) This is the way the young child learns to use her body, relate to others, and develop language; and this is the foundation for later imaginative play. What the child needs at this stage is plenty of opportunities to explore imitation, through watching good examples of basic everyday relationships,

activities, and the 'jobs of life', and a basic, well chosen selection of the universal everyday objects and 'props' of human life, so they can then copy and re-enact what is experienced. What is imitated will gradually transform itself into acted-out imaginative play scenarios. These will be very noticeable by the time the child is 3 years old.

Adults encourage strong imitation by cheerfully carrying out the simple everyday and creative tasks of life around their young child. Television, videos, and computer games are poor and dangerous substitutes. Technologically clever toys and 'early learning' games miss the mark!

How Steiner Parent and Child group settings encourage healthy play

These are the sorts of toys and equipment you will find in a Steiner Parent and Child group setting:

- For the baby and infant: simple everyday objects with different textures and sounds, e.g. rattles, bowls, spoons, boxes, soft balls, preferably made from natural materials. Safe natural objects large enough not to be choked on – e.g. gourds, walnuts in their shells, washed stones.
- Crawlers and toddlers – in addition to the above... simple, sturdy equipment that can be climbed on/in and pushed; safe stepping and sliding structures; push and pull toys. Wooden toys on wheels, wooden people and familiar farm animals. Basic everyday objects.
- Older toddlers – in addition to the above: a home corner with a basic range of everyday objects; soft, simply formed dolls with beds and clothes; veils and blankets and sturdy frames for creating dens; ropes of various thicknesses; a small selection of dressing-up clothes. Baskets of pinecones, wool scraps, and other natural objects.

In Waldorf Parent and Child groups, the importance given to play, and to appropriate toys and play equipment, is based on these main considerations:

- the importance of free movement
- an understanding of the importance of play
- the perspective on child development outlined in Chapter 2

Free movement and the RIE approach

As discussed in Chapter 2, there is a growing movement to encourage parents to allow the free unhindered development of body movement in the young child. Resources for Infant Educarers (RIE), founded by Magda Gerber, is one of the organisations at the forefront of this essential work. Parents with infants are gently instructed in small groups on how to observe their children so that they better understand what they need, to watch and wait before intervening. More than this, however, parents are shown how to talk to their infants gently and respectfully so as to gain their co-operation, and they are shown how to lovingly take care of their infant's basic needs – like feeding, and changing nappies. The Parent and Child groups inspired by this movement are usually openminded parents with children up to the age of 2 years of age. Magda Gerber states that the confidence that the young infants gain through this approach 'leads to independence, in the best sense of the word – helping children become active, self-sufficient, co-operative individuals and members of the family and later of society'.[3]

On the continent, in Germany for example, and in the USA and Canada, the RIE methods have been very successfully fused with the Waldorf approach in Parent and Child groups.

Imaginative play is vital

Many excellent books explore the vital importance of encouraging free and imaginative play in the early years, and they are listed at the end of this chapter. What is attempted here is a brief explanation of why, in Waldorf and other holistic early childhood settings, self-directed and unstructured play is given such a central place. Free and imaginative play is seen as being crucial to children's healthy physical, emotional, and social development.

> 'The way we allow and encourage children to play is of spiritual concern. The health of the body; the life processes; mental, emotional, social and moral competence; and conscience and the innermost sense of self – are all developed through play.'
> *Michael Rose and Martyn Rawson*[4]

Susan Isaacs,[5] a distinguished and pioneering child psychologist in the 1930s, spoke of imaginative play as the starting point not only of cognitive development but also all creative intention, whether it manifests in the work of an artist, poet, or novelist. She also stated that play helps the child to understand the world and to regulate her own responses to life experiences.

Donald Winnicott[6] coined a term, 'transitional space', to describe the mythological consciousness or dream world that a young child needs to inhabit for play to occur, and the necessity that this space should not be impinged upon by adult expectations and agendas. In an important book titled *The Genius of Play*,[7] to these aforementioned benefits of play Sally Jenkinson adds, first, aspects of self-healing and, second, the development of a rich feeling life in authentic play. In a recent article in *Juno*[8] parenting magazine, Jenkinson also makes a plea for parents to resist the 'relentless encroachment of the media into early childhood... to let children loose on the world; to let them live their lives directly, so that they can make their own worlds, real and imaginary, and dream their own dreams'.

There is more and more evidence which points to the link between a child's mental health and the ability to play. 'When play drops out something is wrong', Marc Bekoff of University of Colorado is quoted as saying in Joan Almon's article[9] on the vital role of play in early childhood education.

> 'When young children are ill they often stop playing for a few days. As soon as they are better, their parents notice the spark of play shining in their eyes again. In general, when children are able to play creatively, they blossom and flourish. If they stop playing over an extended period of time, they can suffer a decline and even become depressed or show signs of other illnesses.'
>
> *Joan Almon*[10]

The foundations

The foundations of imaginative play are laid in the first three years through the young child's impulse to explore and imitate. As soon as crawling begins, everything needs to be investigated, tasted, emptied, watched, and copied. Having gained mastery over the physical body so that standing and walking are possible, the young child begins to take an instinctive interest in everyday activities and tasks. Everything is absorbed; the process of learning through imitation and simple repetition is now in full swing. Everything is done with the sense of 'me too'.

The quality of later imaginative play which begins to develop around the age of three is dependant on the richness of this gentle introduction to everyday life. Given space, security, and freedom, scenarios from everyday life will then be endlessly played out and

transformed. What the child needs is a richness of adult activity to imitate and materials that are open ended so that they can easily be adapted for each new impulse.

Early creative play

Creative play can be seen as a 'building up' and 'pulling down' or transforming of materials and scenarios – play as a process of continuous flow from one form to another, the process being much more important than the end-product. It is vital too that at the end of playtime, everything is tidied away so that new impulses can arise afresh. This is much easier if the play materials are 'raw ingredients', rather than finished forms. The processes and cycles of play reflect the inner creative transforming which is building up the physical body of the young child. Free unhindered play helps form a strong physical body – the two are inseparable.

Freedom to explore, imitate, and play in an imaginative way is a necessity in these early years. Our abilities to think, feel, and act creatively and with originality as adults are totally dependant on these imaginative forces unfolding in their natural time in childhood. Perhaps, more than at any time in history, we will need individuals who have vision and imagination. Without a deeper understanding of the importance of play we may be damaging our young children's imaginative gifts, causing them to 'run dry' and become barren, in the process adversely affecting their deep potential to become creative and productive adults.

Freya Jaffke, a very experienced Waldorf Kindergarten teacher, has written two books which explain very beautifully and practically the play and developmental needs of the young child and how we can best provide for them. These books – *Work and Play in Early Childhood* and *Toymaking with Children* – need to be included in any basic Parent and Child group resource list.

The dilemma of too much structure

If the young child is forced into structured activities and ways of being by the adults around her, too early, this natural unfolding cannot take place.

'The child… unites effort, earnestness and eagerness with activity, which of course also includes enthusiasm, joy and delight, and each new step of development is achieved through imitation. I have noticed that children who have not been allowed to learn through imitation but have been brought up through constant appeals to reason and commands to make them behave in a certain way, even in their fourth year, tend to be pale, show little initiative, and have difficulties making contact with playmates.'

Freya Jaffke[11]

TV and computers

A *Times* newspaper article entitled 'It's no fun being a toddler any more'[12] bleakly relates how parental obsession with early learning goals and a reliance on TV and computer games for entertainment and child-minding are affecting young children's ability to develop healthy imaginative play. Quoting a survey by *Mother and Baby* magazine where 2,000 parents of children between 12 months and 3 years were interviewed, the article states that 80 per cent of parents are teaching their toddler to read and write, and 60 per cent are teaching them Information Technology skills before their third birthday! Karen Pasquali Jones, editor of *Mother and Baby* magazine, was quoted as saying that the survey showed that many toddlers were never given the chance to get bored or to explore their own imagination. She felt that the behaviour problems cited were linked to the fact that toddlers free time

'is spent being bombarded with TV, videos, computers and educational books… As a result 21st-century toddlers are suffering from over-stimulation and their volatile behaviour is harder to handle than ever. They are failing to learn the art of inventive imaginative play which is what toddler-hood should ultimately be about.'

Entertaining toddlers

Another issue raised in the *Mother and Baby* magazine survey was the number of 'stimulating' paid-for activities to which parents take their toddlers in a typical week. The average is four. Parent and Child groups would of course be included as one of these types of activity. There is a tendency for parents and carers to think that the more variety they can provide for their youngster, the better for their development. From a deeper perspective and with an understanding of a child's natural unfolding, it becomes clear that it is not quantity of stimulation which is important but the quality. It would be better for a young child's healthy development if the same Parent and Child group were visited every day, rather than subjecting her to change each day. The young child thrives on the security of familiarity and repetition. This is a thorny subject when more and more paid activities are being made available to the under 3's.

Informal play circles

Parent and Child groups can be a place where healthy play can be learnt and experienced by children and their parents. Ideas can be taken back into the home. Informal 'play circles' formed by parents do provide young children with the opportunity to play in a similar way to that provided in the Parent and Child group. The necessity to pay for out-of-home entertainment and early learning can be substantially reduced with imagination, will power, and the company of like-minded families.

Here are some suggestions for play equipment and materials which can support healthy child development, imitation, and play, bearing in mind that a useful motto is 'quality rather than quantity' in all respects!

Play and toys – the first year

A young baby does not need toys in the first few months, despite what we see in the shops, as physically she has enough to do with interacting with her carer and discovering her own body. At a Parent and Child group she will be happiest on the lap of her carer or tucked up in her pram. For older babies, as co-ordination progresses they begin to grasp and explore objects in their surroundings. Tirelessly, actions are repeated until movements are mastered. Laying a baby on her back in a safe place allows her the freedom to explore, move, and exercise her limbs. Gradually she is able to turn her head, then roll over, and finally crawl. Leaving our children to move freely, without interference, we see that they are very competent problem-solvers! As the baby gets used to being put on her back, she can be left to play on her own for short periods of time. This frees mum, as well as allowing the slow process of separation.

Suitable toys for four months and older

The Parent and Child group can provide:

* Simple wooden rattles with bells and things that move
* Soft wool balls of various sizes
* Everyday objects with different textures – e.g. spoons, cups, bowls
* Safe natural objects – that can't be taken into the mouth and choked on, e.g. walnuts, washed stones, gourds, larger shells

These can be kept in a special basket which is brought out when there are small babies in the group. It is nice if a separate area can be designated for parents with babies, away from older and more boisterous children.

Crawlers and climbers

As babies get older, crawling and climbing will take them enormous distances very quickly, and the Parent and Child group setting needs to be laid out in such a way that such investigation is possible with safety. A very mixed group with a large age range of children is going to have more difficulty accommodating these intrepid explorers

Baby toys

than a group dedicated to the under 1's. This is worth bearing in mind if your group is large.

As the baby learns to crawl, sit up, and climb up into the vertical, the range of toys can expand to include those listed in Box 19.

Box 19: Simple baby toys

- Boxes with lids, bowls, and baskets which can be emptied and filled
- Simple everyday objects, e.g. spoon, cup, bowl, pots and pans
- Wooden building blocks of various shapes and sizes, including rounds of sawn branches sanded and waxed
- Simple musical instruments
- Wooden toys with wheels
- Soft balls and other objects that can be safely rolled
- Cushions to crawl through and over
- Strategically placed sturdy chairs and other furniture to hold on to under an adult's watchful eye
- Wooden animals and people

'I'd rather see a busy child actively manipulating a simple toy in a variety of creative ways to see how it works than see a passive child playing with a busy toy that encourages her passivity. A simple toy that allows the child to discover its many possibilities is a good choice – for example, a box that can be opened and shut or a ball that rolls and bounces.'

Magda Gerber[13]

Waldorf Parent and Child group settings do not have baby walkers or baby bouncers as these hinder free movement and interrupt a child's natural progressive development toward walking.

Play, toys, and the toddler years (1-3 years)

It may take 4-6 months from the time a child starts climbing to when he takes his first steps. Once walking is mastered, the young child needs to experience, and thoroughly enjoys, free movement. He slowly becomes agile in body through climbing, pushing, and pulling. The child can play for months with the same movement as he slowly masters it. This is the main way in which the young child fills his first one to two years. It is best if we allow as much unhindered and uninterrupted exploration time as possible.

These needs are catered for in traditional Parent and Toddler groups, where there is often a wide range of larger toys which can be pushed and pulled, climbed into, balanced on, rocked in, etc. These are the push carts and dolls prams; sit in cars and trains, the slides, tunnels, and climbing frames.

The custom of putting all these toys in the middle of a room and assigning safe seats around the edge for parents and smaller children is understandable. There are disadvantages, however. Having a lot of larger moving toys can create a noisy chaotic situation which can be very over-stimulating for young children. There can be a lot of squabbling and upset around who gets what toy, and this can be very difficult for these very young children who genuinely do not understand the 'politics' of sharing! The larger toys just tend to take over the available space. Is there an alternative?

Larger toys in Waldorf settings

In some Waldorf Parent and Child groups, larger toys such as wheeled trains, push carts, and structures with slides are assigned to an outside space where there is more room. Some have only a few well chosen larger pushing toys inside, and many groups will have none at all. It can be a question of space, not only in the session room but also in the available storage facilities.

There are other reasons, too. Public parks and play spaces are often amply equipped with age-appropriate climbing equipment, so there are many opportunities for young children to explore these possibilities. Likewise, most young children will have everyday access to push and pull toys of various kinds. What young children often don't have access to is places where quieter play can be experienced. Without these larger toys in Parent and Child group settings, the children tend to settle down to exploring possibilities for imitative play, and the whole atmosphere tends to be quieter and more harmonious. What are the alternative toy choices for children of this age?

Suitable toys and equipment

There are simple pieces of equipment which can, with the help of attentive adults, provide movement and balance practice for toddlers. Along with the ones listed earlier, the same toys can constitute the raw materials for more creative play as the child gets older. Box 20 sets out some ideas.

Box 20: Appropriate larger equipment for toddlers

- Rounds of logs of various heights and diameters which can be used for stepping and balancing
- Some open-ended boxes which can be used for climbing in and out of, filling up and emptying, pushing around
- Safe step structures used in conjunction with the boxes to make simple slides
- Sturdy play frames (see Freya Jaffke's *Toymaking with Children*), which can be draped with light fabric such as muslin to make houses, tunnels, shops, and dens of all shapes and sizes
- Open carts which can be filled and pushed around
- Toys on wheels with ropes for pulling

Real play for the toddler, as we have said, is about exploration of everyday objects, and the copying and reproducing of everyday activities. The Parent and Child group can be a place where some basic domestic activities are

Toddler toys

Simple everyday objects

experienced by the children, through the group naturally being involved in everyday tasks ('The Living Arts', as described in the final chapter) – such as in the baking and craft activities, the routine shared tasks of tidying away, laying the table for the break time, washing up, the making and mending of toys, and preparing for the various festivals.

Each child will also bring to the Parent and Child group the world she knows. For example, a boy aged 2 is moving large logs from one end of the room to the other. It transpires that he avidly watches his Dad chop wood for the fire and brings the logs into the house! A 2-year-old Chinese girl stacks the simple cooking equipment in the 'home' corner in a way which perfectly replays the steaming of rice in her home.

Everyday objects

There are some simple universally used everyday objects such as a ball, bowl, box, cup, spoons, and brush that are very appropriate for young children from this age, as are objects from nature. In a book titled *The Young Child*,[14] Daniel Udo do Haes talks about the young child's ability to explore and enjoy everyday objects in a very special way because their consciousness is still very connected to the spiritual and archetypal worlds. She explains that young children can experience the soul qualities of objects – the fundamental 'bowlness' of a bowl, for example. The young child experiences a genuine and deep wonder in exploring the most fundamental of our everyday objects. We can give space for this exploration and even draw closer to this special realm in ourselves through our children.

The doll

The doll has a special significance in early childhood play. It is the image of the human being, and therefore helps the young child to develop her own self image. Caring for a doll comes naturally to most young children who have experienced loving warmth and care themselves. There are the so-called 'Waldorf' dolls, made from soft material with simple facial features and limbs. These are favoured in Waldorf early childhood settings because they allow the child to use his imagination to fill in the detail. The younger the child, the less detail the doll needs to have. Some groups have a simple knotted doll made out of a soft cloth, as our grandparents probably knew, for the very young child. Parent and Child groups often have a collection of 'baby dolls' – simple dolls with a clothing body. Older children enjoy a larger, more fully formed doll that can be dressed.

Waldorf dolls

'Waldorf' dolls can be bought but they can also be made very easily. Many Waldorf Parent and Child groups have dolls made by parents in the group. These dolls have a very special place in everyone's hearts.

Houses and dens

Building houses and dens is a universal play theme in childhood – creating secret places away from adult intervention. The building of a little house in some way replicates, for the child, the experience of building the body as house for the child's spirit. Although this sort of constructive play does not really begin to develop until three years of age, a Parent and Child group can provide little places for children to explore. Sturdy play frames draped with muslin lengths and tepee-shaped structures, where the young child can play 'peek- a-boo', are greatly enjoyed.

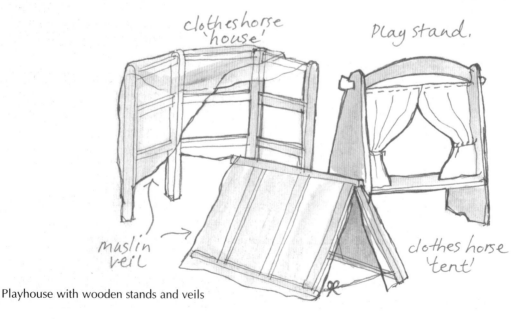

Playhouse with wooden stands and veils

Here, in addition to the lists above, are some ideas for simple materials and toys which can be made available for toddlers in a Parent and Child group.

Box 21: Other toddlers' materials and toys

- A simple wooden home corner house with stove
- A broom, iron, and ironing board
- Soft dolls with a bed and pram
- Wooden or knitted farm animals and people that are not too formed
- Rocking horse
- Ropes of various thickness and length and pegs
- A selection of muslin veils and blankets
- Baskets with a handle
- Simple hobby-horses
- Baskets with shells, pine cones, stones, wool scraps, and other natural objects

---

Play, toys, and the third to fifth year

At around three years of age the child moves more deeply into imaginative play. Most characteristic of this age is the ability to create many different scenarios with everyday objects. Play becomes a continuous stream of enactments of daily life, using simple objects as props. As the child becomes older, play is more and more the outward manifestation of the child's creative imagination. These will include scenarios such as cooking, shopping, changing baby's nappies, going on a train ride, having a picnic, and so on.

The beginnings of imaginative play

There are many commercial toys on the market which perfectly replicate everyday objects and equipment for imitative play – kitchens complete with plastic pizzas and pizza cutters, and perfect replications of carpet cleaners. With these toys it is harder for a child to transform their function

Boys playing

to serve their own purposes and scenarios in play. Perfect objects can hinder richness and depth in imaginative play because their purposes are so rigidly defined. It is hard to pretend that a plastic banana is anything else but a banana. An object from nature, like a slightly curved small branch, can be a banana, a spoon, a fishing rod, a sausage… More is left to the imagination. How deep play can arise with the simplest of materials is wonderfully described in the children's book classic *The Little House on the Prairie* by Laura Ingalls Wilder. Freya Jaffke[15] describes a typical play sequence in a healthy 4 year old child:

'A four year old watches her mother preparing a meal. She fetches an empty basket for a pan, covers the bottom with chestnuts and acorns for potatoes and begins to cook. A little while later she collects the acorns and nuts together in a cloth and decorates the parcel with flowers and ribbons. She presents it with great solemnity to her mother because, "It's your birthday." A moment later she has unfolded the cloth and spread it over the top of the basket, which is now a bath tub. She bathes her doll, using an acorn as soap. Then the cloth becomes a towel, the acorn a baby's bottle.'

This kind of natural play is witnessed less and less these days, as young children's surroundings are filled with many finished toys which make this kind of flowing creative play process difficult. It is often up to adults to show, by example, what is possible – the young child will imitate. In her book *Earthwise*, packed with creative ideas for seasonal crafts with children (3 years +), Carol Pretash suggests one way of encouraging creative play by telling stories with natural building materials and simple wooden toys. Here is an example she gives:

'Spread a large cloth – preferably earth or grass coloured – on the floor or build on the carpet if you have one. Show the children a little river (a long blue cloth) its banks lined with stones. The river flows down out of the mountain (a pile of stones) and runs past a forest (a stand of pine cones) and a farm (a house built of wood pieces, surrounded by a stick fence and perhaps some small wooden animals.) The river flows all the way to the beach (white or sandy coloured cloth and shells and the sea (a big blue cloth). Here comes a little girl or boy (small wooden figure) travelling down the river to the sea. Just imagine (the children will!) all the adventures she or he will have along the way.'[16]

Floor scene with wooden blocks and veil

The range of toys listed above is all that's required for this older group of children, as their growing imaginative faculties will be able to use the materials in new and endless ways. However, every Parent and Child group setting is different, and in the end it is important that there is not a prescribed 'acceptable' list! Here are some other toys enjoyed in Parent and Child groups which stimulate imaginative play:

- Dolls house with simple dolls and furniture
- Brio train track and trains
- Selection of wooden vehicles including diggers, trucks, and boats
- Dressing-up clothes for dolls and children

Making toys

Home-made toys have a very special quality. Many Steiner Parent and Child groups have toys that were made by parents at the beginning of a project. The early vision and enthusiasm seems easily to be channelled into creating beautiful play things for the children. Making toys or dolls can be the focus of the craft activity in the Parent and Child group sessions or can be introduced in craft evenings and workdays. There are several books with patterns for simple Waldorf dolls. These are given at the end of the chapter. Lengths and rounds of wood can be used to create all sorts of simple toys for creative play.

Freya Jaffke's *Toymaking with Children* contains a wealth of ideas for creating simple play structures, toys, and puppets for young children. With some practice in whittling, slightly formed people, animals, and simple kitchen utensils – bowls, spoons – can be made. Jaffke has again come to our help with a wonderful little book on the subject called *Gestalten mit Holz für Kinder* – in German, but still worth buying as the illustrations for the instructions are very clear.

Buying toys and play materials

Several British companies sell natural wooden toys and Waldorf dolls, and these are listed at the end of this chapter. Community Playthings makes very beautiful and sturdy furniture and equipment. Their products are definitely worth investing in, if you are able to find grant funding.

Muslin lengths for play cloths are easily and cheaply available from most fabric shops, as is stockinet for the Waldorf dolls.

Outdoor time

A Parent and Child group is very fortunate if it has access to an outdoor space nearby. A period of free play outside can be structured into the group session, or if weather permits the whole session can be conducted outside.

Some groups have access to an inside or outside sandpit – a wonderful place for rich imaginative play.

'Real tablespoons, muffin trays, metal egg cups, saucepans, and trays, together with wooden cut-offs and perhaps a few trowels for digging have proved invaluable over the years. In the summer months the children can have access to a tap and watering cans too. If parents are close by with their drinks or sewing, then supervision is there. The children need to feel a supportive mantle of awareness and care from all the adults rather than an authoritative adult dominance.'
Kim Billington, Victoria, Australia

'Outside in the corridor I have a sandpit; this has a lid and is closed up at "Ricecake time". I ask parents to sit in the corridor when their child is playing with the sand. It is very popular.'
Jane Parsons, Bristol

Sand and water are ideal materials as they can be continuously moved, formed, and transformed. A large sand pit, in which many children can play at the same time, along with a selection of buckets, baskets, spades, shells, stones, sawn branches, etc. will keep young children very busy and happy. Wooden tree stumps set in the sand pit can be tables, ovens, and landscapes. Steiner early childhood settings sometimes have what are called 'Flow form' water fountain structures which are safe and endlessly fascinating for young children. It is worth exploring this possibility (although expensive) if you have a permanent, well-used venue for young children.

There are many alternatives to filling the outside space with trikes and push carts – see Box 22.

Sandplay

> ## Box 22: Outdoor ideas for the Parent and Child group
>
> - Flower beds or containers where children can help plant and water plants, or just dig
> - Secret areas inside and through bushes
> - Child-size log seats and tables
> - Willow structures
> - Areas of grass for play, picnics, and festivals
> - Simple movable and fixed balancing structures
> - Slide
> - Small slopes that can be climbed up and down
> - Pull carts big enough for several children to sit in
> - Fruit bushes and trees
> - Tree trunks and limbs with branches for clambering over
> - Seats and benches for parents
> - A compost heap
> - Child-size brooms, wheelbarrows, and watering cans, forks and spades
> - Bird table

There are also other options worth considering if the venue does not have an outside space. For example, in Lancaster, UK the lack of a garden next to a Kindergarten venue was solved by renting a nearby allotment. Other groups may be able to use a family garden or public park. In Norwich, the group has access to a little sheltered public garden near to the Community Centre where the Parent and Child group is held.

All is not lost if there is no outside space available. Some Parent and Child groups regularly use some of the session time for a little walk. It is ideal if the walk can pass by natural features such as a pond or stream, hedges or trees. Even in very built-up urban areas there is often a short walk that can pass by back gardens, allotments, or neglected wild spots. The same walk can be done each week, as the children will enjoy visiting and recognizing the same features

again and again, and also seeing what each new season brings. Natural objects – a leaf, a snail, a shell, or acorns – can be collected in little baskets and brought back to the group room to display on the nature table or to be used in craft activities. Parents often enjoy the walk as a time to share questions and problems. The walk can be incorporated with a picnic or swim in the river, for example, as part of a festival or special occasion. At Nokken, a Waldorf family day care centre in Copenhagen, Denmark, the children as young as one year old go out for a walk each day. How strong, well co-ordinated, and agile these little children are!

Play is work for children; adults do their own work

Once a child is settled in play it is best for the adult to withdraw and do 'grown-up' work nearby. Our enjoyment and focus on our work 'carries' the child in a safe mantle, helping them to concentrate on their own work – which is play. In many groups, an adult activity is provided during the play time. *Bonnie Romanow* writes: 'The idea is that if the parents are focused in a meaningful work activity, then the children focus on a meaningful work activity – which for the child is PLAY.'[17]

The question of adult activity during the Parent and Child group session will be discussed at length in the next chapter.

Brenda Watson at Wynstones School, near Gloucester, enjoys having a wide range of ages of children in her group. She says it works like a Steiner Kindergarten in that the older children who are well able to play imaginatively provide a 'holding' for the younger children, who in turn watch and explore. Brenda divides her time between the adult activity and facilitating the play. For the little ones she will set up little play structures out of the various pieces of basic equipment – sometimes a boat or house, other times a fire engine…

Tidying away after play

Freya Jaffke describes playing and tidying up as belonging to each other, like breathing in and out, sleeping and walking. The way the tidying up is done is important, and it needs to be carried out carefully, without rushing. Each toy and natural object has its place in baskets and on shelves. There is a delightful satisfaction in the regaining of order after the freedom of play. In the Parent and Child group, the adults slowly put the toys away, singing a tidy away song and the young children, through imitation, join in the activity. Up to the age of 3, children will help collect things and want to do what we adults do. Beyond that age the tidying away becomes an opportunity for imaginative play. 'The train has to drive to the train station; the ship must sail into the harbour; the delivery man brings the chairs back to the table.'[18] The end of playtime is introduced slowly through the tidying-away song and our own activity, so that the children can come more naturally to the end of their play, without our harassment.

In Waldorf settings we don't have to practise alternating toys in a session – putting some toys away before others are brought out – as this breaks and fragments the playtime. However, there always needs to be a high awareness of safety amongst the adults during the play session, continuously monitoring the how, what, and where of all the toys and equipment.

Main points again

- Free, imitative, and imaginative play is vital for healthy child development.

- Allowing free uninterrupted movement in a safe space encourages self-confident, independent children.

- Natural objects, simple materials, and 'unfinished' toys encourage imitative and imaginative play.

- An understanding of child development informs what toys are appropriate for each age.

- Beautiful toys can be home made.

- Outdoor play is important.

- There are many imaginative outdoor alternatives to push/pull wheeled toys.

- Adults, busy in their own work activity, 'hold' children in a safe mantle where they can feel free to play.

- Tidying away is an important activity.

Useful books

Books on play

Sally Jenkinson, *The Genius of Play*, Hawthorn Press, Stroud, 2001

Heidi Britz-Crecelius, *Children at Play: Preparation for Life*, Floris Books, Edinburgh, 1972

Helle Heckmann, Nokken: *A Garden for Children*, A Centre for Anthroposophy, NH and the Waldorf Early Childhood Association, Md., 1998

Freya Jaffke, *Work and Play in Early Childhood*, Floris Books, Edinburgh, 1996

Donald Winnicott, *Playing and Reality*, Routledge, London, 1982

Susan Isaacs, *Intellectual Growth in Young Children*, Routledge, London, 1930

Christine Macintyre, *Enhancing Learning through Play*, David Fulton, London, 2001

Stephanie Cooper, Christine Fynes-Clinton and Marije Rowling, *The Children's Year*, Hawthorn Press, Stroud, 1986

Toy making

Freya Jaffke, *Toymaking with Children*, Floris Books, Edinburgh, 1988

Freya Jaffke, *Gestalten mit Holz für Kinder*, Verlag Freies Geistesleben GmbH, Stuttgart, 1995 (a book on whittling simple wooden toys – good illustrations)

Carol Petrash, Earthwise: *Environmental Crafts and Activities with Young Children*, Floris Books, Edinburgh, 1993

Making Waldorf dolls

Sunnhild Reinckens, *Making Dolls*, Floris Books, Edinburgh, 1989

Maricristin Sealey, *Making Waldorf Dolls*, Hawthorn Press, Stroud, 2005

Outside play

Bunny Guinness, *Family Gardens: How to Create Magical Outdoor Spaces for All Ages*, David and Charles, London, 1996

Sharon Lovejoy, *Sunflower Houses: Garden Discoveries for Children of All Ages*, Interweave Press, Colo., USA, 1991

Sharon Lovejoy, *Roots, Shoots, Buckets and Boots: Gardening Together with Children*, Workman Publishing, New York, 1999

Waldorf toy/materials companies in UK

Myriad Natural Toys, Ringwood, Hampshire, UK, tel. 01725 517085

Mercurius (UK), P.O. Box 1379, Swindon, SN1 35N, UK; tel. 01793 431480

Waldorf toy websites

www.waldorf-toys.com
www.toyspectrum.com

Children's furniture and play equipment

Community Playthings, Robertsbridge, East Sussex, tel. 01580 880626
www.communityplaythings.com

CHAPTER 5

Shaping the Parent and Child group session

'Rhythm is one of the most useful tools a parent or teacher will ever come across because rhythm helps to contain a person, just like a glass shapes water.'

Jane Winslow Eliot[1]

'Children have no use for and no conception of linear time, but they thrive when their day has a breathing rhythm, a flow between the IN of peace, rest, reflection; and the OUT of activity, action and interest in the world.'

Candy Verney[2]

FOR PARENTS...

Part 5: Shaping the Parent and Child group session (and a young child's day)

Why 'rhythm' and 'repetition' are important words in Steiner Parent and Child groups

We are all subject to the predictable rhythms of the cosmos – the yearly progression of the constellations, the monthly cycle of the moon, the daily rhythm of the rising and setting sun. In our bodies we are also subject to many natural rhythms – the heart pulse, breathing, ovulation…. Young children in particular need to be held and contained by the security of daily rhythms which are predictable and reliable. This is why:

- healthy rhythm in everyday life helps the young child to trust that the world is good;
- in this trust the child can relax;
- in this feeling of safety, the natural growing processes of the first few years can successfully take place;
- in the rhythmic ordering of everyday life the child finds inner rhythm and balance;
- arrhythmical life-styles create a premature wakefulness which can lead to insecurity and anxiety – with ongoing uncertainty about what is going to happen next. This can disturb the growth processes that are forming the physical body, the home of the spiritual individuality.

Rhythm in daily life can be seen as a 'breathing' – a 'breathing out' into activity and the 'breathing in' of rest and quiet. A child's day needs to have a rhythmic movement between these two states.

The activities and their order in a Parent and Child group session demonstrate how this natural 'breathing' can be accomplished.

Repetition of daily activities, and their ordering over time, likewise help to create a deep security in the young child, and she learns through imitation and repetition. The Parent and Child group demonstrates this through the steady repetition of the session structure and its elements, week after week.

How are rhythm and repetition demonstrated in the Steiner Parent and Child group session?

Here are some of the ways:

- Regular ordering of all the activities in the session
- Repetition of verses, stories, and rhymes
- Celebration of seasonal festivals each year
- Crafts and activities that reflect the seasons
- The use of the same songs and verses in the same order, to ease transition times
- Finding a regular timing for the little details

Parents can see how positively young children respond to the strong rhythm and repetition in the Parent and Child session. **Much can be taken back into the home and experimented with.**

This chapter looks at how the Parent and Child group session can be shaped, in terms of the order of activities, so that there is maximum benefit to children and adults.

Superficially it would seem that the 'order of proceedings' would be the most straightforward aspect of a Parent and Child group. After all there is a pretty much universal convention that is generally adhered to in groups, whether they are Waldorf or mainstream which goes like this:

- Playtime/craft
- Snack time
- Songs
- Finish…

Although this format generally seems to work, it is worth taking a fresh look at the 'natural shape' of a Parent and Child session, so that we can better understand what works, what doesn't, and why. It can make the difference between a group with a 'hum' – where the sequencing of the session is smooth and the children and adults leave 'full' and at peace, and a session where there is an awkward disjointedness, the children leaving more fractious – and the adults feeling more hassled than when they arrived! These may seem to describe extreme scenarios, but anyone who has attended Parent and Child groups will know what I mean.

There is an approach to sequencing which fosters a deep harmony and security in young children and helps events and activities to flow more easily, whether in the Parent and Child group or in the home. In Waldorf circles it is known as 'working with rhythm'. Because this understanding is so helpful with any work with young children, I will describe it in some detail.

What we mean by 'rhythm'

We usually understand rhythm in the musical sense – the ordering of short and long sounds. Here, it has a much broader and more fundamental meaning. First and foremost it is to do with remembering that we are, along with all life on this planet, immersed in, and totally dependant on, the interplay of countless natural rhythmical cycles. There is the annual rotation of the Earth around the sun which gives us our seasons, the monthly waxing and waning of the moon as it orbits around the earth, the turning of the earth creating day and night. Even in our bodies we are contained by rhythm – in the pulsing of our hearts and the blood in our veins, in our breathing, our walking and running, our eating and sleeping.

In our technological age it is becoming increasingly easy to imagine that we are free from any restrictions these great natural rhythms may impose. For example, electric light means we can have 'daylight' at any time. Our technological life-styles can leave us feeling less bound to the earth. However, even a little hiccup in the regularity and assumed predictability of these cycles' causes chaos. We forget that a very primal sense of security, as well as our experience of freedom, depends on the reliability of these internal and external rhythms. If we can see how this is true for us as adults we can begin to understand how it is also true for the young child.

The young child and rhythm

The young child needs to be held and contained by the security of rhythms which are predictable and reliable. Healthy rhythm and repetition in everyday life together help the young child to trust that the world is good. In this trust the child can relax; and in this relaxing, the natural growing and unfolding of this crucial period can safely take place. In the early experience of a rhythmic ordering in her world and daily life, the young child finds inner security and balance. The experience of everyday rhythm also strengthens the life forces used in growing a healthy physical body. Unpredictable and arrhythmic life-styles create a premature wakefulness in the young child, can weaken the constitution, and cause a deep abiding insecurity – always an uncertainty about what is going to happen next....

Breathing in and breathing out

A useful way of understanding rhythm is to recognize how it is created out of two qualities: a moving outward and a moving inward, an active part and a still part (like the beating of the heart), a sleeping part and an awake part, a light part and a dark part. Ensuring that these two qualities – 'the rhythmical breathing out and breathing in' – inform the ordering of a young child's everyday life, and in a way which has a synchronicity with the great natural rhythms, lies at the heart of the Waldorf way.

What does all this have to do with the ordering of proceedings in a Parent and Child group? In a world where many parents do not wish to, or find it difficult to, establish predictable rhythms in family life, the Parent and Child group can offer a gentle but profound experience of rhythmical ordering which works. It is the deep heart-beat of the session and it provides security and reassurance for everyone. Here are some of the ways in which this understanding of rhythm and repetition can inform the shaping of a Parent and Child group session.

Harmonizing a Parent and Child group session with the child's natural daily energy cycle

Children's energy patterns are naturally attuned to the rising and setting of the sun. In her book *Let's Talk, Let's Play*, Jane Winslow Eliot describes it thus:

'In the morning young children are full of energy and strength. They are generally more adventurous, more wishing to be physically involved in everyday tasks and they also learn new skills more easily. By mid day as the sun crosses the mid point of the sky, the energy shifts, there is a lull in their energy and they often need a nap. In the afternoon frequently the child's energy is quieter and dreamier, more formless in its expression and better suited to quieter play with other children or helping adults with activities such as painting or baking. As the sun goes down, the child's connection with worldly activity is loosened and their energy needs replenishing. They can become more scattered and out of themselves. Strong evening rituals that contain and allow the child to relax can help to smooth the transition to sleep.'[3]

This basic daily cycle, to which young children are naturally attuned, explains why Parent and Child groups generally work better in the morning, rather than in the afternoon. The morning is more suitable for forays into the world, for more vigorous play, and for meeting others. By lunch time there is a dip. With all the 'breathing out' of the morning a 'breathing in' is required – a quiet lunch and, hopefully, a sleep. Many groups need to meet in the afternoon and often it is more difficult to contain the children – their energy is more fragile and they can easily become fractious. However, the session can be organized so that the whole mood is quieter and more suited to the phase of a child's energy cycle. There can still be a 'breathing', but it is a gentler affair.

Rhythmical ordering within a Parent and Child group session

Within the session itself, the imagination of breathing in and out can be used to help order the activities in a rhythmical harmonious way. 'Breathing in' needs to be followed by a 'breathing out' before another breath in. It is essentially a moving out into the world, followed by a pulling back into the self. A 'breathing out' which goes on for too long leaves a child feeling 'out of herself', over-stimulated, and scattered. If the breathing in is too long (hours in a buggy?) the child becomes restless and unhappy. Here is an example of a way in which a session can be organized around a strong rhythm which allows for deep, full breathing:

Rhythm in the Parent and Child group

Breathing in	Group song and verse on arrival
Breathing out	Playtime/craft activities
...Transition...	Tidy away
Breathing in	Break time around the table
Breathing out	Songs and rhymes
Breathing in	Story
(Breathing out	Walk/play outside)
Transition to breathing out	Closing song and verse

Some groups have a 'rest time' – 5 or 10 minutes when everyone lies down quietly, and for which small cushions and blankets can be provided. Sometimes some lullabies are sung together, making for a lovely intimate time between parent and child – a rare moment of true stillness in our busy lives.

Each group will find its own ordering. Here are some examples of approximate timings:

Wynstones Steiner School

10.00	Play and adult activity
11.00	Tidy away time
11.15	Shared meal
11.30	Songs and finger rhymes
11.45	Walk
12.15	Story
12.30	Goodbye

*Snowdrop Parent and Child Group,
Steiner House, London*

10.00	Start – playtime
11.00	Tidy away time
11.05	Circle time
11.10	Wash hands
11.15	Shared meal
11.30	Rest
11.45	Story time
12.00	Goodbye

'Parenting with heart' California, USA

10.00-10.45	Play time and practical activity
10.45-11.00	Tidy away
11.00-11.15	Circle time
11.15-11.30	Snack time
11.30-11.45	Story time

York Steiner School

1.45-2.45	Play time with practical activity
2.45-3.00	Tidy away
3.00-3.15	Shared meal
3.15-3.30	Circle time with story
3.30	Goodbye

The importance of repetition

As we now know and as already discussed, young children learn everything through imitation. Imitation works when the same activities and routines are repeated consistently. When there is a strong element of repetition, young children also feel deeply secure. They can rest in themselves knowing that their world is ordered and safely predictable.

'Children soon learn there are times to be excited and times to be still, times to sit next to others and times to be alone. They do not need to rebel against doing "as they are told", for the routine of the desired action directs and strengthens their will.'

Kim Billington[4]

A parent reminded me recently how the strong rhythm and repetition in the group was as important for her as it was for her child! She found a great comfort in the consistency of the session, of being able to rest in the predictability of the ordering, the transition songs, and other cues. By experiencing this for herself she was able to foster a wish to bring this quality more into her family life.

In a Parent and Child group there are various ways in which repetitive elements can be introduced at a very basic level in each session (Box 23).

Box 23: Repetitive elements in the Parent and Child group

- Always using the same order of activities in the session
- Using the same songs and verses to introduce different parts of the session
- Doing even the smallest routine activity like tidying away or passing around the food at break time in the same way each time
- Having the toys in the same place each session so that they are easily found
- Repeating songs, rhymes, finger games, and stories for several weeks in the same order – changing them as the seasons change
- If the Parent and Child group meets more than once a week, then having the same type of craft on the same day of the week, e.g. baking on Mondays, sewing on Tuesdays…
- Having the same food and drink at break time

Weaving rhythm and repetition through the years' natural cycle

The strong health-giving qualities of rhythm and repetition can be consciously linked to the turning of the year. This provides yet another dimension to what the Parent and Child group can offer – a living experience and celebration of the great natural seasonal rhythms of which we are all inextricably a part, and a deep sense of connectedness with our earthly home.

Box 24 sets out some of the ways in which the cycle of the year can be worked with.

Box 24: Working with the cycle of the year

- Changing the nature table display to reflect seasonal changes. Using different colour fabric to emphasise the different moods of each season.
- Changing the songs, rhymes and songs to reflect the seasonal changes. In Waldorf groups this may mean only making changes every 4-5 weeks.
- Marking particular festivals throughout the year with special food or a little celebration, either in the Parent and Child group session or at a separate time.
- Using seasonal themes in the craft activities – for example in the use of natural objects or in the preparation for seasonal festivals.
- Using different food and drink at break time depending on the time of the year, for example – fruit salad in the summer, apple sauce and baked bread in the autumn, Advent cookies before Christmas and warming soup in the winter.
- Taking regular walks to experience the changing seasons in the immediate neighbourhood.
- The various aspects of choosing seasonal craft activities, songs and stories and how to celebrate seasonal festivals are described in greater detail in the following chapters.

Songs and the flow of the session

There can commonly be awkward moments in Parent and Child group sessions when one activity has to be cleared away and the next introduced. These are the times when the proceedings can degenerate into chaos. These moments tend to be when:

- Tidying away the toys in preparation for the break time
- Washing hands
- Going to the toilet
- Organizing the children and parents for break time
- Settling down for story or songs
- Doing a job, craft, or baking
- Ensuring that everyone is dressed for going outside
- Ending the session so that everyone leaves calmly

Singing songs at these times, whilst actively engaging in whatever the transition requires, magically creates a mood that can help calm and harmonize the atmosphere. Young children will, in their dreamy way, quickly learn to recognize the songs and rest in the security that each song marks a different but predictable activity. Adults also respond to the songs more readily than to commands! As we sing the tidy-away song, the adults will begin to put things away, and the children will naturally imitate and join in.

These songs can be called *transition songs* – every group will have their favourites, and they are gold! The beauty of these songs is that the children will also respond to the songs back in their homes – the tidying-away song can be used whenever toys need to be put away, the 'putting on the coat song' can be used every time there is a trip out into the world. It is important, however, not to expect the song alone to do the trick – the song signals the activity, and the child carries out the activity through imitating others in his surroundings.

Young children live in sound: from the womb they respond to sound and musical rhythm. From toddlerhood they can pick up the outline of a song very quickly, and children quite simply *love* singing and being sung to. It is now known that singing and movement are fundamentally important in developing memory, speaking, social skills, and writing (see the list of books at the end of the chapter). However, some parents are shy of their voices and don't think to sing to their children. The CD or tape player is certainly a poor substitute for *any* real, human singing voice.

'We accept that physical nourishment is vital for the child's growing body, but are less likely to recognise that everything else the child takes in through his senses has a similar effect. Just as children need and thrive on human touch, human response and love, so they need to hear the sound of the human voice.'

Candy Verney[5]

It is best if the songs are sung without accompaniment. The Parent and Child group leader can give handouts to new adults, showing the main songs that are sung at transition times, but the parents will naturally pick them up along with the children as the weeks pass. All that's needed is an initial willingness on the part of the leader to lead the song and, for a while, perhaps to be the only one singing!

The Parent and Child group is therefore a place where a rich repertoire of songs can be learnt and practised and taken back into the home. Here is a small range of favourite 'transition' songs from various Steiner groups. Many songs have been adapted from well-known songs, and others are made up.

We tidy away

This is sung at the end of play time when adults
and children tidy away the toys, and before the
next part of the session.

This next song can be used while waiting for a
group to become settled at the craft table. Here it
is used as dough is being passed around the table
– it could be used when food or craft materials
are being given out.

Activity at the table song

* Crayons/wool./felt etc.   + Use children's names

Here is an adaptation of an old favourite which is used to ease the putting on of coats and boots to go outside.

Going outside song

In her book *The Singing Day*, Candy Verney has put together a wonderful collection of songs for sharing with young children and which help to ease the transitional moments in everyday life. There are other books now appearing on the market which address the same need, some of which are listed at the end of the chapter.

Length of the group session

One-and-a-half to two hours seems to be a natural length. Children are able to handle a longer session in the morning than in the afternoon. Out of this time three quarters of an hour is often long enough for free play. A two-hour session can include a small walk or play outside.

Setting up and putting away

How this is done will have its effect on the mood of the group. Those who are responsible for opening up and preparing the room can find a sort of invisible support for their work, if they can find a rhythmical ordering in what they do, and if the preparation can be done in a careful, unrushed, and loving way. A quiet warm mood, 'the mantle', can then be created which is welcoming to parents and children as they arrive, providing a transition from the busy world to this more focused space. At the end of the session it is best if the parents and children can leave quickly and quietly, so that the mood can be held as long as possible.

Who organizes and runs the session will determine whether a rota of parent helpers is required. There is a quality of will or 'grit' that is called for, especially if the room needs to be prepared from scratch for every session – which is often the case in the early days and years of a group. (Over time I saw it as 'feeding' the project – our commitment in these matters, over the months, helping to grow the deep roots that a new project needs to thrive and grow!)

Finding the right timing for the little details

Within the broad rhythmical sequencing of the session, thought needs to be given to the placing of the smaller details – for example:

- When do parents pay their fee?
- When are announcements made, newsletters given out?
- Do children take off their shoes and wear slippers, and if so when and how?
- When is a good time to go to the toilet?
- When, if at all, is tea and coffee made available to the parents?
- When is the candle lit and blown out?
- When is the craft activity laid out and cleared away?
- When and how are library books made available?

If all of these events can find a consistent place, then the smooth running of the group will be helped enormously.

Drop-in or a more formal arrangement?

Many Waldorf groups find that a drop-in arrangement, which is common in traditional Parent and Toddlers groups, does not work very well either for the children or for the mood that is being created in the session. It often works better if the families can experience the whole session, as the children very quickly get used to, and enjoy,

the predictability of the strong repetitive elements of the sessions. Some groups start with a song and welcoming rhyme. Paying termly or half-termly means that the inevitable reminding and checking for payment is simplified.

The quality of timelessness

Is this in contradiction to what has already been discussed? – not at all. There is real relevance to the quality of timelessness that can pervade Steiner early childhood settings – this quality is similar to what you would find in a well cared-for garden. It is a quality of life force or 'etheric energy', which helps to grow children, like a warm well-tended garden will grow good flowers. Also, everything has its natural time. This is what we strive for in the Parent and Child group – the natural 'breathing' of the session, held by the adults' presence. The natural structure allows everything that happens within the session time to be unrushed, and there is freedom within the strong form.

Main points again

- We are immersed in great cosmic rhythms as well as the rhythmic inner orderings of our own bodies. We depend on the repetitive and predictable qualities of these rhythms for our own well-being. This is especially true for young children.

- The Parent and Child group session needs to harmonize with the natural daily energy cycle of young children.

- Young children do not experience life in a linear way but in a flowing way. Active periods in a day need to be balanced by restful periods. This alternation creates a natural rhythm and 'breathing' which is essential for the healthy development of the young child.

- There are ways of ordering the activities in the Parent and Child group so that there is a natural 'breathing'. This in turn will help create a harmonious flow throughout the session.

- The young child thrives on repetition. This can be used to great benefit in the Parent and Child group.

- Group sessions can reflect the larger seasonal rhythms in nature through progressive changes in the nature table, songs, seasonal craft activities, and festivals.

- The singing of songs eases the transitions between the 'in breath' and 'out breath' of the various activities in a Parent and Child group session.

- An atmosphere which has a distinctive harmonious 'hum' is very health giving to young children and is eminently possible to achieve, with practice!

- All of these ideas can be taken back by the adults and children into the family home.

Useful books

Rhythm and repetition in early years settings

Lynne Oldfield, *Free to Learn*, Hawthorn Press, Stroud, 2001

Freya Jaffke, *Work and Play in Early Childhood*, Floris Books, Edinburgh, 1996

Singing and poems with young children

Candy Verney, *The Singing Day*, Hawthorn Press, Stroud, 2003

Jane Winslow Eliot, *Let's Talk, Let's Play*, Association of Waldorf Schools of North America, Fair Oaks, CA.USA 1997

Heather Thomas, *Journey through Time in Verse and Rhyme*, Rudolf Steiner Press, London, 1987

Kim Billington (compiler), *Songs and Stories Together*, a Resource Book and Video for Kindergarten teachers, childcare workers, and playgroup leaders. Contact PO Box 4043, Croydon Hills, Victoria, Australia

Shea Darian, *Seven Times the Sun: Guiding your Child through the Rhythms of the Day*, 2nd edn, Gilead Press, Marshall, Wisc., 2001

Mary Thienes Schumemann, *This is the Way We Wash-a-day, Singing with Children Series*, a Naturally You Can Sing Production, East Troy, Wisc, 2003

Music and child development

Sally Goddard-Blythe, '"Music and Movement" – Are these the lost keys to early learning?', paper delivered at the European Conference of Neuro-Development Delay in Children with Specific Learning Difficulties, Chester, 6-8 March 1998

Celebrating the seasonal cycle of the year

Ann Druitt, Christine Fynes-Clinton, and Marije Rowling, *All Year Round*, Hawthorn Press, Stroud, 1995

Diana Carey and Judy Large, *Festivals, Family and Food*, Hawthorn Press, Stroud, 1982

CHAPTER 6

The Practical Activity

'When an adult is working with their hands, he/she is engaging themselves with life, with creative activity. Young children imitate the gesture of the work, and through this they show a greater ability to engage in their movement and play activity. Parents can see how their own activity influences their children in positive ways. The adult is not centred on their children but in work, and the outcome is that children can also do so with their world, therefore getting a better balance in the relationship.'

Lourdes Callen[1]

FOR PARENTS...

Part 6: The practical activity

What is the 'practical activity' in Steiner Parent and Child groups?

In many Steiner Parent and Child groups, a period of the session is allocated for engaging in a practical activity. Some activities are organized solely for the parents, e.g. making and mending dolls and simple toys for the group or home, or making seasonal crafts for festivals. Some are geared to the abilities of the older children, e.g. simple seasonal crafts, crayoning, sticking and gluing; and many encourage parent and child to carry out an activity together, e.g. baking, painting, and very simple crafts, like felting.

The purposes of carrying out a practical activity

The practical activity time can serve many purposes:

- Helping parents to learn new skills
- Providing activities that the children can imitate
- Helping parents to get to know each other, and helping the group to gel
- A sharing time for parents and their children
- Helping the older children to learn simple skills
- Giving children time to engage in free creative play by themselves whilst the adults engage in 'adult work'
- Providing new toys for the group and home
- Making seasonal crafts for festivals and to take home

What are the benefits?

- Parents discover new skills and ideas that can be taken into the home.
- The realization that simple beautiful crafts and toys can be made and don't have to be bought. For example, these can be made with one's own children as they grow, given away as presents, and used in the celebration of family festivals.
- Engaging in practical work provides valuable examples for children to imitate.
- An environment in which adults are engaging in practical work creates an atmosphere that helps children to play.
- Actively engaging in practical and artistic activities on a regular basis both relaxes and energizes.
- Domestic jobs can be seen in this creative light!

Although the 'practical activity' time in Waldorf Parent and Child groups is firmly based on a common spiritual understanding of the young child and of family life, as outlined in the previous chapters each group will work with these understandings in a unique way. Through visiting various groups and questioning Parent and Child group leaders, I have come deeply to appreciate the wide-ranging creativity and emphasis, born out of the artistic and inventive inclinations of the individuals involved. In this chapter I want to give some sense of the range of riches that I have found in the course of researching this book. Hopefully the ideas described here will provide a source of practical inspiration for anyone involved in Parent and Child work and with young children more generally.

What is the 'practical activity', and what is its purpose? Who is it primarily for in a Parent and Child group – the adult or the child – or both? What types of activities are most suitable? Who leads the activity? Are practical activities in the group necessary or should they be explored at a separate time? These questions were asked to several Waldorf Parent and Child group leaders; here is a compilation of their replies.

What do the practical activities include?

Taking the notion of the *Living Arts*, described in Chapter 2, we can divide practical activities into various 'types':

- *Domestic arts* would include, in this context, baking, preparing food for break time, sewing, cleaning, and mending toys.
- *Creative arts* would include painting, felting, sewing, making simple seasonal crafts, toys for the group, and preparing for festivals.

In addition the *social and nurturing arts* can be fostered during the practical activity through the discussions that take place around the activity table; the care taken to create a warm and friendly atmosphere during the activity time; and in choosing activities which do not cause stress for the adults or the children.

Helping adults to be creative and focused

The activity session is a way of introducing adults to a range of simple creative ideas and skills which can be taken back into the home. Many adults have lost their childhood link to their 'making and creating' abilities; and traditional domestic arts and crafts like cooking or sewing may no longer be handed down from parent to child. So parenthood is often an opportune time for the creative flame to be rekindled! As we have said in Chapter 2, having creative outlets as a parent is not only good for relaxing and recharging oneself, but also brings enormous riches to the young child and family:

'…cultivating a sense of achievement, pride, and self-esteem in the parents and how they feel about themselves as creative persons (which will have important "spin-offs" for their children)'…[2]

Lourdes Callen, who runs Parent and Child groups in the Brighton area, UK, described to me how a craft activity helps to calm and refresh parents, providing a focus that naturally allows a feeling of centredness to return. She sees other benefits for the young child, too…

A time to facilitate free play

The practical activity time can be an opportunity for adults quietly to observe their children playing and interacting with other children. If there is a leader of a group, the craft time is often a good time for encouraging and facilitating creative play amongst the children. In this time the leader as well as the parents can get to know individual children more intimately.

Here is *Janni Nichol* from Cambridge, UK:

'The craft activity is generally set out before the parents attend in the morning... They have the opportunity to come to the table when they have settled their child in play, or with the child, and learn a skill of some kind... Doing the craft activity in this way enables... me to spend some time with the children and help them to integrate. If I find there are some children having problems, or some parents who don't know how to play, I ask them to join me in the floor play, and we work with the children together.'[3]

And *Richard House* from Norwich, UK:

'There is a great deal of child-playing during craft activity (they go on at the same time, of course). Sometimes the toddlers bring the toys to the craft table and play with them there, near their mum or dad.'[4]

A sharing time between adults

The practical activity time naturally creates a sharing space where adults, even relative strangers, can feel more at ease and relaxed with each other. Conversation is more spontaneous and heart-to-heart. The activity provides a focus for the hands and mind, which loosens the feeling life of those present. The focus of a practical activity creates a calming and grounding 'hum' in the group which makes it easier for the children to settle to their own independent play.

'I have observed many strong and deep friendships developing between parents in our groups... But there is also something very powerful and nourishing for the toddlers, I think, in witnessing us working away at our crafts in comparative (non-anxious, contained/ing) silence.'[5]

In some groups, the group leader will use the quiet focus of the practical activity time to raise parenting questions and facilitate discussions on different parenting issues.

Can children join in the practical activity?

Kim Billington from Australia:

'My recommendation is that with children under 4, only the adults have prearranged activities. These may be sewing or knitting, little felt or wooden toys, brought out during the first half-hour of each session as the children are busy with their indoor play.'[6]

And *Lourdes Callen* from Brighton, UK:

'The flow... in mainstream Parent and Child groups... can point to thinking that the child needs to be stimulated constantly... [A]dults want to bring the very young to activities (with good intention) but it can generate unnecessary tension and explanations which make the young very tired.... [W]hen the child cannot hold the brush, control water, when they eat the crayons, it simply tells us that it is not yet the time.'[7]

Toddlers in many groups participate in activities such as kneading bread dough, painting, simple felt making, and crayoning. However, their attention spans are short, and there is a danger that attempting craft work with them can turn into a serious early-learning exercise with the outcome being more important than the enjoyment! Many Parent and Child group leaders feel it is inappropriate to have craft activities for under 3s, as their consciousness is not developed to the level of focus and skill that a craft activity typically requires. The younger children are often happy on an adult's lap, watching and listening or doing a simple activity alongside a more complex one that the adults are carrying out. Baking, felting, and painting are all activities in which younger children can easily participate.

The practical activity sessions can be a way of introducing the older children in the group to simple skills which can develop their dexterity and motor skills. Children who are three or more can learn to use scissors, blunt knives, and simple large needles, and are very happy attempting many different activities with the help of a caring and attentive adult. A lot of unnecessary pressure on young children to do things before they are naturally ready can be gratefully set aside. As Kathy McQuillen at Alder Bridge, UK, writes, 'Young children live in the realm of the will. It is the activity they live into rather than the end-result.'[8]

In Waldorf Parent and Child groups, the understanding of the importance of 'Imitation and Example' lies at the heart of all activities with young children. The adult does, and the child will naturally follow, rather than the adult trying to tell the child what to do verbally. The adult gets stuck in first!

Here is *Janni Nichol* again:

'I try and do activities which the older children are able to participate in – drawing, leaf rubbing, some cutting as part of an activity, sticking, etc. I do things which parents will be able to repeat at home… It also gives me the opportunity to reassure the parents that the child is too young, and the activity will be happily acquired at a later stage.'[9]

A sharing time between adults and children

The practical activity time provides a special time when adults and children can share together. In this space, language skills, sharing skills, and

Practical activity in a Parent and Child group, Cambridge

nourishing heart-warmth can thrive. The adults also see what it is possible for them to do with children of different ages. Trying out different practical activities in the group can give more confidence to experiment at home, rather than relying on outside experts in playgroups and nurseries to provide the creative input with young children.

'When we work at a craft together, such as felting…, it enables parents to see what sort of thing can be possible with the children. Baking and painting are bigger and messier activities, but most enjoyable all the same.'[10]

'If the craft is primarily aimed at the adults, then the children either join in their own way or play while the adults chat and enjoy the activity. If the craft is for the children then we all sit round the table and work together.'[11]

'For me it is about… making something beautiful for the children to witness (i.e they are witnessing both "the act of creation" itself and all that is needed in that – perseverance, patience, creativity, skill and dexterity, love, goal directedness, etc.) as well as the beauty of the final product itself.'[12]

Practising the domestic arts

In some groups the adults are given simple domestic tasks to do together. These can include sanding toys, polishing, baking, sewing, and gardening. *Rena Osmer*, Director of the Early Years Department at Steiner College in Sacramento, California, runs a Parent and Child programme. She explained that children are not expected to join in with the adults – though they are of course very welcome if they wish to! The young children are deeply nourished by the presence of adults taking care and joy in doing

meaningful work. The more creative crafts are explored during evening meetings without children, allowing time for greater discussion. 'Washing fleece (to stuff knitted dolls) or dolls' clothes; polishing blocks, dusting shelves and squeezing oranges, are not just fun – they are really useful and honest activities.'[13]

Making seasonal crafts for festivals

Many groups spend time making crafts which have a seasonal relevance, especially around festival times. There are several reasons for this. First of all, materials from nature are freely given: beautiful crafts and presents can be created with very little expense. Secondly, Waldorf groups are based on an understanding of the importance of rhythm and repetition. Linking simple craft work to the seasonal cycle of the year and the seasonal festivals promotes a sense of reverence for nature and a deep feeling of continuity and security in the group, both in the adults and children – especially when the same activities are remembered year after year: 'Parents have… often never done crafts where they can use natural materials either, and assume that everything has to be bought. I tend to use materials from nature wherever possible.'[14]

The activity time can be used to help prepare food and other items for the celebrated seasonal festivals: 'Craft activities can help in the preparation of festivals, encouraging parents to talk about the importance and meaning of the festivals for the young child.'[15]

'It must be remembered that these are… structured activities with… imposed purpose. They should really only be done because the adults are delighted to be involved in them in an artistic and soul-filled way. From this, the child feels free to also joyfully participate.'[16]

Making things for the group or for the home

The practical activity time can be used to make simple toys, dolls, and other items for the group or home. Each parent can have their own project/item that they work on in the group, over a period of time: 'A craft activity is a good way to help parents engage constructively in the group… anything from little gnomes to dolls, they can whittle some wooden toys, make aprons for painting or baking.'[17]

Lourdes Callen described to me how she visited a home-based group where each parent brought their own craft project. The leader was then freer to give attention to the parents and children, and the mood was very relaxed. This could perhaps be an option that could be alternated with more formal craft days – for example, when preparing for festivals.

In *Brenda Watson*'s groups the parents have sewing projects which they choose themselves from the many Waldorf craft books. Some parents may knit; others make dolls or felt balls. Only at festivals will the group make simple crafts together. Sometimes, particularly for festivals, Brenda will do a very easy activity which the older children can join in with. Brenda advocates having time to play, and to really learn what the possibilities for imaginative play are. Crafts can be done at home with their parents.

Who organizes the practical activity?

There is a distinction between groups which are parent-organized and those that have an experienced leader. This is often the difference between a new group, and a more established group with a paid leader – although this is not always the case (see Chapter 11).

A parent-led group will tend to approach the preparation of the practical activity together. In many groups, parents will take it in turns to bring a craft idea, and different adults will have their own interests and skills. In a parent-led group in Bath, for example, the parents decide each half term what activities will be undertaken, and then each parent takes responsibility for preparing one of them. Group leaders usually take the sole responsibility for the preparation of the craft each week.

Brenda Watson leaves the parents to decide what sewing project they are going to tackle; she only takes the lead when making crafts for festivals.

When and where to have the practical activity?

The practical activity is generally carried out in the first part of the session during free play, lasting for about half an hour. Children come to the craft table if they so wish. In some groups, the craft activity is laid out on the table at the beginning of the session, providing a welcome focus for quieter or newer members. Alternatively, the leader may wait until the children have begun to play.

Having a simple craft activity on the floor can work very well when there is a small group. The adults can sit amongst the children, at their level. The children do not feel excluded, and a very gentle atmosphere can be created. Of course, health and safety issues need to be carefully considered.

Some groups that blend together the RIE (Resources for Infant Educarers) and Waldorf approaches spend little or no time on crafts but give the time over wholly to free play. Parents are encouraged to take the time quietly to observe their own and each others' children. These groups are more floor-based, with the parents sitting amongst the children.

Examples of practical activities

Seasonal and festival crafts

Over the weeks and months, the chosen crafts can be planned to coincide with the various seasonal changes and festivals. Specific festivals will be discussed in Chapter 9. The simple diagram below shows the four seasons, and where the main celebrated festivals fall.

There follows a list of craft-activity ideas for the four main seasons of the year, compiled from several Parent and Child groups. Many of the ideas come from a number of Waldorf craft books - where this is the case, the relevant reference is given as an abbreviation. The books are:

AYR *All Year Round*, Ann Druitt, Christine Fynes-Clinton, Marije Rowling, Hawthorn Press

ECB *Easter Craft Book*, Thomas Berger, Floris Books

HCB *Harvest Craft Book*, Thomas Berger, Floris Books

EW *Earthwise*, Carol Petrash, Floris Books

MW *Magic Wool*, Dagmar Schmidt and Freya Jaffke, Floris Books

MMW *More Magic Wool*, Angelika Walk-Gerche, Floris Books

FFF *Festivals, Family and Food*, Diana Carey and Judy Large, Hawthorn Press

CCB *The Christmas Craft Book*, Thomas Berger, Floris Books

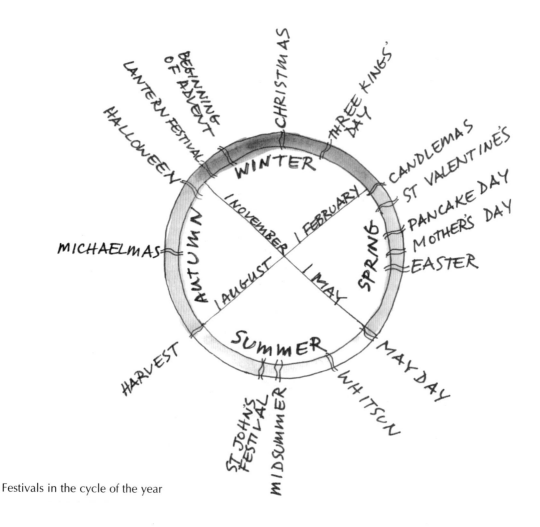

Festivals in the cycle of the year

These books are very popular because many of the crafts are seasonal, simple, and beautiful, and are based on using natural materials. Together they cover a wide range of craft ideas and are generally easy to adapt for young children. These books are truly inspirational – quite essential for your library! Many other books contain seasonal craft activities, but they generally describe crafts of the 'stick and glue', non-natural variety.

Spring crafts

Spring – beginning of February to beginning of May

Candlemas

Floating candles	AYR
Sand candle	AYR
Rolling candles from candle wax sheets	

Valentine's Day

Valentine biscuits	AYR
Valentine cards with cut outs	EW
Valentine mice	EW
Felt Valentine bags	

Pancake Day

Mixing pancakes and cooking them

Spring

Animals and figures out of wool and felt	MW, FC
Washing and carding wool	EW, MW
Wool pictures	ECB, MMW
Felt pictures	MW
Felt flower fairies	ECB, AYR
Bread dough animals	ECB
Salt dough figures	ECB

Easter crafts

Egg dyeing	EW
Easter baskets	FFF
Birds' nests from card or straw	
Seeding cress or grass	
Pom-pom chicks	
Easter cards	
Saucer gardens with seed	
Planting seeds	

Spring crafts

Summer crafts

Summer – *beginning of May to beginning of August*

May Day

Flower crowns	*EW*
Festival biscuits	

Whitsun

White paper doves	*AYR*
Festival biscuits	

Summer crafts

Tissue-paper butterflies and mobiles	*EW*
Pressed-flower cards	*EW*
Alder tree cone bees	*HCB*

Wet-on-wet painting	
Whipper whoppers	*AYR*
Windmills	*AYR, FFF*
Fans	*AYR*
Wooden block boats	
Chopping fruit for fruit salad	
Bark boats	*TM*
Butterfly transparencies for windows	
Potato printing	
Sewing lavender bags	*EW*
Butterfly crowns	*EW*

Midsummer and St John's

Fairy gifts	*FFF*
Golden spiral mobile	*AYR*
Elder flower pancakes	

Summer crafts

Autumn crafts

Autumn – beginning of August to beginning of November

Autumn crafts

Grinding flour and making bread rolls
Leaf and seed mobiles *HCB*
Pressed-leaf transparencies for windows *HCB*
Leaf crowns *EW*
Animals and people made from fir cones, berries, and seeds *HCB, TM, FFF*
Leaf trace drawings
Conker and berry necklaces *HCB*
Conker spiders' webs *HCB*
Conker sling *HCB*
Jam tarts
Chopping apples and making apple sauce *EW*
Corn dollies *EW*
Pine-cone whizzers *AYR*
Walnut boats

Michaelmas

Planting bulbs
Bread dragons *HCB, AYR*
Conker dragons *AYR*

Halloween

Carving pumpkins *EW*
Making pumpkin soup
Gingerbread house *AYR*

Martinmas

Lanterns for the lantern festival
EW, AYR, FFF

Autumn crafts

Winter crafts

Winter – beginning of November to beginning of February

Winter crafts

Pine-cone bird feeders	*ES*
Star windows	*EW*
Gnome gardens	*EW*
Making gnomes	*EW*
Wool dolls EW,	*FFF*
Pom-pom balls	*EW*
Chopping vegetables and making soup	
Cutting out paper snowflakes	*AYR*
Finger knitting	*EW*

Advent and Christmas presents

Making dipped wax candles	
Decorating candles	*EW, CCB*
Wool angels	*CCB*
Advent biscuits	*AYR*
Rolling candles	*EW*
Festive star and candles transparencies	
	AYR, CCB
Pomanders	*EW*
Christmas-tree decorations	*FFF*
Christmas crackers	
Felt finger puppets	
Dressing-up hats	*FFF*
Christmas cards	

Winter crafts

Painting and crayoning with young children and adults

'The little baby first perceives light and colour as differentiated shades of brightness, and it is only when light and colour work upon the eye that it becomes a perfect organ of sight. Children unite with the colours that are drawn towards them from their surroundings, affecting their feelings – one colour a feeling of well-being and another of discomfort... Colour is in fact food for our souls.'

Letitia Costain[18]

The young child's experience of colour is complex because their inner and outer worlds are hardly separated. Rudolf Steiner explains that young children actually experience the complementary of any colour. For example, in the case of the colour red, the young child inwardly experiences the qualities of green; and in the case of blue, it is yellow that they inwardly experience. We can only wonder at how this must be for the young child. But in a deep respectfulness toward this sensitivity, adults are encouraged not to 'school' the young child in the use and naming of colour. *Letitia Costain,* Steiner National Parent and Child representative, explains:

'One of the best ways to experience colour is through painting with watercolours on wet paper. Colours are in their own true element in water. We only have to see a rainbow to realize that we experience wonder and awe. Colour in a thin sea of water can move, mingle, change, lighten and darken, just like our feelings and emotions. ...Pre-school children are totally unselfconscious, absorbing the experience. It is the doing that is important, and not what it is, or how good it is. Just allow the experience to be felt by the child.'[19]

Carol Baker, an artist who helps to run Letitia's group at Rudolf Steiner House in London, shared an approach to painting with adults and young children which she has used very successfully. First, she uses the materials set out in Box :

Box 25: Painting materials for Parent and Child groups

- *STOCKMAR* water-colour paints in the following colours:[19]
  - Vermilion red
  - Crimson red
  - Golden Yellow
  - Lemon Yellow
  - Ultramarine blue
  - Prussian blue
- *STOCKMAR* wax coloured crayons, in the same colours as above. The wax crayons are a rectangle shape that is easily held by little hands, and can make broad marks on paper. The colours are also very pure and blend well together.
- Lining paper – weight 1000/2000gm. This can be bought from any DIY shop.
- Three large jars for mixing the colours (the two yellow water-colour paints are mixed in one jar, the reds in another, and the blues in the third)
- Small jars
- Brushes size 12 (available from Mercurius)
- Bowl of water and sponges
- Kitchen towel or cloth
- Masking tape to hold the paper to the table

First, the paints are mixed – the two reds are mixed together, as are the two blues and yellows, each in a large jar. Some water is added so that the mixtures are just on the thick side of water consistency – not too thin and not too strong!

The lining paper is then unrolled into a large

strip across the table and taped into position securely and flat. Children and adults then sit around the table.

The crayons are used to make large swirling strokes on the paper. The adults begin, and encourage the children to imitate them. The crayoning is continued until the strokes have marked out many shapes on the paper, but leaving enough space for the paint to come through. Then the crayons are put away. The paper is then thoroughly dampened with wet sponges, avoiding any pooling of water.

The three colours of paint are poured into separate little jars (one pot of each colour for perhaps every three children in the group) and distributed along the table. Each pot will have its own brush so that the colours do not get muddied. The children are then encouraged, through imitation, to paint the paper as they will, using the paint directly from the little pots, covering the paper completely on and between the crayon lines. The medium of watercolour on the dampened paper allows the paint to flow, so that the children can experience rainbow colours, as the three primary colours mix together. Nothing is explained, and the children are allowed freely to experience the colour without comment. All the while, the 'Rainbow song' can be sung.

Once the sheet is dry, the art work can be used for other activities, for example cutting up to make autumn lanterns, cards, gift boxes, and baskets.

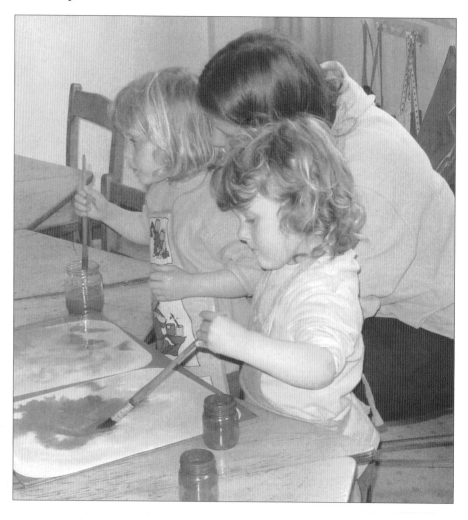

Children painting

The crayons can be used on their own, without paint, to create colour in craft work. For example, a leaf or a cut-out shape, such as a heart placed under a sheet of paper, will, with vigorous (to and fro) crayoning on top, create a shadow of the object on the paper, making lovely cards. Hard-boiled eggs at Easter time can be very successfully coloured using the wax crayons.

Adults do the activity around the table, with the children naturally and necessarily imitating them. The older children will enjoy making animals, nests, snakes – all sorts of shapes. Sunflower and pumpkin seeds or currants can be used for special effects. The children can experience the whole process of baking bread over several weeks (best in the autumn), from

Rainbow

Rain - bow, lov - ely glow, put some col - our in my hand,

then we'll make a fai - ry land

Baking with young children and adults

Here we experience *real* dough rather than 'play dough', with the bonus of being able to enjoy the eating! Many groups will have it as a regular activity, making bread rolls which will then be eaten at the group shared meal. 'I have found that baking works well for *both* adults and children.'[20]

An adult can prepare the dough before the group session, although it is best if the group can witness the whole process. Mix the ingredients at the beginning of the session and then allow it to rise for 15 minutes or so. At a suitable point in the session, when the group is settled, the dough can then be divided among the children around the table and they can knead the dough and then make little shaped rolls. Once made, the rolls are put straight into the oven for 15 minutes or so. Here is a simple recipe (Box 26).

Box 26: Simple bread rolls recipe
(to make 15 rolls)

- 1kg wholemeal flour or 500g of white and 500g of brown mixed
- 2 teaspoons of salt
- 1 teaspoon of honey
- 2 7g sachets of dried yeast
- 2 tablespoons of sunflower oil
- 500ml of lukewarm water

Preheat the oven to 200°C, gas mark 6.

Put the warm water, oil, honey, and yeast in a bowl. Leave for a little while until the yeast is frothy. Then add the flour and salt. Mix until it is soft but not sticky. You can add more flour if necessary. Knead dough for a few minutes and then put in a bowl somewhere warm to rise for $1/2$ hour. When everyone is gathered around the table, the dough can be divided into smaller segments for the children. Each child kneads and shapes their piece. The rolls are then baked in the oven for 12-15 minutes until golden, and they sound hollow when tapped on the underside.

collecting wheat seeds, and grinding (an old-fashioned hand grinder is good to have) to finally making the dough and baking the bread.

The act of making and baking bread is a fundamental, primary human activity – it links us to how we are fed by the earth, and it shows us how we can prepare our own 'daily bread'. Bread straight out of the oven also has one of the best, most comforting smells in our world!

There are many books available that have recipes such as jam tarts, mini pizzas, and seasonal biscuits that are suitable for using with young children. Baking is a wonderful way to prepare for any celebration. A particularly inspiring book called *Festivals, Family and Food* gives many recipes that can be tied to the various seasonal festivals (see end of this chapter).

Singing and the practical activity

There is a very particular atmosphere generated when songs accompany an activity time – a quiet mood descends as everybody comes together. Young children love songs that reflect what they are doing, and it is a way of effortlessly bringing them to the craft table and fully engaging them in the joy of activity. Through repetition, they will soon remember which song to sing, as each song will link to the activity in their memory. 'Of course the adults love to chat, but if it becomes too much or is unsuitable for the young children, then I'll start to sing quietly.'[21]

Each group will develop their favourite songs, often made up to familiar tunes that everyone can remember. There are, however,

Baking in a Parent and Child group, York

different 'doing' qualities that can be experienced in various sorts of activities, and these can be reflected in the song. For example, *Janni Nicol* from Cambridge explained that kneading the bread dough is a very physical activity, and the song can be quite strong and upbeat. Painting, however, is a much dreamier activity, more attuned to the realm of feeling. A quieter song using pentatonic notes (see Chapter 8) might be more in keeping.

The song below, for example, can be adapted for all sorts of activities, just substituting felting with baking, chopping, sewing… 'When we are preparing for a festival I will sing the seasonal songs. In fact, I generally sing most of the time quietly…', writes *Kathy McQuillen* at Alder Bridge.[22]

There are several lovely books I have found with simple songs that can be sung with young children whilst carrying out everyday family activities. Again, these are listed at the end of the chapter.

Main points again

- Practical activities include:
  Domestic arts, e.g. sewing, baking, mending
  Creative arts, e.g. painting, baking, sewing, seasonal crafts, toy and doll-making, preparing for festivals
  Social and nurturing arts, e.g. generating the right social atmosphere

- Practical activity time in a session has the following benefits:
  A time to enable and facilitate free play for the children
  Helping parents to learn new skills
  Providing activities for children to imitate
  Making things for the group
  Making things for festivals
  A sharing time between adults and children
  A sharing time between adults

- Practical activities can be organized by the group leader or by parents and usually last for 1/2 hour.

- In seasonal crafts we make beautiful objects using natural materials when possible. These activities help us to appreciate and feel connected to the cycle of the year and the gifts of nature.

We're baking

We're bak - ing we're bak - ing we're bak - ing all day

long, we're bak - ing we're bak - ing we're sing - ing the BAK - ing song.

ng, felting, and painting are all very
essful activities to pursue in Parent and
d groups.

- Children love to sing a special song with a
  craft activity.

Useful books

Seasonal crafts

Ann Druitt, Christine Fynes-Clinton, Marije
Rowling *All Year Round*, Hawthorn Press,
Stroud, 1995

Thomas Berger, *Easter Craft Book*, Floris Books,
Edinburgh, 1993

Thomas Berger, *Harvest Craft Book*, Floris Books,
Edinburgh, 1992

Thomas Berger, *The Christmas Craft Book*, Floris
Books, Edinburgh, 1990

Carol Petrash, *Earthwise*, Floris Books,
Edinburgh, 1993

Helga Meyerbroker, *Rose Windows and How to
Make Them*, Floris Books, Edinburgh, 1994

Thomas and Petra Berger, *The Gnome Craft
Book*, Floris Books, Edinburgh, 1999

M v Leeuwen and J Moeskops, *The Nature
Corner*, Floris Books, Edinburgh, 1990

Cooking

Diana Carey and Judy Large, *Festivals, Family
and Food*, (also has seasonal songs) Hawthorn
Press, Stroud, 1982

Susan Smith Waldorf, *Echoes of a Dream:
Creative Beginnings for Parent and Child*,
School Association of London, Canada, 1982

General crafts

Sunnhild Reinckens, *Making Dolls*, Floris Books,
Edinburgh, 1989

Freya Jaffke, *Toy Making with Children*, Floris
Books, Edinburgh, 1990

Peter Berger, Felt *Craft-making, Dolls, Gifts and
Toys*, Floris Books, Edinburgh, 1994

Maricristin Sealey, *Making Waldorf Dolls*,
Hawthorn Press, Stroud, 2005

Painting and drawing

Brunhild Muller, *Painting with Children*, Floris
Books, Edinburgh, 1987

Michaela Strauss, *Understanding Children's
Drawings*, Rudolf Steiner Press, London, 1978

Stockmar paints and crayons available from
Mercurius – www.mercurius-
international.com. Also paint brushes
UK contact: Ali Fitzpatrick and Margaret
Campman, 6 Highfield, Kings Langley,
Herts WD4 9JT; tel. 01923 261 646; info@
mercurius-uk.com

Felting and wool craft

Dagmar Schmidt and Freya Jaffke, *Magic Wool*,
Floris Books, Edinburgh, 2000

Angelika Wolk Gerche, *More Magic Wool*, Floris
Books, Edinburgh, 2001

Angelika Wolk Gerche, *Making Fairy-tale Wool
Animals*, Rudolf Steiner College Press, CA,
2002

Christel Dhom, *Making Magical Fairy Tale
Puppets*, Rudolf Steiner College Press, Calif.,
2001

Anne Einset Vickery, *Felting by Hand*, Craft
Works Publishing, Calif., 1987

Singing songs

Shea Darian, *Seven Times the Sun: Guiding Your
child through the Rhythms of the Day*, Gilead
Press, Marshall, Wisc., 2001

Candy Verney, *The Singing Day*, Hawthorn Press,
Stroud, 2003

Kim Billington (compiler), *Songs and Stories
Together*, available from: PO Box 4034,
Croydon Hills, Victoria, Australia

Mary Thienes-Schunemann *This is the Way We
Wash-a-Day*, A Naturally You Can Sing
Production, East Troy, Wisc., 2003

CHAPTER 7

The Shared Meal

'The dinner table has long been considered by experts to be the eye in the hurricane of family life. The ritual bonding of breaking bread together forms the central gathering point where daily experience is shared and enriched, and a sense of security is nurtured in the children.'

Estelle Bryer[1]

'Sharing food is the beginning of sharing life, laughter and love,'

Veronika van Duin[2]

FOR PARENTS...

Part 7: The shared meal

What is the shared meal?

It is an important part of the Steiner Parent and Child group session when parents and their children gather around a single table for something to eat and drink. The 'meal' is usually a simple offering of bread and jam, a fruit salad, or home-made biscuits – a healthy 'snack'. There is juice for the children, and perhaps hot drinks for the adults. More important, however, is the spirit in which this sharing takes place. A candle is lit, and everyone around the table links hands as a little song is sung to bless the food. There is a mood of stillness, followed by the social coming-together as a group. Sharing food and conversation around a table naturally creates a sense of belonging and community. At the end of the meal, a 'thank you for the meal' is given, and the candle blown out.

It all sounds rather religious!

The lighted candle brings a peace and sense of occasion to the meal-time. The blessing expresses thanks to the earth, sun, and rain for our food. The children love the predictability and weekly repetition of the songs and blessing, and also the ritual of eating together. Parents often report that their children insist on having the whole routine, including the lighted candle, at family meal-times. Adults, too, can feel deeply nourished by this simple event, as well as the whole experience of sitting with others around a table. It can be very rare these days to share this sense of community.

Food is shared in many other ways too

Steiner Parent and Child groups excel in finding ways to share food together, whether for a child's (or adult's) birthday or one of the several simple festivals throughout the year. Seasonal food and a specially decorated table all help to mark the occasion.

Shared meal in a Parent and Child group, York

The special quality of the shared meal

The shared meal is a time when the senses and soul life of the young child (and the adults) can be nourished just as much as their physical bodies. The enjoyment of the order and beauty of the prepared table and the experience of good conversation and wholesome food – all of this 'feeds' the group.

For me the shared meal, which comes after the period of play and practical activity, is a very poignant time in the Parent and Child group session. What do I mean by this? There is something very special about the whole group gathering together to share food around a table. But there is more to it than this. In all Steiner early childhood settings, the shared meal is introduced in an atmosphere of quietness. A candle is lit whilst a song is sung, and a blessing is given on the food before it is served. In this moment there is a certain mood which descends on the group which I can only describe as a 'peace'. It is a moment of openness and genuine human community. Everyone is aware of it, even the children, who are often very 'present' and calm.

The shared meal is the part of the session that the children seem to remember most. Parents will often say how their children want the candle and blessing songs sung at home. I feel that in our world where family meal-times are often sacrificed on the altar of television and other activities, taking time to honour the sharing of food and time together has a special significance. A single parent described how important the shared meal was for her and her young daughter, providing an invaluable regular experience of sitting around a table with others and sharing community.

Blessings and songs

In her book *Seven Times the Sun*, which is a celebration of rhythm and everyday rituals in family life, Shea Darian explains for me how the meal-time blessing creates a sense of unity and solidarity in the family circle:

'I have discovered the blessing of our meals to be as important as the feasting. Our familial affection is fertilized as we open ourselves to the gifts of food and companionship. "Saying grace" becomes an invitation for showing grace to all around the table.'[3]

Shea has many ideas for creating simple rituals to celebrate meal-time– for example, learning blessings in different languages, taking it in turns to learn a blessing, making cut-out place mats for special occasions, or making a pot-luck meal where every family member contributes an offering.

An example from York, UK

Each Parent and Child group will have its own songs and little rituals. Here is an example to help inspire you to create your own way:

In York, the table is large enough for all the children and parents to sit around it. A vase of flowers and a seasonal gnome or fairy is placed in the centre as a decoration. At one end there is the break-time food, ready for the meal – in this case a fruit salad prepared from contributions brought by the families, a jug of warm fruit juice for the children, bowls, and cups. The candle is placed on the table – our candle holder is in the shape of an angel.

The children are brought to the table with 'This is the way we wash our hands, wash our hands, and wash our hands…' (sung to the tune of 'Here we go round the Mulberry Bush'). There is a bowl of water, soap, and a towel at one end of the table. They wash their hands and then take their places around the table. Their parents and carers sit next to them, and babies are on laps.

I sit at one end of the table and wait until there is a hush, a pause. This is the moment when the mood changes. I light the candle with an inner focus which honours the specialness of the occasion and we all sing together the following song:

This is followed by a blessing done with hand gestures.

Light the little candle light

Light the lit - tle can - dle light, shin - ing light and bright.

Light the lit - tle can - dle light, shin - ing light and bright.

Light the lit - tle can - dle light, shin - ing light and bright. Shin - ing

light, shin - ing bright, shin - ing light

Blessings on the meal

Bless - ings on the bloss - om, bless - ings on the fruit.

Bless - ings on the leaves and stems and bless - ings on the root.

After this we all hold hands – children and adults – around the table and sing together this song:

Hands, everybody

Now the food and drink is served - both children and parents can have a portion of the fruit salad. Conversation is shared, and news and announcements are given out.

When everyone is done, all the bowls and cups are stacked up at one end of the table, and we all link hands again and sing the finishing song:

Thank you for the meal

During the shared meal

During the shared meal, conversation is spontaneous and free flowing among the group members – including the children. However, there always needs to be an awareness of the level of noise or excitement at the table, as this can throw the younger children into a state of upset. Then the atmosphere can begin to become agitated and the shared meal causes indigestion rather than relaxation! It is good if a harmonious 'hum' in the group can be maintained. The leader needs to be aware of the subtleties of meal-time dynamics, and guide the direction or level of conversation if necessary. A little song can alert parents to the fact that the proceedings are getting a little out of hand!

Some younger children will want to get down from the table before everyone has finished. This doesn't spoil the mood and usually these little ones will happily come back and sing the last song at the end of the meal. Over time, as they get used to the strong elements of rhythm and repetition in the shared meal routine, they tend to settle and stay.

Older children and adults can help in the laying of the table before the shared meal. Children often love to be in charge (with a little help) of placing the cutlery and other items on the table. Some Parent and Child groups, like Sheila's in Clitheroe, have a table cloth every session. A table cloth certainly makes the occasion feel very special

Quality food

It is important that the food that is offered is wholesome and, where possible, organic. In many groups the parents are asked to bring a contribution, and some groups have a rota for making home-made biscuits or buns. With forethought, different snacks can be planned depending on the season – vegetables for making soup, cooking apples for apple sauce. In some groups the children help the adults to make bread rolls or muffins during the craft activity which are then eaten during the shared meal. Biscuits, tarts, and other special treats can also be made during the session, particularly if the group is celebrating a festival. What can be more appetizing than the good smell of biscuits or bread baked in the session! All the children around the table are offered the snack. After a time it is surprising how even the fussy eaters, through imitation, will begin happily to eat along with the others.

Apple juice is often offered to the children at the shared meal. Adding a chamomile, rosehip, or other fruit teabag to the apple juice and topping up with hot water can make a warming drink, which is particularly comforting in the winter months. In the summer, home-made elderflower cordial is a treat.

In some groups a drop of lavender essential oil is added to the water in the washing hands bowl. Lavender has a very calming effect and helps to set the mood for the shared meal.

The shared meal, or 'snack time' as it is often tellingly called, can be a neglected and rushed part of a Parent and Child group session. In the Waldorf approach we recognize its importance as a time when we can acknowledge Mother Nature's wholesome bounty and enjoy the spirit of community and sharing. Preparing for the shared meal is well worth the same consideration we bring to other parts of the session.

After the meal

Some groups will leave the table and sit down elsewhere in the room for the circle time or story. The table can then be cleared quickly by an adult. There can be a conflict here with the need to move on to the next part of the session. If the kitchen is in another room, a parent can be quietly clearing up. Otherwise, the washing or sweeping up does not usually take place until the whole session is over.

Brenda at Wynstones School keeps the families around the table after the shared meal for the songs and finger games. After these the candle is blown out and the group goes for a walk outside in the school grounds before the finishing story. She also has another delightful practice – after the meal, each child is given a warm cloth dipped in water with lavender oil to wipe their faces and hands!

Main points again

- The whole group gathering together around a table for the shared meal fosters a sense of community and belonging.

- The shared meal can be as nourishing to the senses and the soul as to the body.

- Laying the table – with table cloth, flowers, and candle – makes the occasion homely and special.

- Lighting the candle and singing a verse or blessing brings a mood of peace and togetherness.

- The food offered can be prepared in the craft activity time, and can reflect the seasons.

- Children love the candle and songs, and often ask for them in their homes.

Useful books

Veronika van Duin, *Homemaking as a Social Art: Creating a Home for Body, Soul and Spirit*, Sophia Books, London, 2000

Judy Large and Diana Carey, *Festivals, Family and Food*, Hawthorn Books, Stroud, 1982

Shea Darian, *Seven Times the Sun*, Gilead Press, Marshall, Wisc., 2001

CHAPTER 8

The Circle Time

'Wriggle – wiggle – waggle – toes,
Paddy- Paddy - foot that goes,
In the sock slip – slipping deep.
Slip, slipping deep,
Warm, my sweetie, warm must keep.

Wriggle – wiggle – waggle – toes,
Paddy – Paddy - foot that goes,
In the sock slip – slipping deep.
Slip, slipping deep,
Warm, my sweetie, warm must keep.

Boots we pull on any how.
First this one: Pulla-pull!
Then that one: Pulla-pull!
Tie a bow.
For our walk you're ready now.'

Wilma Ellersiek[1]

FOR PARENTS...

Part 8: The circle time

What is the circle time?

The circle time is the part of the Parent and Child group session when everybody comes together to share songs, rhymes, and perhaps a seasonal story with puppets. This may be before or after the shared meal.

Circle time is important

There are many treasures that can be brought to the young child in the circle time in song, movement, and rhyme. The young child has an innate musicality, love of movement and sense of rhythm – these need to be protected and nourished. Shared songs and interactive rhymes can create a very special intimacy between parent and child. What is learned can be taken back into the home to enrich everyday activities, as well as the more potentially difficult transition times like bedtime.

What is special or different about this time in a Steiner Parent and Child group?

There are several aspects which make our circle times special:

- This part of the session is carefully prepared to include songs, interactive rhymes, finger games, and traditional nursery rhymes, that are appropriate for the ages of the children in the group.
- We give thought to how the songs and rhymes are presented, including clear voice and gestures, mood, and humour.
- The songs and rhymes are chosen to reflect the different seasons and everyday activities over the cycle of the year.
- The circle time is repeated for several weeks, so that the children and parents can learn the songs and rhymes. Young children love and learn by repetition!
- Sometimes the songs and rhymes are woven into a little story that is told every week.
- Steiner Early Years education is renowned for its imaginative puppetry. In Parent and Child groups, some leaders use finger or table-top puppets to tell a short story or link the songs and rhymes together.
- We avoid taped songs and music, preferring the warm simplicity of our own voices. We also avoid the written word with very young children.
- Through demonstrating what is possible, parents are often inspired to sing and to tell more stories to their children in the home.

There are many wonderful riches that can be brought to this part of the Parent and Child group session and each group will develop its own unique blend and flavour. Songs, rhymes, touch and action games, simple stories and puppetry are all fundamentally important treasures that can be brought to young children. For adults too, there is a unique opportunity to experience and learn many songs, rhymes and stories. These can be taken back into the home and used to enrich every daily activity and events.

In many groups a circle is formed for this part of the Parent and Child session, with everyone sitting facing into the centre and therefore it is often called 'circle time'. This is how I will refer to it. However, young children do not understand the concept of a circle and in practice it is often easier for parents and young children to sit in what is endearingly called 'a bunch of grapes' around the leader! Older children (two-and-a-half years and older) will generally wish to participate much more readily than very young children under 18 months. Circle time, like all other elements in the Parent and Child group, has to be sensitively re-created in each particular group, taking into account the general age range of the children and the skills of the leader. What works in one group may not work at all in another. Some groups bypass circle time altogether, except for special occasions!

Here I will outline and discuss the various categories of songs, rhymes, puppetry, and stories which are appropriate for the Parent and Child group and then give some examples from different Waldorf groups. Although this chapter is quite long, actual circle times tend to be very short – perhaps only 5 minutes for very small children!

Movement

'Movement is interwoven with sound for the young children. Neurologists have found that a child who is unable to make certain movements is unable to make certain sounds.'

Rahima Baldwin[2]

Children live totally in the realm of movement and gesture. The young child is a sense being. The senses of touch, movement, balance, and life are in particular being developed in the first few years. As adults and carers, one of our tasks is to ensure that these are protected and enhanced in healthy ways. Much of this is achieved in the natural rhythms and activities of everyday life, which include providing suitable examples for imitation and plenty of time for active and free play both inside and out. But there are quieter, rhythmical, and musical ways in which the young child's need and love for movement and music can be met, and this is through movement, rhymes, and songs.

In addition, finger and hand movement games develop dexterity and help with brain development. Songs and rhymes about everyday jobs and tasks which are accompanied by clear 'truthful' gestures help the young child to come to language as the actions surround the word with meaning. They also provide strong examples for imitation.

Music and rhythm

'Every child is a musical instrument and inwardly feels a kind of well-being in the sound.'

Rudolf Steiner[3]

Young children are strongly drawn to rhythmical and musical songs and games because their experience of their own movement is intimately tied up with the rhythms that they are establishing in their own bodies. The rhythm a young child responds to is not the fixed beat or fixed note value but more that of a pulsating activity – 'elastic in its constant alternation of stress and relief'. In her article entitled 'Music in relation to the young child', Joan Holbek explains that it is not until puberty that it is possible to appreciate and digest our full scale of 'adult' musical intervals and beats. Not all music is good music for young children, and we need to be discerning about what we bring to them.

'A baby's first instrument can be a simple wooden rattle, and later they love to play with pots and pans, and wooden spoons, banging them like drums. …Small children really should have "instruments" that produce sound that they create by their own movement, so electronic books, toys, squeaky toys etc. really have no place in a baby's world. I have watched babies react quite strongly, whether with shock or some type of nervous reaction, when surrounded by noisy toys.'

Joan Holbek[4]

Rudolf Steiner stated in a book on child education:

'For early childhood, it is important to realize the value of children's songs as a means of education. They must make a pretty and rhythmical impression on the senses; the beauty of sound is to be valued more than the meaning of words… Dancing movements in musical rhythm have a powerful influence in building up the physical organs and this should likewise not be undervalued.'[5]

The young child has an innate musicality born out of the sensory openness in the first few years. 'The small child hears music… less with the ear than his whole being, which vibrates and lives in the musical element.'[6] Children as young as two will often sing while playing, the songs mostly being in rhythm to the actions of the play – a living song intimately related to movement and gesture.

Music from television, radio, and tapes is of questionable value with very small children. Much better is the heart-warmed singing voice of a caring adult. More appropriate are those instruments which are simple and gentle in their sound – like wooden block xylophones and lyres. (Apparently different instruments resonate with different parts of the human body. For example, the violin can sound like caressing under the skin, whereas a wooden xylophone penetrates almost to the skeleton. The harp or lyre has a soothing and healing effect on their nervous system.)[7]

The Pentatonic Scale and the mood of the fifth

The young child is most at home with steady slow rhythms and a simplified scale – the pentatonic scale, which is a five full-tone scale rather than our Western seven-tone scales, which include half tones. (This is like playing only the black notes on a piano, or whole tones on the white notes, like CDFGA.) Ancient cultures from the childhood of humanity used the pentatonic scale, and it is still evident in countries such as China and in some old Celtic tunes. Tunes played using a pentatonic scale are always harmonious. The tunes do not have an end note, and therefore possess a dreamy quality of going on and on for ever.

The scale magically creates a sense of security and protection. Pentatonic lyres are available from Waldorf suppliers, allowing young children to experience very directly the harmonious sounds of the pentatonic scale.

The 'mood of the fifth' – a term used in Waldorf circles – refers to tunes in the pentatonic scale which revolve around the central tone of A. Every note in a scale has its own special quality, and the note A above middle C has a particularly harmonious resonance in the young child, and is often used as the starting note. 'This musical mode forms a protective shelter in which the child can feel secure.'[8] Many lullabies and songs used in Waldorf Parent and Child groups and Kindergartens use tunes which are pentatonic and in the mood of the fifth.

The healing quality of hand gesture games or 'caresses'

'Children incarnate through bumping up against the physical world. As a complement to this they need to experience tender, gentle caressing touch.'

Wilma Ellersiek[9]

'Caresses' are rhythmical finger, hand, and touch games that parents or care-givers can share with very young children. The term comes from a particular body of therapeutic work pioneered by the German educator and Waldorf eurythmist, Wilma Ellersiek. To quote:

'In many children we find a great yearning for objective, loving touch, for bodily awareness and bodily limits which help them to incarnate entirely, right down into their fingertips and toes. Only when a child feels comfortable in his or her body and is well incarnated can healthy contact with the outside world be established…. The touch games nurture, above all, the sense of contact, the sense of well being (life) and the sense of the child's own movement. Much that serves later life depends on these senses' wholesome development.'[10]

The gesture games developed by Wilma Ellersiek can be profoundly healing. Language is used in a musical way, with attention given to the forming of sounds. The corresponding gestures are soft and fluid, and the touch is very tender. The rhymes are shared with the young child in a spirit of reverence, free of subjective emotions. Wilma's book *Giving Love, Bringing Joy* is listed at the end of this chapter.

There are many Waldorf programmes which bring these touch games to pregnant mums, babies, and young children up to 3 years of age.

Interactive songs and rhymes

One of the best musical things which can be done with the young child is to sing with them. Singing involves the breath and the middle chest region of the body. A young child's growth is particularly concentrated here and singing therefore helps to harmonize and foster healthy development in this area. It also, of course, makes for a quality of relating and bonding that is particularly warm.

The Mother Goose Program is a Waldorf-inspired organisation in Canada which promotes and teaches the singing of interactive songs and rhymes with parents and young children. The programme is dedicated to strengthening the bond between young children and the adults who care for them. 'Babies and toddlers sit on their mothers' laps, older more independent children may choose to sit nearby, but "doing the rhyme" is always a joint activity with lots of eye contact, gentle physical contact, smiles and laughter'.[11] The rhymes and gestures are done slowly so that the children can keep up. One of the programme's booklets recommends the following types of rhymes for different ages.

Birth to 6 months

Right from birth, soothing songs and rhymes, along with eye contact, smiles and gentle touch, can nurture and strengthen the soul bond between mother and child. Although they do not yet understand language, young babies respond instinctively to the rhythm, rocking, and gentle touch of lullabies and baby rhymes.

4-5 months plus

A baby who is 4-5 months old will understand and be thrilled by songs and rhymes which have a tickle or a hug as a climax.

Sitting-up babies

As the child gets older and can sit upright on a parent's lap, the possibilities expand enormously, and gently rhythmic bouncing, patting, and tickling songs and rhymes come into their own.

Walkers

Once a child can walk there are many possibilities for songs and rhymes which have simple arm and leg gestures, bending over or 'falling down'. Attention span is short but there will be definite favourites!

Talkers

Children learning to talk love rhythmic songs like traditional nursery rhymes. It is not the meaning of the rhyme so much as the rich visual images which can be conjured up in their newly discovered imagination. They also love recognizing words in action rhymes which, for example, identify parts of the body. Songs with strong gestures help them to surround words with meaning.

Two year olds

This is the golden age of songs and rhymes with a climax – claps, tickles, 'falling down'…. Their moods can easily be soothed or diverted by a carefully chosen rhyme!

Three years old and older

By this age children love to join in and to be in a whole group, enjoying a singing and action game or rhyme with other children and adults. They also love to pretend to be people doing various jobs and to be animals.

Ring games

These are songs and rhymes which are done standing or moving in a ring. Many of our traditional ring games are too complicated for a group of very young children and adults. However, there are a few classics like 'Here we go round the Mulberry Bush' or 'Here we go Looby Loo' which are enjoyed very much by the group. These types of songs are more appropriate if the majority of children are over 2 years old. Circle dances and ring games naturally lend themselves to moving toward the left (toward the heart) and are more appropriate if they avoid marching beats.

Seasonal songs and rhymes

In Steiner Parent and Child groups, a celebration of the seasons of the year is brought to the adults and children in song and rhyme, as well as through craft activities and festivals. There is a wealth of songs and rhymes from all over Europe which have been passed down through the Waldorf Kindergarten movement; these are now available in several books (listed at the end of this chapter), in which there are enough short verses and songs to make a group purchase worthwhile. Gestures and interactive actions can be improvised for most of them. There are more mainstream book favourites like *This Little Puffin*, which also has a wealth of poems and verses for every occasion.

Traditional nursery rhymes

Many traditional nursery rhymes have a richness of imagery and rhyme that make them firm favourites with young children and parents alike. Some of our very ancient nursery rhymes may

Circle time, Cambridge

tell, in picture language, of the descent of the young child to the earth – 'Ring a ring of roses' telling the fall from a heavenly paradise to earth; 'Hush a bye baby' telling of the safe cradling in the mother's womb and then the rude birth. Rhymes like 'Sing a song of sixpence' are full of the rich imagery of a dream. Although their meaning may be totally lost to us, young children seem very nourished by a hidden wisdom. Many Parent and Child groups include one or two traditional nursery rhymes in a ring time session.

Story-telling

Parents are encouraged to read to their children from a very young age, but there are many more benefits to be gained from the telling of stories to young children. This is why. For the tiny baby – even whilst still in the womb – the warm weaving of the human voice provides a deep security and bonding. As the child gets older and language begins to develop, story-telling takes on new meaning apart from the loving intimacy it engenders. Words are learnt by being recognized again and again, listening skills are honed, the developing memory is fed with rich pictures which encourage the imagination. But not any story will do! Most of all the soul of the young child is deeply nourished by archetypal themes that are recounted in simple everyday stories about the natural world.

'…it is not the mother or grandmother, or even the teacher who brings the child his first stories: this task is performed by none other than Mother Earth…. [I]t is this greatest mother of all who tells, though in tales which may only be read by the dreamy soul of the child, that the source of all that she surrounds us with lies in the spiritual world. The soul of the little child resounds with everything which Mother Earth "tells" him. This resonance of quiet wonder is, in fact, the deep reverberation of this prenatal sound.'

Daniel Udo de Haes[12]

It is not appropriate to bring fairy stories to the Parent and Child group. These very young children, still so close to the spiritual realms, are naturally and, of necessity, totally open in their senses and soul to earthly life. Daniel Udo de Haes explains that we can only resonate to beauty and truth because we have God within us. For the very young child this resonance is greatest when meeting the ordinary things and events of life – 'these simple things which in their own earthly appearance can speak to him in the language of their heavenly origin'.[13]

In some Parent and Child groups, a little nature story, only 3-5 minutes long, will precede the songs and action rhymes. In others, the story is woven, like the thread, through the songs and rhymes, linking them together like beads on a necklace. The story usually focuses on a family – a boy/girl with one or both parents or grandparent or different common animals who go about their daily lives within the changing seasons. Nancy Mellon, trained in Waldorf education and in psychotherapy and a master story-teller and workshop leader, is the author of

the book *Storytelling with Children*. She writes, 'To speak of the consistent roles of natural things gives children a sense of trust in our universal journey, throughout which all are related and must give to one another'.[14] She explains the archetypal themes that can be woven into story-telling with the very young child.

In the autumn, for example, creatures begin to create their winter coats and collect and store things. We also have these deep instincts and longings, and the little stories can reflect them – watching squirrels collecting nuts, our need to wrap up snugly in warm coats and hats, collecting wood for winter fires, planting little seeds which will sleep over the winter but awaken in the warm rays of the spring sun, picking fruit and making jam.

As winter approaches, the little stories can weave in elements that reflect the growing darkness and the hibernating of the earth's creatures. The stories can be about the resting of Mother Earth, animals snug in their warm dark homes and the delight of making pumpkin lanterns, or later the Martinmas lanterns, to create our light in the darkness. Winter is a natural time for gathering close around a candle to sing and tell stories. Advent has its own special mood of preparation and expectancy and then fulfilment of the great light of Christmas. The Christmas story with the special baby in the manger and the animals, who are close, can be told in a simple way. There is also the experience of frost, snow and ice, cold breath, feeding birds…

As spring comes, there are many stories that can be told about the returning sun, the awakening bulbs, the new lambs and other animals in the fields, the stirring of creatures from their winter sleep, and the budding of trees. At Easter, stories can describe nests and eggs, butterflies being released from chrysalises, seeing hares. In the summer, the full range of outdoor activity and adventuring can be explored from the activities of farmers and other workers, to what can be found in nature on walks or trips to the seaside. All the stories can tell in some way of our gratitude for Mother Earth's abundance and our knowing that the world is guided by spiritual beings.

As children move toward their third birthday, they are ready for the simple fairy stories such as Billy Goats Gruff, The Gingerbread Man, Goldilocks and the Three Bears, and The Enormous Turnip – stories that have a strong element of rhythm and repetition. In Waldorf early years settings, particularly for children from four years of age, the Brothers Grimm stories are widely used. This is because the stories are very old and their imagery and themes are archetypal.

The use of puppets

Puppet stories, beautifully and simply performed, are a very important part of the work with young children in Waldorf early childhood settings. Appropriate puppetry can be very successfully used to tell a story or weave the threads of a song and rhyme time together. ***Bonnie Romanow*** describes the puppet play or story as a balance between the 'in breath' and 'out breath': 'The space between the inhalation and the exhalation is a place where God resides. It is the space where the soul forces live. Stories and puppetry speak to that aspect of the child.'[15]

Finger puppets

Suzanne Down, a Waldorf puppeteer who runs her own School of Puppetry in Colorado, USA is a great advocate of the use of puppets with small children. I was lucky to be able to attend a course on puppetry for young children with her in 2003 and to learn about the magic of her work.

'When a young child sees their first ladybug on their fingers, they open their hearts to the world of nature. This is a powerful force of

Finger puppets

beauty and peace for their entire lives. Animal and nature puppets, especially when made of natural materials, can enhance this connection, weaving it with song, poems, tales, and movement that help the young heart and head enter the natural world with glowing imaginations.'[16]

Finger puppets create a very intimate space between the story-teller and child which can be filled with love and humour. Suzanne describes how finger puppets can magically add a visual element to stories, poems, and songs but there are certain things we need to remember. It is important, for example, to find the natural movement or gesture of the animal we are depicting. This is where the skill lies – in the subtle indication of the true nature of the animals with our finger! This is best learnt by closely observing how different animals move and then practising in front of a mirror.

It is also important to use slow and subtle gestures, as sharp gestures that are too quick are difficult to follow and can break the 'mood'. The puppets need to be 'ensouled' and this is possible when the story or rhyme is told through the heart. With all story-telling, it also helps if the story is visualized in picture form as it is told, rather than just thinking in words.

Suzanne suggests making the finger puppets from wool felt and wool fleece. Silk lengths are used to create a scene on her lap – green for a field, blue for the sea. Little creatures can be hidden under the silk and brought out as a surprise during the story.

Suzanne's books on the subject are listed at the end of the chapter.

Table-top puppets

In Waldorf early childhood settings, where puppetry is given much importance, 'table-top' puppets are very popular, particularly for using with children of 2 years and older. These puppets are usually around 4-7 inches (10-17 cms) high and can be made very simply with wool and material or dry felted. They can also be simply knotted from material or made from wood.

Fabric garment — Head – cotton knit over wool ball — unspun wool hair — wrapped unspun wool body — .12cm — Felt animals

Table-top puppet family

The story-teller uses her lap or a low table to move the puppets as the story is told. Coloured veils and natural wood shapes usually create very adequate settings. As the children progress beyond 3 years of age they will take great joy in retelling the stories themselves, or in making up their own stories using the puppets.

Kim Billington creates wonderful rhyming puppet stories for her Parent and Child group using simple felt puppets and scenery from veils – her video shows some of these.

A puppet story, Kim Billington and a group

Patricia Rubano who runs a group for 3 year olds in the USA explained to me how she told the Giant and the Gnome story:

'The giant is simply a scarf or cloth with a ball of yarn inside for the head and the hands and feet knotted. The gnome is a little knitted gnome. I tie the giant in front of the parents and children so the parents can see how simply a story can be done.'[17]

Sheila Clarkson in Clitheroe, UK uses a table-top puppet family and woollen and wooden animals to tell seasonal stories that are interwoven with songs and rhymes.

Knitted gnomes

HAND PUPPET   SUZANNE DOWN'S ROD PUPPET

Hand puppet and rod puppet

Hand puppets and Waldorf-style rod puppets

These are sometimes called 'heart' puppets because the gestures of our hands are very related to our heart feelings. Because of this, the hand and simple rod puppet can carry and express enormous warmth and intimacy in an unselfconscious way. They have a large range of movement in their arm area, and because of this their gestures can be wide and free. Because young children inwardly imitate these free gestures, these puppets help children to breathe more rhythmically and fully in their own bodies. Apparently these puppets also help young children to sleep well! Children love them, and will often relate to them more openly and freely than to an adult.

A simple rod puppet out of dry felted wool and wooden pegs can be used to tell short stories to young children. These puppets tell the stories directly – *they* are the story-tellers!

Waldorf marionettes

The type of marionette puppet, used in Waldorf Kindergartens for older children, is very simple and easy to make, being basically a square of silk, shaped to form a head, body, and arms, and three strings, one from the top of the head, one from the back, and one that connects the hands. These tend to be used for the older children – 5 years and over – to tell fairy stories such as from the Grimms' collection.

The story apron

The story apron has been developed for Waldorf education by *Suzanne Down*. Several of her students – Jennifer Aguiree, Karen Viani, and others – have focused on apron telling in their work. It is another wonderful way of sharing stories with young children, both in everyday Parent and Child group settings and on more special occasions such as birthdays and community celebrations.

Marionette

One of Suzanne's apron styles for children aged 3-6 is made from a linen table cloth and has embroidered pockets of various sizes. Bells and feathers on ribbons give the apron a magical quality, and inside each pocket is a little character or object whose story can be told – a gnome, a mouse, a star, or flower. Children can take it in turns to point to a pocket – each time this elicits a song and a story with the help of the little inhabitant of the pocket. Individual stories can be told, or the story apron can hold all the characters for one particular story. The characters gather on the story-teller's lap or on a nearby table. Extra puppets, props, and cloths can be kept in a basket nearby.

There are many enchanting possibilities – a handkerchief discovered in a pocket can be knotted during a story to make a little rabbit, a little fairy can unexpectedly appear from inside a flower embroidered on a pocket. Suzanne has created a simple 'one pocket' seasonal story apron for the very young, with just one soft unveiling story image. Jennifer, Karen, and others have also developed the idea of a themed apron story

Janni's story apron

where, for example, an autumn apron is decorated with a tree, and within its roots and branches are little pockets holding birds, squirrels, nuts, and other objects. A birthday apron can hold various treasures which can be put together with a simple story to make a gift for the birthday child. In Chapter 9 on 'special occasions', I describe a birthday apron story in detail.

Letitia Costain, who runs a Parent and Child group in Steiner House, London, has recently developed a story suitcase. She keeps her little puppets and veils inside the suitcase and brings them out at story time. She uses the top of the suitcase as a stage, and says this works better than the floor as, sometimes on the floor, the younger children want to hold the puppets when they can reach them.

The voice

'I can't sing' is a sad reminder of how easily we were put off singing as children. It can take confidence to lead the songs and rhymes for the first time – but only for the first! We all have a singing voice, and the Parent and Child group can be a place where we can learn, slowly and without embarrassment, to enjoy our voices – perhaps even so that we start singing spontaneously, during the day, to our children. A couple of things to remember: children sing in a higher range than most adults, so we need to be sensitive to our child's pitch and try to match it. More important than a perfect voice is one that is heart warmed. This simply means singing and telling stories and rhymes from our hearts rather than from our heads or throats.

It is best if there is one leader 'voice', meaning that one person takes responsibility for this part of the session over a period of time. In some seed groups where there is no leader, the parents often take it in turns to lead the circle time – each taking responsibility for the three/four weeks for which a particular circle time is used.

Engaging the children

In her information leaflet for parents, **Bonnie Romanow** describes very clearly how the circle time can reflect how young children learn. She explains that young children have a 'local memory' – they remember events only if they are reminded by similar ones in the present. The next phase of memory building is rhythmic – doing things repeatedly through the body. The third phase is the forming of the picture memory. Young children do not have a picture memory, so our focus needs to be on building up the rhythmic memory through repetition. The movement triggers the memory. 'The circle engages the body first and then memory follows – which is a very natural process for the young child.'[18]

Bonnie also makes the observation that if the children have really had a strong experience of play – 'out-breathing' – then they tend to sit more calmly during the circle time, which is an 'in-breathing' time.

Janet Parsons shared her experiences with me:

'I find the children respond to the singing rhymes more than the spoken verses, and they love the nursery rhymes. Sometimes they all sit and dream through it all, content on their parents' laps. Other times they are active and moving about. This can be disturbing, and I ask parents with very active children to sit at the back of the circle so that they can play if they prefer. (They do join the circle, when they have passed that 'move at all costs' stage.) I don't demand that the children sit still but encourage them to do so, sometimes sitting them on my lap, and sometimes I give them something to hold.'[19]

Repetition – how the young child learns

All songs and rhymes tend to be repeated in Waldorf Parent and Child groups. Bonnie repeats all her songs and rhymes three times. She explains that the first time allows observation, the second time encourages integration, and the third time helps the action to be learnt – which is the sequence in which the young child learns.

'In the beginning, the first time the children watch, the second time they begin to integrate, and the third time is the echo, the action. Often you will see that this third time is when the children seem to "get it", so to speak.'[20]

Bonnie gives hand-outs after the third week, so that parents have an opportunity, through their own learning of the rhymes, to understand how their young child naturally learns.

Engaging the adults

It is important that the leader of the circle time presents the songs and rhymes clearly with clear gestures. It is also important that all the other adults are imitating the leader as precisely as possible. Bonnie says:

'If your child isn't participating it's important that you (the parent) are. The children are watching us, deciding if they should take the leap out of themselves and imitate our activity. If mom or dad is doing the activity, then even if the child is not yet ready to do it, they experience it as something worth doing.'[21]

Putting the circle time together

Every Parent and Child group will use song, story, movement, and rhymes in a unique way, depending on the strengths and interests of the parents or leader and the ages of the children, although in all groups a circle time will be repeated over a period of three to four weeks.

In a group with the majority of children under 2 years of age, a few interactive rhymes and songs will be enough – perhaps aiming for 3-5 minutes maximum. For older children a very short story using puppets followed by a number of seasonal interactive songs and rhymes, or the other way round, can work very well. Bonnie separates her circle time (which she has before the shared meal) from the puppet/story time which she has at the end of the session. Each group needs to find its own way.

What I give you now is a small selection of examples to show how different Waldorf folk have developed their own circle times.

Acorn Parent and Child group, Clitheroe

Sheila Clarkson uses puppets to tell a seasonal story which incorporates songs and rhymes. All her stories revolve around the day-too-day life of brother and sister – Patrick and Sally. She uses table-top puppets and felt animals to tell the story. The scenery is created with veils and natural wooden blocks. This is a winter circle time. On the floor, or low table, some wood blocks are arranged on a veil to indicate the house space. A green veil laid next to the house denotes the garden. There are simple table top puppets for Sally, Patrick, grandma, and grand-dad. There is a wool bird and some white silk veils for snow.

Sally and Patrick were snug and warm beneath their blanket. Outside the snow fell on their garden and it fell on the trees. It fell on the hills and mountains. When Sally and Patrick looked out of their window they loved to see the white snow.	*Lay a white silk cloth over the garden area.* *Cover a twig with strands of combed sheep's wool.* *Move the puppets to upright.*
Sing together a snow-flake song.	*Sally and Patrick sway to the song.* *Everyone sings.*
Sally and Patrick went downstairs. Grandmother had made hot porridge. They had their breakfast.	*Sally and Patrick are joined by grandma.*
We can stir the porridge; we stir it in the pot; *We can stir the porridge till it's nice and hot*	*Use stirring gestures with arm.* *Everyone says…*

Sing the nursery rhyme 'Pease porridge hot,
pease porridge cold…

Then they put on their warm coats, hat, and
boots, and grandmother gave them some food for
the birds. Sally and Patrick fed the birds.

The birds from high in the sky flew down

They pecked, pecked, pecked at the food, and
then flew away over the trees and over the
garden and house and far, far away

The north wind doth blow,
And we shall have snow;
And what will the robin do then, poor thing –
He'll sit in the barn,
And keep himself warm,
And hide his head under his wing – poor thing.

Sally and Patrick then played in the snow.
They played at sliding, snowballing, and then
they built a snowman

I can build a snowman,
I can build him high;
I can build a snowman reaching to the sky.

Sally and Patrick began to feel cold so
they made their way home. Grandmother
and grandfather had made them a hot
drink. They all sat by the fire.

Polly put the kettle on,
Polly put the kettle on,
Polly put the kettle on –
We'll all have tea.
(They've all gone away.)

Puppets sway to the song.
Everyone sings.

Sally and Patrick move to the white silk veil.
With clear gestures Sheila puts food down for the
birds.

Use birds made out of wool. These can circle
down to the ground.

Birds fly away.

Everyone sings.
Use appropriate arm gestures.

Use small gestures with Sally and Patrick and
make a small mound with a silk veil

Use appropriate gestures to make a snow man
Everyone sings.

Puppets go back to house space

Snowdrop Parent and Child group, Steiner House, London

Letitia Costain told me how she first shares some songs and rhymes with the group, and then tells a little story with veils and very small puppets which she keeps in a basket. Below is an example of how she starts the circle time after the transition and settling songs.

After the songs the candle in a lantern is passed around the whole group and everyone sings 'Candle light'.

Sing:	*Use appropriate arm gestures.*
Rock-a-bye baby on a tree top, etc…	*Everyone sings.*
Sing:	
Row, row, row your boat, gently down the	*Use appropriate gestures.*
stream, etc…	*Everyone sings.*
Say:	
Round and round the garden like a teddy bear, etc…	*Use appropriate gestures.*
	Everyone sings.
Sing:	
Daddy and Mummy and Aunty Con	
Got on a horse and rode along.	*Use appropriate gestures.*
Mummy fell off (lean to one side),	*Everyone sings.*
Daddy fell off (lean to the other),	
But Auntie Con rode on and on (sing again	
slowly and then quickly)	

Candle light

Can - dle light,   can - fle light.   come - ing down to ear - th.

Shin - ing here ab - ove our tab - le.   oh so nice and bright!

This may for example lead into an autumn story, like the one below.

An autumn-time story

Here is a field and a river, and in the field there is a house [place the house], and in the house there lives a family – Mummy, Daddy, children, other relatives. In the field there lives a cow/horse/cat/dog/duck

Sing a song like: Five little ducks went swimming one day…

The children are looking for their friends of summertime – the butterfly and bumble bee, who visit them before going for their winter's rest. They see a hedgehog getting ready for winter, and a squirrel collecting her nuts.

There are little songs and rhymes that can be sung as this happens.

The story ends with the parents and children feeling tired and going back to the house where they go to sleep.

The last song can be 'Twinkle twinkle little star', and then she puts the candle out with a snuffer.

Finally, a goodbye song is sung.

Take a cloth and spread it on the ground.

There are little puppets which come out of apron pockets.

Make a suitable gesture and noise as each animal is taken out of the pocket.

Parent and Child group, Nailsworth, UK

Deirdre Pyzer runs a small Parent and Child group from a Camphill Community. Her group meets for 1¹/₂ hours in the afternoon. After an indoor playtime they go for a walk. On return everyone sits around Deirdre and she first sings a seasonal song with gesture and a few finger games. This leads on to the uncovering of the story basket.

'The simple story unfolds as things are taken out – a green silk "field", a house (curved log), a stream (blue silk) a bridge over it (curved log), a mother, father, boy, girl, cat, and dog. The children always go for a walk appropriate to the season – paddle, collect conkers, see fallen leaves, a squirrel, etc.… Then home again. I round off the story, we say goodbye to the family, and all the things as they are put in the basket in turn. Then I say "goodbye" to everyone in turn.'

Deirdre told me that she makes it clear to her parents that they do not need to stay for the circle time, if, for example, they have an adventurous crawler. They can go home straight after the walk.

Parent and Child group, Bristol Steiner School, UK

Janet Parsons shared with me her 'singing time'.

'The length and content of the singing time depends on the age and mood of the children that day. We always begin with "Who's under the blanket? Who can it be? Lift up and see. It's............' This is a fun method of calling everyone together without having to orchestrate it, and the circle forms in a natural and relaxed way. We then sing "Rinka, Ranka, Rosy, Ray" from *Gateways* (see end of chapter for book details), followed by "Build your house up very high, point the chimneys to the sky. Put on the roof and lay the floor. Open up your big front door", with appropriate actions. We finish with "Row, row, row your boat" and "Ring a ring of roses". In between I include at least one seasonal song with actions (mainly for the parents), nursery rhymes, and finger rhymes. I use puppets quite a bit, and find finger and glove puppets very successful as the children respond to them in an intimate way. The standing puppets are more successful at story time. I find 10 minutes for singing time enough, some mornings 5 minutes is too much and other days you just have to abandon all the pretty things you have planned!'[22]

Parent and Child group, Wynstones School, near Stroud, UK

Brenda Watson, shared her story time. The story always revolves around the family of table-top puppets and what is happening in their garden (which is the top of the nature table). For example, every spring the frog comes to the pond, then around Easter there is a chrysalis which turns into a butterfly. As summer comes the bees arrive to visit the flowers, and then at Whitsun a dove comes to the garden. A little robin lives in the garden all the year round! There are songs for all these happenings. After the story is finished and the session over, the children are welcome to play with the little animals and puppets before they are safely put away.

Managing the transitions at the beginning and end of the circle time

The transition from the preceding part of the session needs to be managed calmly so that the group is settled and focused for the story, songs, and rhymes. The circle time, which is often the end of the whole session, also needs to finish smoothly.

In preparation for the circle time, the toys would have been cleared away with the help of the clearing-away song and a space created in the centre of the room. Sometimes cushions are placed on the floor for adults to sit on, and the children can then sit on their laps. The older children may want their own cushions. There may be a circle or a 'bunch of grapes'.

Letitia told me that she has the circle time at the end of the session. Before the circle time, and after the shared meal, she has a 5-10 minute rest time when lullabies are gently sung to the children. After this time a song is sung to call the children to the circle time, which is given in another part of the room. She says that this short rest beautifully soothes and quietens the group. She also told me that when she had only babies, with no older children in the group, she had wondered whether even a very short story was appropriate. But the parents had asked for the story anyway because they enjoyed it so!

The circle time is often carried out near the nature table. Sometimes a candle is lit or taken from the meal table (if the ring time is done after the meal) and placed on the nature table, quietly signalling the shift of mood. In other groups, special songs are used to gather and quieten the group. For example:

Sheila Clarkson in Clitheroe uses the following sequence to introduce the circle time once the group is settled. First of all she lays the story cloth on the floor in front of her, and then everyone says together:

'Down is the earth,	*(arms down)*
Up is the sky –	*(arms up)*
Here are my friends	*(hold hands)*
And here am I:	*(indicate oneself)*
Two eyes to see,	
Two ears to hear,	
Two feet to walk and run.	
Here are my hands –	
Give yours to me,	
Good morning everyone.'	*(everyone holds hands for a moment)*

She then sings a welcoming song to welcome all the children (and adults as well) to the circle. The little story gnome, called Tomten, is taken by Sheila around the circle to acknowledge each child as their name is sung.

She then lights a candle (to the same song used in the York shared meal) and passes it around the group. During this time she sets up the puppets for the story/song time.

In York I always sing a lullaby as the last song of the circle time. The parents can rock their children gently in their arms, and the song is sung twice a term. Gradually the parents are building up quite a repertoire!

In Waldorf groups there is usually a final special song sung each time to signal the end of the circle time. This song is as important as the songs and rhymes that are used to introduce the beginning of the circle time. The children will, through repetition, trust the ending and will feel secure in its predictability. The ideal is to finish the circle time with a group mood which is quiet and at peace, as for many groups this will also signal the end of the whole Parent and Child session. It is then easier for the children to make the big transition of putting on outside clothes and leaving the group, without upset.

On the next page are the songs which indicate the end of the circle time and of the session in York.

Here we are together

Goodbye now

Good bye now, good bye now, we say good bye and

home we go. Good bye now, good bye now, it's time to say good bye. It's

time to go or we'll be late let the chil-dren lead us to the gate. Good bye now, good

bye now, good bye to all of you.

Blow out the little candle light

Blow out the lit-tle can-dle light, shin-ing light and bright.

Blow out the lit-tle can-dle light, shin-ing light and bright.

Blow out the lit-tle can-dle light, shin-ing light and bright. Shin-ing

light, shin-ing bright, shin-ing light

Main points again

- There are many riches that can be brought to the Parent and Child group circle time. Appropriate elements include, and can be a combination of:

  * movement, gesture, and interactive rhymes and games
  * songs in the pentatonic scale and 'mood of the fifth'
  * classic nursery rhymes
  * simple ring games with gesture and imitation
  * seasonal songs and rhymes
  * seasonal stories and, for older children, some very simple fairy tales
  * puppetry

- Themes in the circle time need to reflect the goings-on in the real world of the young child and the changes in the seasons.

- The length of the circle time will be dependant on the age of the children – perhaps only 5 minutes for toddlers, and 6-10 minutes for older children.

- Thought and preparation needs to be given to the transition times before and after the circle time to ensure that they are as smooth and harmonious as possible.

- Because young children thrive on rhythm and repetition, a circle time will usually be repeated for 3-4 weeks or even a half term before being changed. Some groups keep the same songs all the time, or introduce songs in a rotation.

- Every group will use the circle time in a unique way. Important factors include the age of the children and the strengths and interests of the circle-time leader.

Useful books and resources

Songs and rhymes and stories for the very young child

Mary Thienes-Shunemann, 'Singing with Children Series', CD included. A Naturally You Can Sing Production, East Troy, Wisc., USA; available from mary@flowformsamerica.com
  * *The Wonder of Lullabies*
  * *Sing a Song of Seasons*
  * *The Singing Baby*
Candy Verney, *The Singing Day* (CD included), Hawthorn Press, Stroud, 2003
Parent–Child Mother Goose Program series, available from mgoose@web.net 720 Bathurst Street, Suite 402, Toronto, Ontario (Canada), includes:
  * *Zoom, Zoom, Zoom and Other Rhymes to Play with Your Child*
  * *The Moon is Round and Other Rhymes to Play with Your Baby*
  * *Bounce Me, Tickle me, Hug me*
  * *Lap Rhymes and Play Rhymes from around the World*
  * *Favourite Interactive Rhymes and How to Use Them*
Wilma Ellersiek, *Giving Love – Bringing Joy: Hand Gesture Games and Lullabies in the Mood of the Fifth*, available from the Waldorf Early Childhood Association of North America, Spring Valley, NY, 2003
Sheena Roberts, *Playsongs, Action Songs and Rhymes for Babies and Toddlers* (CD included), Playsongs Publications, London, 1991
Carol Gnojewski, *Songs and Games for Toddlers*, Totline Publications, Calif., 1997
National Youth Choir of Scotland, *Singing Games and Rhymes for Tiny Tots*, the Mitchell Library, 201 North Street, Glasgow, UK, 2002; available from SPPA (Scottish Pre-school Play Association)

Seasonal poems, songs, and stories for Waldorf
Kindergarten teachers – Wynstones Press,
Gloucester, UK, 1983; series includes:
* *Winter*
* *Spring*
* *Summer*
* *Autumn*
* *Spindrift*

Elizabeth Matterson (compiler), *This Little Puffin*, Puffin Books, Harmondsworth, 1991

Shea Darian, *Seven Times the Sun: Guiding Your Child through the Rhythms of the Day*, Gilead Press, Marshall, Wisc., 2001

Kim Billington, *Stories and Songs Together*, book and video available from P.O. Box 4034, Croydon Hills, Victoria 3136, Australia

Puppetry and story-telling

Seasonal collection of poems and stories for early childhood teachers and parents. (Finger puppets) Collected by Suzanne Down.

Available from Jupiter Tree School of Story and Puppetry Arts, storyartpublications@juno.com – PO Box 17666, Boulder, CA (USA).
Includes:
* *Spring Tales*
* *Autumn tales*
* *Around the World with Finger Puppet Animals*

www.junipertreepuppets.com

Janni Nicol and Estelle Bryer, *Nursery Rhymes and Stories*, glove/theatre or table-top puppet plays for solo or more puppeteers (special occasions). Available from Jannisteiner@aol.com

Roy Wilkinson, *Plays for Puppets* (glove puppets for older children), Rudolf Steiner College Press, Calif., 1993

Nancy Mellon, *Storytelling with Children*, Hawthorn Press, Stroud, 2000

CHAPTER 9

Special occasions

'In the modern world [festivals] have, to a far reaching extent, lost their substance, …but rightly understood, rightly celebrated, the festivals can become a source of healing for the individual and society, a harmonising, community building power… Through living with the festivals and seasons… we can learn to experience ourselves in the world, and the world in us.'

Pamela Johnson Fenner and Karen Rivers[1]

FOR PARENTS...

Part 9: Special occasions

What special occasions are celebrated in Steiner Parent and Child groups?

The Festivals celebrated in Waldorf settings are mainly Christian in origin, but they use symbols and activities which transcend partisan religious practice and appeal to what is sometimes called 'the universal human'.

- They are a way of acknowledging our connectedness to nature, the great cosmic cycles and spiritual truths;
- They provide a sense of goodness and security for the growing child, not only through seeing that we as adults care about our world, but also simply in the rhythmic repetition and re-experiencing of these special high points, year after year;
- Celebrating these little festivals in community and in the family home brings many riches in terms of sharing, sense of meaningful occasion, and fun.

In the Steiner Parent and Child group, festivals will be celebrated in a very simple way – often with a special shared meal and particular songs, rhymes, or a puppet story. For the more important festivals like the Harvest Festival in September, the Lantern Festival in November, Advent, and Easter, there may be a separate gathering organized outside the Parent and Child session, with a little activity and shared food.

Nothing is explained to the children, and only the older ones will have any sense of the occasion. Adults, however, are often deeply nourished by these simple events. An information sheet which explains the background and spiritual meaning of the particular festival and time of year is often given to each parent beforehand, for their own reflection. For many parents, attending a little seasonal festival in the Parent and Child group will be a first-time experience – it can be very moving. It often inspires parents to create family festivals throughout the year in their own homes.

Birthdays are celebrated very simply – often with a cake and special song. However, in some groups the Rainbow Bridge birthday story is told.

In this chapter I will look at how festivals and birthdays can be celebrated. As with the other components of a group session, what happens differs widely from group to group, depending on the age of the children and the confidence and interests of the leader. Most group leaders I have spoken to agree that the proceedings need to be as simple as possible. A sudden change of rhythm in the session can cause very young children distress rather than pleasure. Some leaders would argue that these special events are primarily for the adults to enjoy – they are soul food. We try and demonstrate in a simple way how festivals can bring delight, reverence, and a special sense of occasion into family life. Many groups celebrate the festivals outside the session time as a separate community event.

Festivals in the round of the year

Festivals are celebrated in all Steiner educational settings. They are occasions when teachers, parents, and children come together, and they bind community in a joyful way.

The festivals that are marked in the Waldorf calendar are mainly Christian, and arise from more ancient times when the changes of the seasons were acknowledged and worshipped. Each significant point in the cycle of the year has its own quality and deeper meaning.

The four main festivals – Advent, Easter, St John's, and Michaelmas – fall near the four significant solar points of the year – the winter and summer solstices, and the spring and autumn equinoxes. The other main festivals cluster around what are known as the Celtic Cross Quarter Days – the beginning of Spring at Imbloc (at the beginning of February); the beginning of Summer at Beltane (beginning of May), and the beginning of Winter at Samhain (beginning of November). The other cross quarter day which heralds Lammas, the beginning of Harvest and Autumn, which falls at the beginning of August, is in the summer holidays so is not celebrated in school communities in the UK. There are other traditional festivals which are also acknowledged during the year. The chart below shows the sequence of the festivals of the year.

Circle showing seasons and festivals

At first, the smallest children will only dream their way through these festivals, but over the years these rhythmical high points of the year provide a deep security to the growing child. As well as being celebrated in the group, they are often taken into the family home, where they become permanent family events. For many parents, attending a little seasonal festival in a Parent and Child group will be a first time experience, and it can be very moving.

There are some excellent books which describe in detail the festivals celebrated in Waldorf settings, The book *All Year Round* is an excellent place to start learning about them. (See also the book list at the end of this chapter).

Multiculturalism and festivals

Parent and Child groups are open to families of all or no religious persuasion. These days many of us live in multi-cultural communities. How do we honour the richness and validity of each spiritual path? How do we avoid the dangers of being exclusively Christian, on the one hand, and of 'trying to be all things to all men' on the other?

I spoke about this to *Lynne Oldfield*, who runs the Waldorf Kindergarten teacher training in London. The great festivals from all the religious traditions are embedded in the cycle of the year, and their timing is often determined by the sun, moon, or star constellations. The festivals speak of spiritual events, but these events are placed at the particular time of the year where the deeper meaning is reflected and shared by the mood and rhythm of the earth and the cosmos. The collective spiritual experience, which lies at the heart of all festivals, unites us with heaven, earth, and each other. Rudolf Steiner himself said that we need to create new festivals that express eternal truths in a contemporary living way.

This understanding makes it possible to create uncomplicated family festivals using simple symbolism and the qualities of each season to touch and express the essential mystery of our place in the cosmos. Lynne explained: 'Young children do not in any case live in "differentiation" – to them everything is united and whole, so it is even more appropriate that we celebrate what we have in common rather than our differences.' With these thoughts in mind we can transcend the 'particular' of a certain religious tradition and look for ways to create festivals which express universal truths that everyone ('the universal human') can appreciate.

Out of an inner reflection on the particular qualities of different times of the year, images can arise which can be used to create simple celebratory events which are both joyful and spiritually enriching to people from all sorts of religious backgrounds. Some festivals have spread and become established throughout the Waldorf world – the Advent spiral being an example.

Festivals in the Parent and Child group

In this section I describe briefly the meaning of the main festivals celebrated in Steiner Early Years settings and how some Parent and Child groups celebrate them. Ideas for craft activities for the various festival times are given in Chapter 6.

Candlemas, 2 February (or Snowdrop Day)

The Celtic Festival Imbolc (Festival of Lights), dedicated to the Goddess Brigit, is held on the 1st February – the beginning of Spring. This Christian Festival (dedicated to St Brigid) marked the occasion when the Holy Child was presented to the Temple. In many parts of the world, the new candles for the coming year are taken into the churches and blessed on 2 February – hence the name 'Candlemas'.

Candlemas comes at the time of year when the darkness of winter is beginning to be noticeably replaced by lighter mornings. New life is stirring, and the first bulbs of spring – the snowdrops – are beginning to make their brave appearance in our British gardens. It seems that the earth is beginning quietly to breathe out after the pause of mid-winter. It is a time when the old, dead year meets the new life. Using these indications, the Parent and Child group can celebrate this festival very simply and beautifully. Here are some ideas from various groups.

Making candles

In London, **Letitia Costain** helps her parents and children to make candles from sheets of beeswax, rolling a wick in the middle, and then decorating the outside with coloured wax. These can be taken home.

In Clitheroe, **Sheila Clarkson** told me that she melted bees wax (from old candles) and made (new) walnut shell candle boats, which the parents and children then floated in a tub filled with water, rocks pebbles, and shells. She also put little lighted candles in the ground outside where bulbs where beginning to pop their heads up.

Waking up the bulbs

In York, the parents and children have made rolled candles and then taken them into the garden in jam jars (for protection from the wind) and laid them near emerging bulbs. There is a little song that can be sung to the tune of 'Frère Jacques' which goes:

> Are you sleeping, are you sleeping
> Little bulbs, little bulbs,
> Spring time is coming, spring time is coming
> Ding, dang, dong, ding, dang, dong.

Little bells can be rung by the children to help wake up the bulbs.

The nature table

In the group room, snowdrops can be displayed on the nature table where the dark cloths of winter can be uncovered, perhaps in one corner, to reveal a pale green cloth, representing the return of spring. In circle time there is a song about snowdrops that can be sung and rhymes which reflect the emergence from winter.

Candlemas celebration

Shrove Tuesday (the day before the beginning of Lent)

The tradition of making pancakes comes from the practice of needing to use up certain food items including butter, eggs, and milk before the beginning of the Lenten fast. On the Continent this day is celebrated in a more frivolous manner with an event called Carnival (translating as 'goodbye to meat'!) where there is dressing up and general fun. Our pancake races are probably an echo of this.

In many Parent and Child groups, pancakes are made for the shared meal, and songs about pancakes are sung. The little story can be told about pancake making and tossing.

Mothering Sunday (fourth Sunday in Lent)

Mothering Sunday is a medieval English festival; a day when the austerities of Lent were relaxed and people were given time to visit the church of their Baptism and for children employed as servers in the Michaelmas Fairs to visit their families. It was customary to bake Simnel cake and to give violets.

Sheila makes small cakes with the parents and children in the week before Mothering Sunday. These are gift wrapped and presented to each parent.

Easter (first Sunday after the full moon after the Spring Equinox)

Although Easter Sunday is in school holiday time there are various ways in which this special time can be celebrated. For the young child the mood of Easter is of new growth and renewal, rather than the crucifixion. There are many seasonal elements at this time of year which symbolize in a simple way this special time.

Decorated Easter eggs

The egg, a very ancient symbol representing the cosmic egg of creation, resurrection, and new birth, is the traditional symbol of Easter. Egg decorating can be done with the children in the weeks leading up to Easter. One simple way is to find coloured tissue paper which bleeds colour if dampened (you need to test to be sure!). The eggs are blown and then covered in tissue paper which has been wetted. The wrapped eggs are left to dry. When the tissue paper layers are peeled off the colour will have made marvellous patterns and shapes on the egg surface. There are many other ways of decorating eggs and at the end of the chapter some craft book references are given.

The Easter hare

The hare also has ancient lineage, featuring in stories from Pre-Christian times as well as from Buddhism. The hare represents the archetype of the Self who has overcome personal ego and is capable of devotion and sacrifice. Although he does not lay the eggs himself, he is permitted to decorate them and bring them on Easter morning. The Easter hare motif can be used in different decorations.

The Lenten and Easter garden

On the nature table, the 40 days of Lent can be marked by a simple vase of branches in bud, and some bare soil in a bowl. During the Easter Festival when the group meets again, the nature table is transformed into an Easter Garden. The coloured eggs are used to decorate the budding branch, which then becomes the centre-piece of a spring display complete with nests, chicks, and flowers.

Easter crafts

The Easter Egg hunt

This carries the symbolism of seeking and finding. Many groups meet on Easter morning to enjoy an egg hunt together, perhaps with a shared meal afterwards. Sheila makes grass nests with the parents which, on Easter morning, are filled with Easter eggs and placed in hedges and trees. The parents bring biscuits and cakes to share with a hot drink afterwards.

Craft activities and story

The chrysalis transforming into the butterfly is another symbol of the mystery of Easter, and butterflies can adorn the Easter Garden. Tissue butterflies can be made by wrapping pipe cleaners around rectangular strips of coloured tissue paper and then hung on thread lengths Growing grass seed, started a week before Easter, expresses in a magical way the new growth of spring, and this can also be placed on the Easter Garden.

May Day – May 1st (Beltane)

May Day is the Celtic Festival of Beltane, heralding the beginning of summer. The trees are now in full blossom ('may' is a country word for hawthorn blossom). The natural world is bustling and bursting with activity and growth, and the earth breathes forth her abundance. Watching the sunrise on this day is a wonderful experience for adults and children alike.

The Maypole

Originally a tree stripped bare, apart from some new growth at the top, the Maypole still stands in some village greens. The tradition is to attach coloured streamers to the pole and to dance around the pole in formations that weave the ribbons together in patterns. The Maypole and the dances that take place around it accurately express the exuberance and sheer potency of this time of the year. A queen of the May is chosen, and adults and children alike wear garlands of flowers. 'To the rhythm of lively music, the Maypole dance works its magic, translating the invisible weaving of colour and light in the streaming summer air...'[2]

In Clitheroe, UK, Sheila Clarkson will start preparing for May Day a few weeks earlier, by making head garlands, either out of long grass woven together with binding string, or out of card. The grass garlands can be decorated with real flowers on the day, the card garlands can have crêpe paper flowers. She also starts singing the Maypole songs so that the parents know these by the time the festival arrives.

On May Day, all families gather around a Maypole erected for the occasion. Little Maypole dances are danced by all – parents with their children (often the first time for adults as well as children!). There is a shared lunch for everybody, and at the end of the festival each of the children takes home a small posy of flowers which are handed out during a song sung by all the families in a large circle. The Maypole is not just used on May Day but also on several sessions throughout May. A similar event takes place at Letitia Costain's

group in London. Here, the Maypole has been made from a broom handle and is used inside!

Whitsun (Pentecost) (50 days after Easter)

In the Christian tradition, Pentecost is the time when Christ's disciples and Mary were filled with the Holy Spirit, which descended upon them in tongues of fire. Through this experience, they were able to speak in a way that made them understood in every language. Pentecost is experienced as a festival of community and a celebration of unity in diversity. In England, Pentecost is also called Whitsun, from the term 'White Sunday', as it was once the custom to wear white on this day.

Whitsun is celebrated in some groups as a community picnic, where everyone is invited to wear white. The food can be white as well! Poems and songs and music from different cultures are shared.

Before Whitsun, parents with their children can make Whitsun doves from white card and tissue paper to hang as a mobile in the family

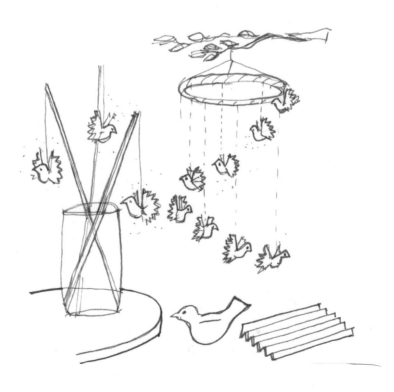

Whitsun doves

home. The nature table is decorated in white, and twelve candles are arranged around a central one, to represent the twelve disciples around Christ. The stories and songs around this time can be about doves and about other cultures.

St John's Festival – 24 June (Midsummer)

Midsummer is the high point of nature's abundant outpouring. Days are at their longest; the air is filled with warmth and we expand and relax in the great outdoors. This is how families celebrate this festival. For adults, wishing to go deeper, however the festival of St John is, in contrast, a reflective time. John the Baptist (whose festival it is) warns us against totally losing ourselves in 'midsummer madness', but instead asks us to find and keep hold of an inner discipline and nobility that will carry us through the darkening months. At the point of maximum abundance and frivolity in the cycle of the year, we are asked to think consciously about our own life direction, and look toward the coming decline in the natural world.

'Jumping the fire'

Fire rituals, which are a traditional aspect of this great festival, echo back to ancient times when huge fires were made to burn bones and the unwanted dross of life, the smoke cleansing the neighbourhood of evil influences. The custom of driving animals over or between fires was to drive out parasites. Today in Steiner schools, 'jumping the fire' lives on, a chance to be prepared, by an act of courage, for the darker months ahead and to have fun! Some groups will make a tiny fire with tea lights which the parents and older children can symbolically jump over.

Even if there is no outdoor space, celebrating St John's festival is still possible. Letitia Costain lights a tea light and everyone jumps over it, to the rendering of 'Jack be nimble, Jack be quick…'!

Jumping the 'fire'

with the four elements

Families sometimes gather for a picnic where the elements of water, air, earth, and fire can be experienced. A small fire is lit, and older children (6+) can 'jump the fire' with their parents. A shared meal is cooked over the fire, and grass wreaths are made, and saved for the base of the Advent wreaths.

In Clitheroe, in the Parent and Child session prior to St John's, the parents and children make paper 'whippa-whoppers',[3] which they can take home. Sheila (Clarkson) also gives each child a posy of lavender.

A midsummer fair

When the Lancaster Parent and Child group was started in 1990s, we organized a little 'Fair' in a group member's garden. There were very simple tasks for the willing little children to perform – for example, pouring water from a jug into a vat, hanging washing on a line, rolling balls along the ground. There were flower garlands to be made and worn, and elderflower pancakes to be eaten.

Other simple craft activities

Letitia Costain suggests making bee mobiles (from pom-poms or from alder cones), fans, and rose water.

The nature table

The nature table can be decorated with objects which represent the four elements – for example, a large golden sun motif for fire, bees and birds for air, pebbles and flowers for earth, and sea shells for water. There is a large candle to signify the importance of this festival. A rose and a lily can be placed on the nature table – the rose symbolizing inner transformation and the lily symbolizing innocence.

Harvest (Autumn Equinox) and **Michaelmas** (September 29)

By the time the summer holidays are over at the beginning of September, there are signs that the earth is beginning to 'breathe in' after the out-breath of the first half of the year. Plant growth is coming to a halt, the yellow grain fields have been harvested, and the berries and fruits are full and ready to be picked. Harvest can be celebrated over a number of weeks with various practical activities such as grinding wheat (a coffee grinder is good), chopping fruit to make jam, chopping vegetables to make soup, and making simple corn dollies. Some groups have a harvest meal with a large loaf of bread in the shape of a wheat sheaf.

The Feast of St Michael and All Angels starts on 1 August. Michaelmas Day is on 29 September, and comes very shortly after the autumn equinox when day and night are in balance. Archangel Michael is usually depicted with sword in hand, subduing the dragon, or else he is holding a set of scales with which he balances the soul deeds of man after death.

Michael helps us find inner spiritual strength, which makes it possible for us to move through nature's season of darkness and death, and all difficult periods of life. He protects those who strive to do the good. Michaelmas stands in balance to Easter: there, the festival celebrates the resurrection and victory of life over death; while here, we are challenged to dig deeply to find our own forces that will counter the dying of natural life.

Simple ways to celebrate

The background and meaning of Michaelmas can be given to adults in the form of a hand-out, as can every festival as it arises. For the young children in a Parent and Child group, it can be sufficient to give them bulbs to plant outside; these will emerge in the spring, thereby linking this festival with Candlemas and Easter. Other ideas might be to make bread buns in the shape of dragons, or make dragons out of strings of conkers.

Letitia Costain makes this suggestion:

'A beautiful crayon/painting can be done by old and very young alike by placing leaves (vein side up) underneath the paper, crayoning over the leaves, then wetting the paper and painting it with primary colours. The paint flows together making a wash of colour around the leaf vein shapes.'

Sheila Clarkson celebrates the Harvest Festival and Michaelmas together. The week before the festival she makes bread in the shape of a harvest sheaf. On the day of the festival the table is decorated with lots of flowers and each child over 18 months is given a plate and knife to spread their own butter, honey from the comb, or home-made jam. Produce from gardens is shared amongst the group. After the regular little walk, each child plants a bulb in a pot, and these are kept until the following Candlemas when the children can take them home. On this festival each child takes home a shiny apple.

The Apple Lady

In Lancaster the tradition of the Apple Lady was started. On Michaelmas Day the children and parents go for an autumn walk, collecting conkers and leaves to make neck garlands. On their way they meet the Apple Lady, dressed as Mother Earth in her flowing robes and carrying a basket. She offers each child a shiny apple whilst singing a short song. The autumn walk ends with a puppet story and shared meal.

The nature table

The nature table at this time, draped in flaming reds and oranges and displaying the natural harvest of autumn, can have a candle – perhaps decorated with a dragon – as the centre-piece.

Halloween (31 October) and Bonfire Night (5 November) (Samhain)

Halloween, All Saints Day, All Souls' Day, and Remembrance Sunday all cluster around the Celtic Cross Quarter Day called Samhain (2 November), which announces the beginning of winter and the Celtic new year. All of these festival days are concerned one way or another with remembering the dead. It is at this time of the year that the veil between the visible and invisible worlds is thought to be at its thinnest.

Halloween is an echo of folk customs which respected the closeness of the 'wee people' and made sure they were given their due respect. Turnip lantern faces warned off the more menacing visitors! Many people disagree with the commercialism and dark connotations of Halloween, and some Parent and Child groups do not celebrate this festival.

There is, however, another way of approaching this time of year and the qualities that these winter festivals bring. As the light fades in the natural world so we are challenged to find our own inner light. The turnip and pumpkin lanterns mirror this need to create a light inside a physical shell to compensate for the lengthening outer darkness. This theme is repeated a few days later in our Bonfire Night, an echo of another ancient fire festival which marked an important transition in the year. (Apparently at the end of the Celtic year all old fires were extinguished and new ones kindled from the ceremonial bonfire on Samhain.[4]) We still gather together at this time to share light and warmth in the increasingly dark and cold world.

In some Parent and Child groups, there will be pumpkin carving and the making of pumpkin soup or pie. Songs, rhymes, and stories about pumpkins are told.

Families will often come together for Bonfire night to create a little festival complete with fire, fireworks, sparklers, Yorkshire parkin cake, and hot juice.

The nature table

The autumn colours will now have moved into darker, earthier colours like brown and blue. Bare but interesting shaped pieces of wood can make a centre-piece. Teasel hedgehogs, felt squirrels, and other little animals can shelter around the log. The spoils of late autumn – conkers and acorns, leaves and berries – are still around. This is also a time when gnomes of various sizes and descriptions tend to make their appearance.

Martinmas (12 November)

Martinmas is commonly celebrated on the continent, though it is unheard of in the UK apart from in Waldorf settings. It is the festival of St Martin of Tours (316-397 AD) who helped to establish Christianity in France, and speaks to how we can provide warmth and hope to each other in the darkening days.

'When we make a paper lantern, we may feel that we are giving protection to our own little "flame" that was beginning to shine at Michaelmas, so that we may carry it safely through the dark world…. Every light brings relief to the darkness.'[5]

Martinmas lanterns and the lantern walk

The festival is commonly celebrated with a lantern walk through the local neighbourhood, with accompanying special Martinmas songs – an activity which is very successful in Parent and Child groups. In *Letitia Costain*'s group, the children and adults have done wet-on-wet

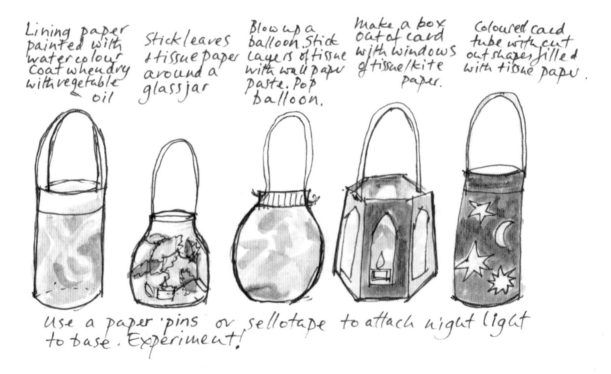

Lining paper painted with watercolour. Coat when dry with vegetable oil

Stick leaves + tissue paper around a glass jar

Blow up a balloon. Stick layers of tissue with wall paper paste. Pop balloon.

Make a box out of card with windows of tissue/kite paper.

Coloured card tube with cut out shapes filled with tissue paper.

Use a paper pins or sellotape to attach night light to base. Experiment!

Martinmas lanterns

painting on a large sheet of lining paper a couple of weeks before the festival to make beautifully coloured paper for the lanterns (as described in Chapter 6). When the paper is dry, it is cut up to make paper lanterns with handles. Another of many possible ideas is to blow up balloons and stick coloured tissue paper to the outside, using home-made flour-and-water paste. When the glue is dry, the balloon is popped and taken out. Holes are made near the top rim and string threaded through to make a handle. A night light can be safely stuck inside the base of all these lanterns.

Sheila Clarkson also starts making the lanterns with her group at least two weeks before the festival. She told me:

'Last year we met at 4.30 p.m. on a Sunday. We did a short walk singing lantern songs. When we arrived back in the garden, Tony, my husband, had a bonfire burning. We had pumpkin soup – which parents and I had made – with bread rolls and apple cakes. It was a great success.'

The nature table

A lantern can be displayed on the increasingly bare table. Traditionally, red and blue are the colours for this festival

Advent (begins on the fourth Sunday before Christmas)

Advent means 'preparation for an important event' – the birth of the Christ child. Unfortunately, by this time of the year, Christmas commercialism is in full swing in the shops, and it is easy to see December as just a mad rush. However, Advent as it is celebrated in Waldorf settings allows us to move into a quieter, more contemplative place, which is much more in keeping with the silence and darkness of the resting natural world.

The Advent wreath

Advent wreaths are made and used in the weeks running up to Christmas. Traditionally, the Advent wreath is a ring of cut evergreen, on to which four candles are placed. An additional candle is lit on each of the Sundays leading up to Christmas, so that on the last Sunday all four are lit. Grass or straw wreaths stored from St John's Festival can be brought out and used as the ring, on to which the greenery is attached. The advent wreath can be used during the shared meals during Advent. It is another way in which the theme of 'finding the light in the darkness' is brought to expression, a way which acknowledges the steps of the journey to the greatest light in the darkest time of the year – Christmas.

Advent wreath

The Advent Spiral

This is now a fairly established tradition in all Waldorf settings. The Advent Spiral is literally a spiral of greenery laid on the floor of a large room with a single large candle on a tree stump in the middle. Stones and crystals are set into the greenery and the room is lit with only a few candles. This gives a wonderful atmosphere of peace. In the silence and awe that the scene engenders, each child with a parent, in turn, is given an apple, which has an unlit candle securely embedded in it. They slowly walk into the centre of the spiral, light their candle from

An Advent spiral

the big candle, and then place their smaller candle where they wish on the evergreen spiral as they walk back out. The only sound is the soft singing of Christmas carols. No words are spoken, and the placing of the apple candles continues until all children have had a turn and the room is filled with the soft glow of candlelight. Everyone leaves the room as quietly as they arrived and it is only when safely away from the Advent Spiral room that food and drink are served and conversations begin.

This is truly a festival which reaches the 'universal human': it speaks of our path into the darkness of this world, of our light which is the same as the true light, and how we take this light and place it where we will on our life path.

Sheila Clarkson usually holds the Advent Spiral – to which all families and grandparents are invited – on the first Sunday of Advent at 2.30 p.m. The Advent spiral has been set up in the group room, which is lit with only a few candles. Parents are given candles in jars to illuminate the carol sheets. As great care always needs to be taken with festivals where there is candlelight; minded buckets of water and fire blankets are close at hand.

Other Advent activities

During the weeks running up to Christmas, there are many simple practical activities which can be shared – for example, making Christmas cookies (a continental custom) and Christmas presents like decorated candles, wool angels, and tissue-paper transparencies.

The Advent Garden

The winter nature table can be transformed into an Advent Garden, complete with stable. Over the weeks leading up to Christmas, Mary and Joseph – who can be made out of wool or felt – can slowly make their way across the garden to the stable.

For non-Christians who don't celebrate Christmas

It is no coincidence that the festival of the birth of the Christ child is placed near the darkest day of the year. Seeds, which are full of the potential of new life, need to be planted in the darkness of the earth; our spirits are encased likewise like a seed in the depths of our souls; we are conceived in the darkness of our mothers' wombs. The birth of a special child to a mother in the depth and silence of midwinter speaks of something universal. I feel that even for non-Christians there is something in the Christmas story which can be related to on a non-literal level, if we can take the time to listen to the essential qualities of midwinter.

Other ways to approach the festivals in the group

Janet Parsons in Bristol celebrates the festivals through discussion and practical activities:

'I use the seasons, my nature table, and the activities to give parents a view of what they could do at home. During Advent we made transparency windows, folded stars, and fruity bread, and I held an Advent Calendar workshop in the week before Advent... Later in the year I am planning a "Celebrating Together" workshop, where we can discuss how families can celebrate...'[6]

Birthdays

So often birthdays, for adults anyway, are quiet hidden affairs! What if we recognized that on this one day of the year we are closest to our spiritual identity – that we truly stand in our own unique light on our special day? Birthdays are about celebrating the day we decided to start our life adventure. On our birthdays, those who love, encourage, and support us on our life

journeys are drawn to celebrate with us. How important birthdays are! But how can we bring the real significance of birthdays, simply and beautifully, to the young child, whilst avoiding the worst excesses of consumerism and entertainment?

The Thomas's *Children's Party Book*[7] makes the point that a child is not really ready for a proper birthday party until they speak of themselves as 'I'. This is a huge stage in a young child's development, and occurs in the third year. It reflects the child's early discovery of their own consciousness separate from those around them. Until this time, a child will not truly be aware of their birthday occasion and may even be disturbed by the change of routine and the level of fuss and surprise. Even when the young child is seen to be ready for a party, the Thomas's suggest a very simple affair – perhaps with a puppet show and a few simple circle songs and rhymes. So should birthdays be acknowledged in the Parent and Child group, and if so, how?

Birthdays need to be approached with sensitivity and flexibility. In some groups, no special story is told, but there may be a birthday cake brought in by the parent. *Janet Parsons* in Bristol keeps birthdays simple this way:

'I make a small gift to give at singing time – a little stuffed felt ball for one year olds, a small pouch containing a pretty shell for two year olds, and a butterfly for the three year olds. I sing "What is in my basket? – let us see...". And as I take the gift from the basket, "Lucy has a birthday...has a birthday. Lo and behold, a little parcel for the birthday child." The parents bring a cake if they want to.'[8]

Brenda Watson at Wynstones School also keeps her birthdays very simple. She has a special candle and holder which she will put in front of the birthday child at the meal time, and the child later extinguishes the candle with a special

Birthday

snuffer. She also makes each child a birthday present: on their first birthday, they receive a decorated candle; when 2, a knitted kitten; at 3, a standing puppet; and at 4, some finger-knitted strings for play.

There is a birthday story told in Steiner Kindergartens that many Parent and Child group leaders have adapted for the very young child and their parents. This following version is told by Letitia Costain, who uses a story apron.

The Rainbow Bridge Birthday Story

Letitia's story apron has a top pocket decorated with blue felt, and the pocket is embroidered with the sun, moon, and stars. In this pocket are kept two angels made from wool fleece – a big guardian angel and a little angel who wants to be a child. There is also a baby in the pocket made out of wool and swaddled in a felt blanket. Finally, there is a 'rainbow bridge' made of coloured paper folded to represent rainbow steps. Letitia sits on the floor, and around the base of her apron she arranges a wooden house with a felt family, a field, and animals, as she sings a song about a rainbow. Then she starts the story. As she tells the story, she takes the angels out of the pocket.

> ## Box 27: The Rainbow Bridge birthday story
>
> Once upon a time a big angel and a little angel were travelling round the sky because the little angel wanted to go over the rainbow bridge to a baby girl/boy. They fly to the Sun for a golden gift, and then to the moon for a silver one, and to all the stars for a crown of star-light to take down to earth.
>
> When they get to the rainbow bridge *[here she takes out the rainbow bridge]* the little angel looks down at the earth and says 'Where shall I go?' Then other little angels join her *[this is only spoken, not represented by other angels!]* and they go down together to their mothers and fathers where they can play together. And one day they can give back their gifts to the sun and the moon and the stars.
>
> *[The little angel is put back into the pocket and then the big angel takes the baby to the family waiting by the house.]* The big angel says, 'I will always be with you' *[and flies back to the pocket, leaving the baby with the mother and father].*

At the end of the story, Letitia sings 'Twinkle twinkle little star'. A card is given to the child, and a little present of a narrow golden crown and a little wool baby. If the child is to be 3 years old or older, Letitia may say something like, 'When you were a baby you smiled and cried. When you were 1, you sat up and crawled and began to walk. When you were 2, you ran and laughed. And now you are 3, you are talking and playing'. If another brother or sister has been born into the family, Letitia will mention that too.

In her Parent and Child group, *Sheila Clarkson* also tells the birthday story, but uses a blue story veil pinned to her shoulder as the sky. She only tells the story if the child has a birthday on a Parent and Child group day, and only after asking the parents if they feel comfortable with the story. For other birthdays she gives the child a card and present from the group, and sings 'Happy Birthday' to them during the circle time.

At the shared meal, the child will have a birthday cake made by the parent. The first candle, in the centre of the cake, is lit while Sheila says, 'Her mummy and daddy named her.......'. For each additional candle, the parent relates something important that happened to the child in that year.

It is also fine if birthdays are not acknowledged at all in the group. There are, in the end, no fixed ways of approaching birthdays at this tender age. The only important thing is to be sensitive to the situation and very gentle in the rendering.

Creating the mood

As we have seen, festivals and birthdays need to be very simple affairs in the Parent and Child group. However, this does not mean that they do not have substance. On the contrary, these festivals and birthday celebrations can touch participants very deeply and offer a real renewal of spiritual experience. The quality and depth of the occasion, however, has much to do with how the adults and leaders approach the festival.

Giving parents some background information before the event is important, as the right mood will be created more by the adults' reverence, understanding, and joy for the occasion, than by any props.

Main points again

- Festivals are important family events. They connect us to spiritual truths embodied in the cycle of the year and create a strong sense of community. They provide a deep sense of security and connectedness in the young child, especially if they are repeated over the years.

- The festivals celebrated in Waldorf settings are mainly Christian in origin, but they use symbols and activities which transcend partisan religious practice and appeal to the 'universal human'.

- Festivals for Parent and Child groups need to be very simple.

- They are best celebrated outside the group session as a special family event.

- The mood of the festival is created by what is done, but also by how deeply the adults can enter into the essence of the occasion.

- The theme of each festival can be reflected in songs, rhymes, and stories told in the Parent and Child group session. The nature table can be specially decorated, and festive food can be brought to the shared meal.

- It is helpful to give some written information to the parents about each festival beforehand.

- Birthdays are acknowledged in a gentle way. Sensitivity to the situation and the child's needs are paramount.

- A favourite birthday story is an adapted version of the Rainbow Bridge told with simple wool puppets.

Useful books

Ann Druitt, Christine Fynes-Clinton, and Marije Rowling, *All Year Round*, Hawthorn Press, Stroud, 1995

Ann Druitt, and Christine Fynes-Clinton, *The Birthday Book*, Hawthorn Press, Stroud, 2004

Brigitte Barz, *Festivals with Children*, Floris Books, Edinburgh, 1989

Diana Carey and Judy Large, *Festivals, Family and Food*, Hawthorn Press, Stroud, 1982

Sue Fitzjohn, Minda Weston and Judy Large, *Festivals Together*, Hawthorn Press, Stroud, 1993

Anne and Peter Thomas, *The Children's Party Book*, Floris Books, Edinburgh, 1998

Ruth Marshall, *Celebrating Irish Festivals*, Hawthorn Press, Stroud, 2003

Noorah Al-Gailani and Chris Smith, *The Islamic Year*, Hawthorn Press, Stroud, 2003

Rudolf Steiner, *The Festivals and Their Meaning*, Rudolf Steiner Press, London, 2002

Evelyn Frances Capel, *The Christian Year*, Floris Books, Edinburgh, 1991

Adrian Anderson, *Living a Spiritual Year*, Anthroposophic Press, New York, 1993

CHAPTER 10

Supporting parents

'Parenting is a journey – a spiritual journey – a path of transformation… for which we are rarely ever prepared. Remember the moment your heart stirred for your child with affection different than you ever experienced before?... At that moment, perhaps, you recognized that your life as you knew it was dramatically changed forever. And that thought held both joy and trepidation.'

Bonnie Romanow[1]

FOR PARENTS...

Part 10: Supporting parents

Parenting as a spiritual journey

In Steiner Parent and Child groups we recognize that when our children are born to us, we embark on a new journey of learning – about how to be a parent in the practical sense; but also a journey which takes us back to our *own childhoods*, confronting us with our deeper anxieties and questions, and providing many opportunities for healing and inner growth. Rudolf Steiner explains that we are collectively living in the time of the 'consciousness soul': we are becoming more self-aware, and in our self-consciousness we move ever closer to the threshold between the sensory and the spiritual worlds. We often feel alone in our struggle as we are forced to question our roles as parents, and to find our own source of inner confidence and wisdom. Parenting is, indeed, a spiritual journey.

The Steiner Parent and Child group as a learning community

Understanding that our anxieties and questions as parents are natural, rather than judging them, we can see parenting as a learning journey which can be shared with others. In fact, adults learn best in a supportive environment with others, and the Parent and Child group can provide an ideal 'learning community' in the most positive sense, because the group is founded on a shared warmth and respect for each individual. Everyone is free to form their own judgements and to make their own choices as parents. However, the spiritual understandings that underpin the Steiner perspective allow a deeper, freer exploration; and our individual inner quests enliven and enrich each other.

There are many ways in which Steiner Parent and Child groups support parents' individual learning journeys:

- Through the experience of the group session
- The 'warm mantle' of the group
- Friendships
- Study groups
- One-to-one conversations
- Parenting workshops and courses
- Lending library
- Festivals and other community events

How do we support parents in their task of protecting the early healthy development of the young child? How can we, in Parent and Child groups, support individual parenting journeys? What are the ways in which we learn and grow as parents? This chapter offers a perspective from which to understand these questions and some ideas and examples of the different ways in which Waldorf groups meet and work with them.

Parenting as a conscious path

Many of us today can feel unprepared for parenthood, uneasy in our new role, unsure of what our small children really need. We can be reluctant to call on our own experiences of being parented as a model for our own parenting; and the extended families, which in the past shared the responsibility and the wisdom of parenting, are dissolving. We are left in our aloneness to find our own way.

The 'consciousness soul'

Rudolf Steiner understood and described this sense of aloneness that we feel as human beings and the deep personal dilemmas that it creates. He explains that we live in the time of the 'consciousness soul', where, collectively, we are becoming more self-aware as human beings. More and more we need as individuals to question everything, have facts, form our own judgements, and do things our own way – which in turn means that we cannot simply rely on what has gone before. The promise is that the development of a much more awake and aware relationship to ourselves and the outer world will, in time, give us a new freedom – freedom of choice. We realize that we can stand in our own uniqueness and make our own choices, and through this process we develop a new sense of ourselves and our connectedness to the whole. At this time in human evolution, however, we stand individually and collectively at a kind of

threshold to the spiritual worlds, no longer able to rest in instinct, not yet able to see beyond our sense of physical, emotional, and intellectual separateness to more subtle realities. And this is as true in our parenting journeys as in any other areas of our lives.

How the 'consciousness soul' manifests in our roles as parents was addressed recently by *Lourdes Callen*, an experienced Waldorf Kindergarten teacher, counsellor, and Parent and Child group leader, at a national UK conference for Waldorf Parent and Child group leaders.[2] Leading the conference theme entitled 'Working with Parents', she explained that we may decide as parents to 'go with the flow', to unthinkingly succumb to the many influences that are affecting our children, repeating automatic ways of doing things because of a fear of being different. Or we begin to question – and, through this process, to find a new inner guidance that gives us the courage to be creative in our parenting. Here is a list of what parents from today's world commonly bring to Parent and Child groups, compiled by the participants at the conference:

- Parents wanting something different for their child but are not sure what.
- They are isolated in the home and wish for company and stimulation
- Lives are hectic and rushed. Wanting to slow down, but how?
- Parents needing to control and direct our children's development.
- Wanting children to be well adapted to society.
- Belief that children are miniature adults.
- Parents wishing to learn about parenting skills.
- Wanting facts and information.
- Parents needing the support and company of other parents.
- The question of TV, media, technology – does it need to be addressed?

- How to be with a young child.
- Parents being very aware of their child as an individual.
- Wanting the warmth and sharing of community.

Anxiety and parenting

As we begin to look at our life-styles and the influences to which our children are subjected in the world, there arises a level of self-consciousness which can lead to uncertainty and doubt. We can feel somewhat unsure of our abilities to parent our children, to find the right way. In an article entitled 'Beyond "Paranoid Parenting"' in a recent edition of *The Mother* magazine,[3] Richard House explored some of the ways in which we can easily begin to feel disempowered as parents, and look more and more to 'experts' to tell us what to do. House discusses the work of Frank Furedi, author of the book *Paranoid Parenting*,[4] who suggests that there are many pressures these days that can contribute to a sense of disempowerment. For instance, we live in a 'surveillance culture' where we feel we have to monitor our children continuously. There is also a growing 'professionalization of parenting and child rearing' which can leave us feeling dependant on outside sources of authority. In addition, contemporary theories of and fashions in early learning demand that we give our children this or that experience, in order to stimulate or develop their abilities. There is a real risk in all this of what we can call 'over parenting'.

As part of our own waking up and inner reflection, we can also get caught in the erroneous but inevitable assumption that we are the victims of our parents' failings and therefore will inevitably fail our own children. This is what Frank Furedi terms 'infant determinism' (the view that early experience determines future development), and 'parental determinism' (the view that parental intervention determines

children's future fate). The profound mystery of individuality, resilience, and self-determination of the young child is overlooked, because the spiritual dimension is overlooked, and we can end up trying to carry the impossible responsibility of being the sole dictators of our children's personality and fate.

Furedi's solution is that we resist the pressure to subject our children to our own anxieties, that we ignore the 'experts', and instead use our own instincts. But what if the access to our instincts seems a little shaky and unreliable? Rather than see our anxieties as symptoms of being a 'neurotic parent', it may be more helpful to see them as the initial effects of becoming more self-aware, of standing at the threshold.[5] We need continuously to acknowledge the feelings to which our anxieties give rise, and see them as a learning process. As Lourdes Callen says, 'Let's see what can be learnt from this situation'. As our independent thinking is activated, and with this the voice of our inner guidance, we find the courage to be creative and to recognize new ways of doing things. All this is the awakening of the 'consciousness soul'.

Parenting as a conscious path of learning

In our increasing self-consciousness, we are learning more 'consciously' how to be parents to our children in these complex times. And this 'learning' is perhaps the key to how we can begin to find a new confidence and surety in our task. We realize that we want to question, develop, and grow in ourselves so that we can better understand our children and 'meet' them in healthy ways. Susan Weber, director of Sophia's Hearth in the USA, puts it like this: 'We have to change to become who our children need us to be!'[6] This is particularly true in the first three years of life, when our children need the most protection from harmful influences.

In California, **Bonnie Romanow** has worked

with parents and young children for over twelve years. Through experience she has learnt that it is much more important, as a parent, to strive to be as conscious as possible, to hold ourselves with love and compassion, rather than to try to have a perfect home and do all the 'right' things. For Bonnie, 'respect' is the key – true, deep respect for each other:

'When I stay out of the way, and support parents to become more conscious and aware, communicating respect and honour for their own knowing and individuality, amazing things happen for the parents and the family. Their confidence allows them to take up ideas and suggestions in a much more powerful way that is appropriate to the unfolding destiny of their lives.'[7]

There are other realisations that can help us on this journey toward an inner confidence. One key is the acceptance that our children are spiritual beings and that there are certain truths and natural laws that direct their development. As parents we need knowledge that addresses these more subtle realities. If we work with these understandings, we can better 'meet' our children and allow them to unfold naturally in their own timing. This in turn gives us an inner confidence. Another key is reminding each other that our children chose us, and that we are also spiritual beings on a journey of our own unfolding. This larger context for viewing our children, as well as ourselves and other adults, brings a new freedom – the freedom to undertake our own journey in our own way, the freedom to share and learn from each other, the freedom to create in our lives what we know out of an inner strengthening and awakening to be important and good.

Lourdes Callen summarized it this way:

'Developing a capacity to learn, we can transform experiences into inner richness of soul. When we can work with parents from a learning attitude, then we can accompany them on a path of personal development. To see ourselves on a path of learning has liberating effects beyond guilt or perfection. Self-judgement is an obstacle. However, working with these obstacles opens the way for developments now and in the future. Working with one's own learning attitude will help others to do the same.'[8]

I can recommend a wonderfully empowering and life-changing book titled *The Reluctant Adult* by Jill Hall.[9] In one reading I was finally able to understand my own personal struggles from a wider spiritual perspective, and to realize that only by accepting subtle-spiritual realities and our own spiritual nature can we individually and collectively move forward, beyond our existential angst!

The way adults learn

When we work together with other adults, it helps to know a little about the nature of adult learning from a spiritual perspective. In Chapter 2, Rudolf Steiner's teaching of the threefold human being was briefly introduced. To summarize again – the human soul has a three-fold nature – we are thinking, feeling and willing beings. Whereas the different soul aspects are addressed in turn in the three phases of childhood – the will in the first seven years, the feeling soul in the period between 7 and 14 and the intellect in the teenage years to 21 – in adulthood we need to be able to engage all three aspects. However, it is primarily through the engagement of our will that we as adults learn.

In his book *Awakening the Will: Principles and Processes in Adult Learning*,[10] Coenraad van Houten explains that for adults it is the drive for knowledge, self-development, and self-improvement that creates the conditions for learning. But for learning to take place, two conditions must be met: the independent will of the individual needs to be deeply involved, and there must always be the freedom to form independent judgements. It is through the active personal engagement and enthusiasm with learning that the 'inner teacher' is awakened: 'We can find inner security in ourselves, only if we manage to awaken it through our own effort of will. The spirit of the times demands an awakening of the will.'[11] Van Houten explains that there are always resistances to learning – these can be intellectual, emotional, and in the realm of the will. The three-fold nature of the human soul (thinking, feeling, and willing) needs to be continually addressed and balanced in the learning process.

Learning is a process which includes various stages or steps. If any of these are missed or become obstacles, then the learning process is affected. Adult education, or learning as adults, is about facilitating this process of learning. It is in our life crises that most change, learning, and growth is possible. The path of parenting brings us very strongly in touch with our own inner struggles and inhibitions. Through the cultivation of a safe sharing space in the friendships made in a Parent and Child group, we can help each other to move through resistances, come to new realizations, and contact new strengths. Not least, we can facilitate each others' learning.

'Working in groups is tricky because of the many subtle and not so subtle ways people are affected by authority (the facilitator, teacher, expert, etc.). Parents seem to be as vulnerable as their children are at this age, filled with concern for what is the best for the child, "Can I do it?", "What do others think?", the disillusionment of what they thought parenthood would be, and so on. It is essential to build a sense of trust and safety. Parents want to share their experiences with their children, both positive and

difficult, but are susceptible and fearful of others' judgement. People respond well, however, when we cultivate a capacity to deeply listen and empathize with them. Reminding parents of their strengths is essential, for all of us have strengths. Be they daily challenges of caring for a little one, or tackling inner behaviours and habits, coming from a position of knowing one's own strengths makes a huge difference in the outcome. This also builds a sense of community, so sorely lacking in today's world. …New friends are made with others of like-minded intentions, which form a supportive network of solidarity against the onslaught of cultural and environmental influences parents choose to mitigate. A mantle of warmth around the parents and children develops.'

Bonnie Romanow[12]

In Parent and Child work it is very possible to work strongly and well in the three soul realms. Through discussions and study, the faculties of thinking and independent judgement can be engaged; through the respect and care taken in human relations, the feeling soul can be nourished, and through the experiential 'doing' activities of the group session, the will is fully engaged. It is primarily through experiencing the session, and in practically participating in the warmth and enthusiasm of the Parent and Child group, that parents can be gently supported, if they so wish, in their own inner journeys, in their own time. As *Lourdes Callen* says: 'There is more to a Parent and Child group than first meets the eye and it is not possible to see the effects early on – the process takes time. There are different levels of experience as parents gradually open.'[13]

There is something that happens when adults come together to learn and share in trust and non-judgement. The enthusiasm and commitment of even one adult will, over time, inevitably stir the inner life of others. The warmth that is generated makes it easier to open to change. It is our actions and attitudes that create the nourishing environment where each other's inner growth is possible. The journey is a shared one. This is community in the true sense.

Ways to learn together in the Parent and Child group

If parenthood can be a path of inner growth and development, in the context of sharing and community, then the Parent and Child group is, in many respects, an ideal setting for this learning community of parents to develop. But how do we go about creating this community, and what does the Parent and Child group offer?

There are various ways in which parents in Parent and Child groups can be supported 'in a mantle of warmth'. Some of these have been described in different chapters on the various aspects of a group session. However, sometimes a more formal educational element is also offered to parents, either as part of the session or in addition and separate from it. What I wish to do now is describe some of these ways, using examples from different projects, so we can get a sense of the range of possibilities.

'Experiential' learning

Parents who attend Waldorf Parent and Child groups mostly learn about new ideas and ways of parenting through experiencing the sessions. Apart, perhaps, from a simple introductory handout given to new parents, little will be explained and the adults – like the children – will learn through participating in rhythm, repetition, and imitation. The leader, if there is one, will answer any questions which may arise, but the adults are left in freedom to find out more and form their own judgements.

Richard House, with long experience of running Parent and Child groups, explains that

he does not offer any information in a formal way.

'Informality has been the basis on which we have worked with parents in the past. By this I mean that during sessions, parents will and do ask questions – often about why we do things the way we do – which then gives the leader the opportunity to say something about the pedagogy or philosophy – to mention imitation or rhythm, for example, or the reason why we use pink or strictly exclude plastic toys. When a question like this is answered at the craft table, it will tend to be overheard by several parents, and can lead to interesting discussions and sharings.'[14]

Kim Billington in Australia explains that in setting up a new Parent and Child group, she will lead it for the first year, slowly handing over the responsibility to other parents in the group. Learning how to the run the group is achieved through practical experience. In this same way, what is learnt 'experientially' in the group can also be taken into the family home. She regularly runs what she calls 'Open Parenting Seminars', arranged in the evenings when parents can bring questions about contemporary parenting issues and day-to-day challenges.

Actively working with parents

The merging of the Resources for Infant Educarers (RIE) approach (discussed in Chapter 2) and the Waldorf philosophy has created a form of Parent and Child group where parents are encouraged to allow their children to move freely, to observe their children actively, and to be very mindful in their relationship to their child. There is more instruction or direction from an experienced leader. The parents attend because they wish to learn a new way of being with their child.

In some of these projects, pre-natal classes have been developed for pregnant mums that are separate from, but run alongside, groups for parents with older children. Again these may be divided into separate age groups for parents with infants up to the age of 1, groups for parents with children aged 1–2, and groups for parents with children who are 3 and over. The particular developmental stages of the young children can then be closely experienced and catered for. The Waldorf School in Portland, Oregon USA, is one such example. At the school the parent-child classes also include two parent-only evenings per term. These 'same' age groups seem to work well in established settings but are often not appropriate for new initiatives where numbers are small and of very mixed ages.

An innovative family centre in Frankfurt, Germany, called 'der Hof', which has brought together the work of many early childhood researchers including Emmi Pikler and Rudolf Steiner, offers a wide range of groups for parents with children from babies to Kindergarten age.

At Sophia's Hearth Family Center in New Hampshire, USA, *Susan Weber* provides a programme for parents with infants and toddlers up to two-and-a-half years of age. There is an emphasis on the Waldorf philosophy and RIE-inspired free movement and play, with readings for parents, discussion time, songs, and games. Courses are also offered on infant massage and for expectant parents. These classes are part of a long-range vision to create a centre, which will also incorporate full-time child care in a family setting for a mixed-aged range of children.

Lourdes Callen has developed her own particular way of working with parents and young children. The special qualities she offers in her group are possible because of her personal training and experience in group work and counselling. Her groups are shaped in an informal way with the adults suggesting themes, contributions, and questions. Themes can include anything from exchanging books, understanding tantrums, to sharing discoveries and concerns. All the themes can also be discussed further in evening meetings. Lourdes also does craft activities and concentrates particularly on creating nourishment in the group. She achieves this by:

- building a warm atmosphere around the child
- listening and being interested in each other
- respecting differences
- balancing the needs of the adults with the needs of the children
- creating community through sharing struggles and noticing achievements
- creating a healing trust between parents.'[15]

Lourdes describes her work like this:

'Where does nourishment come from? A vessel can be created working with these qualities and balancing tendencies where the working of the spirit can be felt: creating an outer environment together with the inner work of understanding both parent and child… The adults have a direct experience of how to treat, care for, and embrace young children. We acknowledge, trust, and celebrate childhood. In doing so together, new forces and insights are developed which help us keep to the aims of providing the special start in life that each parent would like for their children.'[16]

In California, *Bonnie Romanow* has similarly developed her own work with parents and children called 'Parenting from the Heart'. She has a background in Waldorf education, RIE training, and counselling/group facilitation. One main intention of her programme is to help parents develop skills of observation so that they can objectify their own experience with their child and so better identify the latter's needs. This is how, in a leaflet, she describes her approach to working with parents:

'Many feelings and attitudes regarding children and parenting either come from our parents or are a reaction to our parents. We identify some of the things that do not serve you, your family or your child. Articles and exercises augment experiences in class and at home, providing intellectual understanding. Parenting from the heart… enlightened with knowledge and experience… – that is the aim of our class.'[17]

In the first half of the session the parents learn to manage the delicate balance between interacting with their children, who are free to play, and focusing on their own craft work. Bonnie likes the parents to sit in a circle enclosing the space where the children play – 'a sacred circle'. Time is taken to slow down and observe what is going on in the room. As trust is built between Bonnie and children, she works with parents directly on the difficulties which arise between parent and child. There are three main ways she does this, always asking their permission first:

1. coaching them in situations with their children when appropriate, in order to try out new ways of responding and interacting;

2. making suggestions and posing alternative scenarios when certain topics arise; and

3. interacting with a child once the child has established a connection, to help look at new ways for parent and child to be together.

Parents are given readings outside the classes which can help them better to understand how they can objectify their responses to their children and become more sensitive to their needs. If there are questions or concerns, the parents are encouraged to express them.

Bonnie also gives much importance to the circle time, teaching strong imitation of gesture through the songs and rhymes.

Ann Strauss in Cambridge, UK, runs an informal weekly mother and baby group from her home. Pregnant mums and parents with babies up to a year old are invited, and there are about 6–7 regular families who attend. The session is divided between adult time for reading and discussion on topics to do with parenting and child development from a Steiner perspective, and the sharing of songs and rhymes. There is a variety of simple toys for indoor play and also an outdoor space. Once the children can confidently walk, the family can join a local Waldorf Parent and Child group. There is no charge for the group, but everyone shares in the practical organisation and running of the group.

Kate Pigeon-Owen is a qualified instructor with the International Association of Infant Massage, who offers baby massage as part of her work with parents in Suffolk. She combines nurturing touch with the other passion in her life – Steiner education. Baby and toddler massage is an option for parents at the Raphael Steiner Parent and Child groups in Suffolk, UK. Children who then enter the Raphael Kindergarten and school are offered the massage. Working alongside *Sylvie Hétu* (see Chapter 11), who is also a qualified massage instructor and Waldorf teacher, their experience and expertise is offered on various parenting courses, including Sure Start and other government training schemes.

Supporting parents with 'special needs' children

Kathy McQuillen, who is a trained Steiner Kindergarten teacher and Parent and Child group leader, has a special needs child called Laura. In a telephone conversation she told me how the Steiner perspective has helped her in her own journey with her child, and how she feels it can help other parents.

'All children are different, and you can say that all children have special needs that are their very own. From a Steiner perspective, each and every child is an incarnating being, who has chosen a particular incarnation and intention. We as parents, by acknowledging the essential divine spark in our child, can find a deep well of love and respect for the child who has chosen us.

Steiner settings do have a deep respect for the spiritual individuality of each and every child, and therefore can offer a special quality of support for parents. It is about *being there* for parents – to listen and support and answer their questions if we can (or talk to colleagues and others if we need help to answer their needs). There is a wealth of knowledge in the Steiner world – for example, through the established experience of the Camphill Community movement and the curative aspects of anthroposophical medicine. In addition, the whole way in which parenting is approached is deeply helpful to parents with special children – not only the elements of rhythm and repetition, but the gentleness of the whole approach, and the fact that the senses are particularly cared for and protected.'

'Adult only' study/craft/discussion groups

These are meetings where the parents who attend a Parent and Child group are invited to attend additional group time, once a fortnight or so, usually in the evening, without their children. The aim of these groups is primarily to give parents time to discuss and share their concerns and learn more about the Waldorf approach. These groups help friendships to strengthen and a close sense of community to build.

Reading texts:

'Study groups' can be developed to supplement the Parent and Child group session, or sometimes as preparation and introduction for parents, who may wish to set up a group in the future. Some groups may take a text, written by Rudolf Steiner, or by a more contemporary author, and read it together over a number of months, leaving plenty of time for discussion. In other groups, parents themselves supply the topics, even taking it in turns to do the necessary preparatory work. A very popular book used in the USA is called *Mitten Strings for God* by Katrina Kenison. It is a Waldorf parent's heart-felt reflections on being a mother, with all the pressures and speed in today's world. All parents can relate to the challenges and simple joys which the author describes. I list some other suggestions in Appendix 5 at the end of the book.

Craftwork:

Some groups come together to learn craft skills, make dolls and toys, or prepare for festivals. While the craft work is being carried out there is much opportunity for sharing and discussion. These groups can be very warm and sharing spaces.

Experiential classes:

Rena Osmer, director of the Caldwell Early Life Centre at Rudolf Steiner College, Fair Oaks, California, described to me how in her work with parents she sets up 'hands on' (my term) experiences. For example, dividing a group and asking one group to play with Waldorf 'open-ended' play materials and the other with highly finished toys, or comparing the watching of a video with watching a puppet story of a well-known fairy tale. The experiences are then used as a basis for discussion. Other groups have experimented, for example, with experiencing for themselves, in floor work, the various stages of movement and body co-ordination in the first few years of life.

Biography work:

Some groups have found it helpful to work with each others' life biography, as a way of gaining clarity about what may be brought to parenting from one's own childhood experiences. This work needs to be done separately, away from our children. From these explorations, a new freedom of choice in the way we relate to our own children can arise. These groups need a skilled facilitator experienced in biographical work.

Parenting workshops

These can be run at many levels of organisation. They provide the opportunity for parents, whether they are part of a Parent and Child group or not, to learn about various aspects of parenting from a spiritual perspective. Because they can be run over a whole day or several days, rather than just an evening, they can include a mix of formal lectures, craft and artistic activities, and plenty of time for discussions.

In York and London, I organise a series of workshops called the *First Three Years* for parents and Parent and Child group leaders which are run every year, once a month for ten months. Experienced speakers and early years practitioners are invited to come and share their knowledge and wisdom, and there is time for singing, movement, and craft activities. The singing in particular is a wonderful way of bringing the group together. These workshops have proved to be very popular, attracting participants from all over England, and many parents have gone on to form their own initiatives.

Joy de Berker, mother and Kindergarten teacher in Bath, UK, runs an annual series of ten parent development morning workshops – called 'Education for a Happy Childhood' – for parents and for people working with young children.

Emma Tyer, mother and trained Kindergarten teacher, runs workshops, courses,

and evening classes for parents on a variety of topics, ranging from festivals and rhythm to inspirations for parents. She has just founded and facilitated an annual weekend for families at Hawkwood College, Stroud. Through her work, Emma wishes to nurture a greater recognition of the spiritual mission of parenthood and to encourage parents both to support each other and to request that society should honour this sacred role. Emma lives near Stroud.

Susan Weber, director of Sophia's Hearth, has described her participation in a 5-day workshop offered by the School for Body –Mind Centering:

'I have just had the experience of the infant before it learns to crawl (and afterwards, in those other moments the young child spends in the horizontal when we enable her to do so). What a powerful position from which to get to know the world! It is a gentle time, a magical time with no goal, not even that of reaching for a plaything. It is the child's birth-right to get to know peacefully her own body and the world around in her own time, at her own pace: is that my leg, my stomach, my hand? Never again will the world be so simple, and never again will there be the same possibility for uninterrupted time to get to know oneself.'[18]

Another example is the development of workshops on biography work, which give adults valuable time to explore more in-depth aspects of their own life journey. For example, Malcolm Daniels runs Destiny Learning workshops in the UK, which explore life themes from a spiritual perspective.

Lourdes Callen has developed her own parenting workshops called 'A Time for Childhood', which she runs in Barcelona, Spain, and in England. In an information leaflet she describes how the workshops 'facilitate the processes of learning, leading to an understanding of the time of childhood in an experiential way, covering biography work and personal development'. In a self-published booklet called 'A Time for Childhood' (details at the end of the chapter), she explores this approach to working with parents.

The one-to-one conversation

This is where 'two equal human beings are meeting in a way in which healing or inspiration can come.' This is not therapy, as such, but can, if conducted in a sensitive and caring way, help enormously to gain clarity over a particular problem and come to a new step. Parent and Child group leaders will often find themselves in this position. It is, in a way, the most profound way in which parents are supported in their individual journeys. There are specific skills which are important in this aspect of parenting work, such as 'selfless' listening, empathy, and non-judgement.

The Parent and Child library

This is a very important part of a Parent and Child group, allowing parents the freedom to explore aspects of the Waldorf approach in their own time. A list of possible core books is given in Appendix 5 at the end of the book.

Main points again

- Parenting is a spiritual path of self-development and learning.

- There are many questions that parents bring to the Parent and Child group – questions which form the basis for shared learning and growth.

- Adults learn in a particular way. Individuals need to feel enthusiastic, safe, and committed. There needs to be complete freedom to form individual judgments.

- Groups of parents coming together to learn create 'learning communities'. Parent and Child groups are ideal learning communities.

- There are many ways to support parents. These include:
  * Through the experience of the group session
  * The 'warm mantle' of the group
  * Friendships
  * Active working with parents
  * Study groups
  * One-to-one conversations
  * Parenting workshops and courses
  * A Parent and Child group library
  * Festivals and other community events

Useful books

Some Anthroposophical books on adult learning and community

Margarete van den Brink, *More Precious than Light*, Hawthorn Press, Stroud, 1996

Coenraad van Houten, *Awakening the Will: Principles and Processes in Adult Learning*, Temple Lodge, London, 1999

Tom Stehlik, *Each Parent Carries the Flame: Waldorf Schools as Sites for Promoting Lifelong Learning, Creating Community and Educating for Social Renewal*, Post Pressed Flaxton, Queensland, 2002; www.postpressed.com.au

Margarete van den Brink, *Transforming People and Organisations: The Seven Steps of Spiritual Development*, Temple Lodge, Forest Row, 2004

Useful organisations

Some Parenting-relevant Anthroposophical adult learning centres and courses

Emerson College, Forest Row, East Sussex RH18 5JX, UK; info@emerson.org.uk; www.emerson.org.uk; tel. 01342 822238.

Hawkwood College, Painswick Old Road, Stroud, Glos. GL6 7QW, UK; info@hawkwoodcollege.co.uk; tel. 01453 759054.

Biography and Social Development Trust, 1st Floor North, Hillside House, Lewes Road, Forest Row RH18 5ES, UK; Biogsoctru@aol.com; www.biographywork.org; tel. 01342 822907

Education for a Happy Childhood, Parent Development mornings, Joy de Berker, tel. 01225 891730

The First Three Years early childhood course, for Parent and Child group leaders, childcare providers and parents at York and in London. Tel. 01904 612683 or www.steinerparentandchild.co.uk Email: info@steinerparentandchild.co.uk

Faculty of Education, University of Plymouth, Douglas Avenue, Exmouth, Devon EX8 2AT, UK; Abi.mccullough@plymouth.ac.uk: tel. 01395 255325; (Steiner Education degree and Foundation degree in Early Years education)

Part-time early years and kindergarten teacher training diploma in London, Woodbine Cottage, Harescombe, Stroud, Glos GL4 0XD, UK; lynneoldfield@lineone.net

Steiner House, 35 Park Road, London W1 6XT, UK; tel. 020 7723 4400. Many workshops and courses.

'A time for childhood' courses and workshops – Lourdes Callen; www.atimeforchildhood.com; lcallen@atimeforchildhood.com

'Parenting from the heart', Bonnie Romanow, Novato, Calif., USA; heartfulparenting@yahoo.com

Sophia's Hearth family center, an Educational Resource Center for families and educators offering parent and professional courses and seminars: 36 Carpenter Street, Keene, NH, USA; info@sophiashearth.net www.sophiashearth.org

Lifeways North America, Caldwell Early Life Center, Rudolf Steiner College, 9200 Fair Oaks Blvd, CA; seminars and training for those involved in the care of the young child; info@lifeways-center.org

Part-time early childhood teacher education program, Sunbridge College, 285 Hungary Hollow Road, Spring Valley, New York 10977; www.sunbridge.edu info@sunbridge.edu

Seminare zur Leitung von Spiel Gruppen, Waldorfbildungswerk. E.V. Mergelteichstrasse 59, 44225 Dortmund, Germany; PSZD-Middelkamp@t-online.de

The first three years – courses and Parent and Child groups, Freie Bildungsstätte, Dalt Niederursel 51, 60439 Frankfurt, Germany; www.der-hof.de

Emma Tyer – 'Practical Parenting with a Spiritual Heart', Stroud UK rtyer@freeuk.com

'Childways' – Infant massage training. Kate Pigeon Owen. www.childways.co.uk tel. 01379 677 335 Email: katepigeon-owen@freeserve.co.uk

Infant massage, International Association of Infant Massage – promoting nurturing touch right from the beginning – www.iaim.net

Massage in schools programme – www.massageinschools.com

CHAPTER 11

Working and growing together

'Parent and Child groups can be seen as "flowers for the present time" that provide seeds for the future. That future can be consciously looked at, and "worked" for by the community of parents and teachers of the group – and then a new garden for the children will surely emerge.'

Sylvie Hétu[1]

FOR PARENTS...

Part 11: Working and growing together

Starting a Steiner Parent and Child group

Deciding to start, or become involved in the development of, a Steiner Parent and Child group is a journey in discovering the true spirit of *community*. Steiner-inspired groups are natural situations for new forms of community to develop, fulfilling our needs to join with others in freedom to build new educational forms, develop co-operative ventures, create enriching experiences for our children and ourselves, and grow in the company of like-minded others. The Waldorf model is a healing force in the world.

There are practical aspects and stages to developing a Parent and Child group venture, and although each initiative will find its own unique way, there are some guidelines that can prove useful. These are explained in the chapter that follows, and include:

- Understanding what sort of 'seed' your project is
- Creating a vision
- What you need to know if you are starting in someone's home
- Making the transition into a public space
- Stages in group life
- When to introduce formal structures, e.g. committees, business plans, bank accounts, setting fees, paying a leader

Appendices list practical aspects of fund-raising, publicity, and other 'nitty gritties'.

The joys and challenges of group endeavour

The concept of 'the learning community', outlined in Chapter 10 on 'Supporting Parents', is taken to a new level when practically embarking upon a pioneering venture like starting a Steiner Parent and Child group. We find talents and skills we never thought we had; we experience the reality of parent power; and we experience the satisfaction of knowing that we have taken full responsibility for creating what we deeply aspire to for our children.

We also occasionally encounter the unavoidable frustrations of working with others in a co-operative way both in the group and in the wider community. We ourselves are changed through these challenges, and our lives can be both transformed and immensely enriched. Luckily, others know the terrain of spiritually founded group endeavour, and have created 'maps' for us – some of which are referred to later in the chapter.

Case histories briefly describe the journeys of some pioneer projects, and illustrate how Steiner Parent and Child work can be taken into 'mainstream' situations.

If any of the ideas in this book inspire you, you may wish to think about starting your own Parent and Child group and creating a community of families. What I wish to do in this penultimate chapter is to share why and how forming Parent and Child groups fulfils many of our needs for 'belonging' and community. I also want to give a practical overview of how to move from a 'vision' to a reality as smoothly as possible, using examples of how individual Waldorf groups have made their way. It is a question of having one's head in the heavens, one's feet on the ground, and one's heart in community!

Parent and Child groups and the birth of community

Sylvie Hétu, experienced teacher and workshop leader, has described how 'Steiner'-inspired groups are natural situations for new forms of community to develop.[2] In this time of the 'consciousness' soul (a notion introduced in the previous chapter), we gain the gift of freedom consciously to decide our lives and actions. In the sense of aloneness which this can engender, we seek new ways of joining with others. Sylvie explains that the Parent and Child group naturally fulfils our social-community needs in four main ways. Firstly, parents come to Steiner education out of a freedom of choice. We are 'met' by others who have made similar choices – the 'I' meets the 'we' in a shared sense of purpose. Second and relatedly, it is only really possible to express our individuality when in relation to others; we need to be with others in order to effectively know and express ourselves. This truth is expressed in a verse, the so-called Motto of the Social Ethic, which Rudolf Steiner created to be read at the beginning of group meetings:

'The healthy social life is found
When in the mirror of each human soul
The whole community finds its reflection,
And when, in the community,
The virtue of each one is living.'

Thirdly, as parents we have a wish to share with others, to be reaffirmed and reassured in our choices. The Parent and Child group easily becomes a place for support and friendships. Lastly, there is a need in individuals to learn and to develop, and the Parent and Child group can fulfil this need in many different ways.

Many can testify to how a more spiritual perspective on childhood and parenting has changed our lives, starting us on an inner journey which we can share with like-minded others. As long as the wellsprings of the spiritual perspective are tapped in all the various activities of the group, there is an 'aliveness' which pervades the endeavour. It can create a continuing sense of exploration and renewal.

In addition, there are many ways in which we can 'consciously' nurture new forms of community life. These have been touched on already in the book and include study groups, craft groups, and festivals and special events.

Tom Stehlik[3] describes in detail, with the example of Mt Baker Waldorf School in Australia, how Waldorf schools naturally promote adult learning, community, and social renewal. On a smaller scale, the same can be said for Parent and Child groups.

The threefold nature of groups and communities

There is a very helpful book titled *Vision in Action*, providing a wealth of insight and wisdom for new initiatives. A description is given of the human being as a threefold being – the *body*, made of the earth; the *spirit* (or, as Steiner described it, the Ego), which is our eternal higher being's connection to the spiritual world; and the *soul*, which is the psychological stage on which we experience ourselves (through willing, feeling, and thinking). This picture of the threefold human being is then applied to communities and groups. The first realm is the 'body', the physical premises, the equipment, the money. The second realm is of the 'soul' and involves the qualities of relationships between people, communication, working conditions. The third realm is of the spirit or identity, and includes the vision, goals, and name. Each of these realms needs to be nurtured if the group is going to thrive.

> 'Seeing the relationship between the spirit, soul and body of our own being and its expression in institutions, in the dialogue with the spirit, in the dialogue between people and the dialogue with the earth is an important aspect of building healthy organisations. It awakens us to an ongoing sense of which area of organisational life needs attention.'[4]

Our ventures need to be nurtured and balanced in their expression of vision (spirit), relationship (soul), and practicality (earth). The more consciousness we can bring to our group endeavours, especially at the inception stage of a venture, the more freedom we have to choose what we wish to create.

What sort of a 'seed' are you?

The image of a new venture being a seed is a very useful one. The initial vision for a Parent and Child group is like an acorn, full of potential and possibility. Its fully grown magnificence is already, somehow, complete in the acorn. What we need to do, like a good gardener, is to name the seed as accurately as we can, and then to give it the particular conditions it needs in order to be able to grow into a strong and healthy plant. It also helps if we know what the various stages of growth may look like along the way!

The parent 'seed' group

This is probably the most common way in which a Parent and Child group comes into being – a few parents, usually friends with young babies, decide to meet on a regular basis in their homes and experiment with Waldorf ideas. Over time, the group grows until it is large enough to be held in a public space, and to welcome the wider community. Many groups go on to start Kindergartens and spawn fully fledged educational projects. Lancaster is one of several projects that have started in this way.

The parents are often new to parenthood and inexperienced in group work, and the project evolves as the group members gain new skills and confidence. For many parents involved in this type of project, the experience is one of self-empowerment and tremendous personal growth.

These groups tend to move through a succession of stages of organisation:

- The informal group – the session is parent led
- Gradual polarizing of roles and responsibilities within the group
- Formal constitution with steering committee and committee roles
- Employment of Parent and Child group leader

The vision gradually meets the soul life of the individuals who, through working together, ground the venture in the real world.

Some groups may decide to stay at any one of these stages of development for their whole existence.

The 'seed' planted by an individual

Groups are sometimes started by an experienced early years' teacher who has the time, energy, and commitment to pioneer a new venture. These projects tend to be most successful where there is already a Waldorf educational presence and parent community in the area. Initially, the group is commonly run on a fairly informal basis, with the individual initiator shouldering responsibility. Over time, however, different parents may take on many or all of the responsibilities of running the group. Kim Billington in Australia has successfully seeded many new Parent and Child projects in this way (see Chapter 10).

The 'seed' in warmed ground

In this category are included groups set up in existing Early Years Centres, where there are Kindergartens, nurseries, and schools. Here, a strong parent community will probably already exist. It is usual for a group leader to be employed by the organisation, and this may be the end place for a project which initially started as a parent-led group. The group leader is released from many of the practical and administrative duties shouldered by more independent groups, but has more of the teacher, counsellor, and facilitator role within the group. The work may also involve encouraging new parents to join the school/Early Years Centre and being an active member of the teacher body. Consequently it is usually only those experienced in work with young children and adults in a group setting who gravitate toward this sort of work.

The need for a vision

It is important, even if the group in the beginning consists of just a couple of friends, to formulate aspirations into some sort of founding Mission Statement. This would incorporate the kinds of matters set out in Box 28. A group attracting interested families needs to have a strong vision, so that it is not pulled in different directions by each new view. This is particularly important for groups who wish to go the Waldorf way, as the approach used in the group may be unfamiliar, or may not necessarily provide the kind of education that some are looking for.

> ### Box 28: Aspects of a group founding mission statement
>
> - A shared vision of the needs of early childhood and parenthood
> - What the aims of the group are
> - The hoped benefits of the group for children and adults
> - What the sessions will include
> - The range of toys
> - The types of snacks
> - Choices for activities
> - Health and Safety
> - Inclusion – racial, religious, special needs
> - Level of organization and task allocation

An important way to deepen the vision is to spend time in study and discussion together. Many seed groups will meet weekly or fortnightly, exploring various themes and issues, discussing what to bring to their children and for themselves. This activity alone creates a warm 'heart core' of shared commitment and friendship – essential if the group is to weather the inevitable challenges of growth and development.

Another way of creating and filling in the vision is to visit other projects – both Waldorf and mainstream – and attend relevant workshops and courses. The Pre-school Learning Alliance (PSLA) and Scottish Pre-school Play Association (SPPA) run very practical courses on setting up and running Parent and Child groups. Various Steiner schools and centres around the country run inspiring workshops on the Waldorf approach to parenting and childcare.

The initial founding vision will inevitably change, and hopefully enlarge as time progresses. A once-a-year – or even more frequent – review is one effective way to keep the vision alive, and will be relevant, too, to the group's overall development. It is important, however, not to be too ambitious in the beginning, as there is the necessity for a down-to-earth, realistic assessment of what is possible in the early months and years.

The early months

This is like a gestation period. In the early months it is wise if the Parent and Child group session is held in the homes of the involved families. This ensures minimum monetary outlay and plenty of time to learn, gain confidence, and establish routines and roles. There are a few guidelines that can be helpful:

- *Find a good name and logo for your group.*

- *A good starting number:*
  Patsy Collinson, who recently started a Parent and Child group in Sheffield, told me that although she thought it best to start small, she realized after a few mornings that the session 'worked' much better when there were 5-6 children and their parents. Too few and it was more like a normal social morning. What is the difference? Perhaps it is the 'hum' which is evident in group situations when there is harmonious play and activity. The Mayflower in Barton on Humber, UK, started with eight families; Lancaster started with six.

- *Finding interested families:*
  Word of mouth is obviously the most effective way at this stage. If, however, there are very few of you and you would like more families, then try some of the following:
  * A well-presented poster in appropriate shops
  * A public talk
  * An article in the local paper
  * A poster in your front window or car
  * Produce an information sheet that you can give out to new parents explaining simply what you are wishing to do in your sessions and why.

- *Finding the right venue:*
  You need to choose a home or homes were there is a good-sized, uncluttered room, preferably near the kitchen and toilet, and with easy access to a usable outdoor space. Other considerations are the same as outlined in Chapter 3 on choosing a setting.

- *Health and safety:*
  Every home used for a Parent and Child group needs to be checked so that the rooms used are hazard free. It is worth working through a check-list. Make sure there is a good first aid box, clean towels, fire extinguisher, and fire blanket near at hand. You will also need to have a fire procedure.

- *Insurance:*
  Check home insurance for third-party accidents and public liability, or think about getting insurance, especially if new families are joining your group. The Pre-school Learning Alliance, for example, offers insurance for Parent and Child groups. Morton Michel Ltd. (London) is used by many British Steiner early years settings.

- *The question of toys:*
  Some groups use the toys that belong in the home being used. I personally found it was better to build up a small separate collection; not least, this pre-empts the understandable difficulties to do with sharing and ownership.

- *Thinking of money:*
  Even at this early stage, *think 'money'*. Have a kitty box and ask for an amount from each parent at every session. This can go toward food, drink, and materials. Think about simple fund-raising events which can help pay for larger items – you may want to charge a proper sessional fee. Many groups advise that it is 'best to start as you mean to go on', and charging too little undervalues

the high quality and commitment of the work we do. Some groups have also found that paying half-termly, or even termly in advance, is preferable to operating a more casual drop-in group, as this not only helps with much needed financial stability but also creates a more solid community of committed parents, and greater continuity for the children.

- *Study groups and planning meetings:*
  Hold regular study and planning meetings, and make sure everyone is involved in some way in planning and running both the sessions and any other events.

- *Celebrate the festivals:*
  Invite relatives and friends to these special and frequently moving occasions.

- *Take photos:*
  Start to build up an album. This will one day be worth its weight in gold.

- *More sessions:*
  If the group begins to expand, but you don't feel ready to move into a larger space, then arrange more sessions during the week.

Moving into the wide world

There may come a time when the group is large, ready, and 'strong' enough to move into a public space. Support for the project will need to be steadily increasing. This phase opens the possibility of the venture eventually turning into a well-founded early childhood initiative. Even if the project is started by a lone individual, there are many advantages to involving parents, thus spreading the load as the project expands. I am therefore addressing groups rather than individuals in this section; and you will need to pick and choose here to find what is relevant to your particular needs.

Sylvie Hétu lists the following as important points to consider once the group reaches a stage where more organisation and structure is needed:

- Defining mission and goals
- Identifying human potential and resources
- Creating an official legal organisation
- Identifying steps or actions to reach mission and goals
- Creating evaluation processes, including that of conflict resolution

These points are 'archetypal' in the sense that they are relevant to any group wanting to bring more conscious organisation to a community endeavour. Each community needs to create its own unique 'colours' and ways. Sylvie warns of the dangers of trying to imitate what others have done: '… the process of creating the organisation is often what gives it strength. We need to insist on the word "creating" here. Creating means to start from a clean page. "Who are we?" is the first question…'[5]

She also reminds us that if we are to create new forms, we must not be afraid to establish new structures, new ways of doing things: that the main priority is to create a structure which is 'living' and suits the purposes of the group rather than trying to fit into the norm. Likewise, the structure needs to be flexible, able to change over time:

'A created so-called "structure" should be in the service of the human beings who created it, and should be "alive". A structure can evolve, can be adjusted, and should be clear, yet breathing. Unfortunately, many groups of people strangle themselves within the structure they created. If a structure does not serve any more, it is appropriate, even necessary, to modify it, to assist it to evolve.'[6]

The main point is that each group needs to find their own way. However, the knowledge that other groups have gained can be helpful. Below I list some suggestions based on experiences of existing Waldorf Parent and Child groups.

Forming a committee and adopting a constitution

Adopting a constitution allows your group to be recognized as a charity, which means that you can fund-raise outside your group. Moreover, some Community hall committees will only rent space to groups who have a constitution. It also means you may be able to get grants from charitable trusts, and that you won't have to pay tax on income from gift aid donations. Model constitutions can be purchased from the Pre-school Learning Alliance or Scottish Pre-school Play Association and most local authority Early Years Development Departments. With a constitution you need to arrange an annual general meeting (AGM) each year and have regular, minuted committee meetings. The committee members need to be elected. The PSLA, SPPA, and local authorities give advice on all these aspects of running a group.

Defining committee roles

Such definitions are needed for a constitution. As the project gets larger, it is much healthier that roles are defined and shared. The danger otherwise can be that one or two dynamic individuals end up doing everything. Box 29 gives a selection of roles that you could consider choosing from when forming a committee.

Please don't imagine that the list needs to be 'in place' right from the outset! – for in practice, it just doesn't work that way, and it's very important not to be discouraged by such lists, which at the outset can seem rather daunting. Every new group will have its own path of development; and as you grow organically, the requisite steps will become apparent and fall into place, given the appropriate effort and commitment.

Box 29: Parent and Child group committee roles

- Chairperson
- Secretary
- Treasurer
- Session leader/s
- Health and safety person
- Equipment and materials officer
- Experienced person to be a new parent 'welcomer'
- Publicity person
- Events person
- Information and library keeper
- Grant applications and fund-raiser
- Refreshments organizer
- Setting out and clearing away person

Finding the right premises to rent

There are always compromises that have to be made. You can use the ideas in Chapter 3 to help make your choice. Arrange a simple tenancy agreement with the owners and see if one of your members can become a member on the premises' committee. Ask a Fire Officer and Health and Safety Officer to advise you on the suitability of the premises for a Parent and Child group. Unless you are very lucky you will have to set up and clear away every session. This takes time and commitment. You need to have access to a phone – either in the premises or via a mobile phone.

Taking out insurance

This is available, for example, with the Pre-school Learning Alliance or SPPA, and it typically covers the issues listed in Box 30.

You will need to start keeping an up-to-date inventory of all toys and other equipment.

Box 30: Group insurance needs

- Public liability
- Personal accident cover
- Employer's liability
- Loss of money
- Equipment cover
- Personal effects
- Group money
- Employer's liability insurance if you pay someone to lead the group

---

Group rules and guidelines

It is also very helpful if the group has rules and guidelines on how various day-to-day aspects of Parent and Child group work are to be dealt with (Box 31).

Box 31: Guidelines for running a group

- Maximum numbers and age range
- Inclusion
- Dealing with unacceptable behaviour
- Special needs
- Child protection
- Confidentiality
- Parental involvement
- Safety
- Smoking, vegetarianism, and healthy food
- Study and craft groups
- Festivals
- Equal opportunities
- Waiting lists
- Who is responsible for what

The rules and guidelines will need to be reviewed on an annual basis.

Developing a three-year business plan

The *raison d'être* for a business plan is to help give direction, vision, and strength to the venture. This can be presented as a document, and it needs to be worked out and agreed by the committee. *Vivienne Morpeth*, a founder-member of the Mayflower Parent and Child group and Steiner Educational Initiative in north Lincolnshire, UK, told me that the group found their business plan an essential reference source – helping the project to stay on track, stay true to original vision, resolve disputes, and provide something to pass on to new members. It also gave the group a sense of community, equality, and group ownership. The plan could include the matters listed in Box 32.

Box 32: A sample group business plan

- The purpose, aims, and objectives of the group – this would come from the original mission statement and the aims and objectives written into the constitution
- Group legal status
- Ground management structure
- The constitution
- Short- and long-term strategy (who, what, when, how, for whom, why, what if?…)
- Financial plan
- Marketing plan
- Contingency plan

Help and advice on creating business plans is available from local authorities, the Pre-school Learning Alliance, and SPPA.

Opening a bank account and keeping accounts

This will be necessary as part of the adoption of a constitution. You will need two signatories for the cheques, and the treasurer's job will be to oversee income and expenditure. At the end of every year an independent person will need to do an audit of the accounts for the AGM. You will need a petty-cash float and also to keep all relevant receipts. There needs to be someone in charge of day-to-day money concerns. An annual budget is an important way of keeping control of the money flow, and also helps to plan ahead. The PSLA and SPPA have courses and booklets to help you with these practical essentials.

Setting fees

If you have a constitution, the fees will need to be set for the year at the AGM. You need to decide the level of fee, whether families or individuals pay, and whether they pay in advance. Generally, as a group gets more established, the 'pay when you drop in' arrangement becomes more problematic. It is helpful for the children to have the strong rhythm and continuity of the session over the weeks, and 'a pay in advance' arrangement helps parents to make a firm commitment to the group. A payment for each half term in advance, for example, also makes it much easier to budget.

There is the difficult question of how much to charge. Independent Waldorf Parent and Child groups tend to charge more than groups attached to early years centres or schools. Generally, parents are happy to pay higher than average fees (compared to mainstream groups) because of the quality and distinctive nature of the sessions.

Paying a leader

Much depends on whether there are the funds to pay a leader. Traditionally, groups have been entirely voluntary. But what value do we place on a committed and responsible leader? Each group needs to look at this question at regular intervals, and to find a solution that suits their particular situation. There are new responsibilities for the committee in paying someone. A paid employee cannot be on the committee, and they need to be paid at least the national minimum wage, and also registered for National Insurance. There needs to be a job description, contract of employment, and clear management procedures. The PSLA and SPPA can help with these aspects of running a group.

There are three appendices which look in more detail at various aspects of setting up a group, namely:

- Appendix 1: Marketing and publicity strategies
- Appendix 2: The practical 'nitty-gritty' of running a Parent and Child group in a public space
- Appendix 3: Fund-raising

Working in groups, working on ourselves

'When one lives in a community, one senses more and more what it means to live on the threshold of the spiritual world. What does this mean, to live on the threshold? It means to experience ever more consciously that we are being "seen". We are being seen by the spiritual world, by our colleagues, and more and more, thereby, we are seeing ourselves in a new light. We come to know ourselves as like the others, wrestling with our shortcomings and with our insufficiencies, trying to live up to ideals that are just beyond our grasp. This is the self knowledge we need.'

Robert Schappacasse[7]

Initiatives are a training ground for our faculties of soul.'
Christopher Schaefer and Tyno Voors[8]

Working in groups is not easy. In initiatives that have formed out of a spiritual impulse there is often a wish to work co-operatively, with equality and consensus. We want to experiment with new ways of decision making and dialogue. Our high ideals are often disappointed, however, because we still encounter conflict and dissent! We realize that working with others in a more spiritually aware way actually requires more of us – that we may need to 'work' on ourselves. In short, we are called to grow and become self-aware.

There are organisations and trainings that encourage groups to develop new ways of working and dealing with the inevitable conflicts, and some of these that are Steiner inspired are listed at the end of the chapter. I outline some very basic concepts that may be useful starting-points in your own venture.

New initiatives and soul-building

Those involved in starting a new initiative will discover new abilities and talents which they didn't know they had. It is important that each person has the opportunity to develop and shine. Sometimes a 'queen bee' – highly competent and with many skills – can take charge; but the group as a whole may then become weakened and can flounder if the queen leaves.

There are also particular skills that are needed in the various phases of the initiative. In the book *Vision in Action* they are described like this:[9]

- *The Pioneer phase* – courage, initiative, will
- *The Administrative phase* – clarity, rationality, planning, and attention to detail
- *The Mature initiative* – wisdom, insight, compassion

People who are strongly active in the first phase may find the transition to the more practically administrative phase difficult. Others who are better equipped to carry the second phase need to be made room for. There is also the tendency for a split to develop between the visionaries and 'feelers' of the group, on the one hand, and the 'doers' who can feel they end up doing all the thankless tasks, on the other. Over time, this can cause ill feeling. Inner work and awareness in the group can allow a flexibility and movement between thinking, feeling, and willing, both individually and collectively.

Group life and inner development

All of the skills and conscious awareness that need to be developed in Parent and Child work need also to be practised in group work which is orientated around planning and management of the venture. Meeting with others in a group will sometimes highlight our anti-social tendencies. Our critical and judgemental attitudes, our likes and dislikes, our selfishness and egoism – all these are aspects of our 'shadow', those tendencies we would rather not own but only ascribe to others! These aspects of ourselves can be reflected on individually as the 'stuff' of personal growth and self- knowledge. However, the group also grows and transforms if meetings can be reviewed in the same way – recalling what happened, what worked, what didn't, where the group lost consciousness…. It is through the sharing of these reflective processes that the group is deepened, strengthened – and grows.

Rudolf Steiner said that in this type of group working, tolerance 'of a truly heart-felt kind' is needed to a much greater degree than in any other situation. *Vivienne Morpeth*, told me that it was goodwill and humour which were the fuel of their project, particularly in the difficult times…

Radical group working: the art of consensus

Sylvie Hétu, who runs workshops on Consensus and Dialogue, describes consensus as a radical way of decision making in groups where the aim is to 'find the best solution for the given situation, a solution that everyone in the group feels comfortable with'.[10] She describes how, in consensus, we use our perception abilities in the service of the group to 'hear' what the best solution might be. We listen to cosmic thoughts; in a way we listen with anticipation to 'what is coming out of the future into the present', and *the whole group* becomes the ear. Individual preferences, 'band wagons', and early judgements of right and wrong need to be laid aside.

Hétu describes how, in consensus, there is, ideally, a moment of 'grace' when a 'collective yes' provides a clear way forward for the question that was asked. Yet the timing of this moment is unpredictable. The whole process ends with evaluating, choosing, and deciding the 'best'. In each stage of the process everyone has the freedom to express themselves. Consensus is a way of working which itself comes out of the future – an ideal which is as yet generally difficult fully to achieve in group life, but which shows a way of working more directly with the spiritual worlds.

Keeping strong and steady

New initiatives require grit, determination, patience, and a strong will to survive. We live in a materialistic culture where many people have a resistance to the spiritual perspective that Waldorf initiatives embody. Misinterpretations and misunderstandings of our intentions are common.

Steiner stated that inner strength for any new project is forged 'by fearless knowledge and a really strong will'.[11] The book *Vision in Action* also gives sound advice:

'In taking an initiative, we are going into the unknown with only ourselves as resources…. So a threshold of fear needs to be crossed, not only once but repeatedly. In other cases the fear of success may play in…. I believe that fear is the cause of many aborted initiatives and of many which die in infancy.'[12]

And in reality we do not have to depend only on our own strength. We are supported by the spiritual worlds in our work, and Rudolf Steiner states that a spiritual being, who will oversee the endeavour, will come into being by our conscious group work.[13]

The Waldorf model as a healing force

As Tom Stehlik writes, the whole Waldorf educational movement arose 'out of a quest for new social forms and a desire for freedom to learn in an environment of creativity'.[14] That ethos is still the driving force in the expansion of this movement on a world-wide level, and it provides an example of organisational, educational, and social forms that can be offered as a model carrying a healing force into the world.

Similarly, the Waldorf approach offers a model which can be experienced as a force for healing in family and community life. Each parent does carry a flame – a burning wish to provide the best for our children and, like the imagery of the Olympic torch, we can pass it on to others in the heart-warmth of community endeavour. Steiner Parent and Child groups, so often born out of the enthusiasm and commitment of a few families who share a flame, provide the seed beginnings for new forms of community and group life.

Registering with the Steiner Waldorf Schools Fellowship and the Steiner Waldorf Early Years Steering Group (UK)

If you wish to go the Waldorf way, it is important that you register your interest with the Steiner Schools Fellowship and the National Parent and Child group representative on the Steiner Early Years Steering Group. You will then be put in touch with a regional representative who can keep you informed about training courses, workshops, and advice in your area. Speakers and workshop leaders can also be arranged – useful contacts are given at the end of the chapter; and more details are given in Appendix 4.

Some project case histories

New Parent and Child group, Sheffield, UK

For a number of years, *Patsy Collinson* ran a large conventional toddler group (30+ children). She discovered Waldorf Kindergarten education in Sheffield for her own children, but realized that there was a need for a Waldorf Parent and Child group too. In 2003 she came to a short Parent and Child leader training course I organized at York Steiner School, and started to visit different Waldorf Parent and Child groups. Patsy was encouraged by parents to get something going. She has subsequently set up her own group and wrote to me about her experiences.

After looking at the issues and costs of renting a public space, Patsy decided to have the group in her own home. Most of her parents found a morning session best. Charity shops supplied wooden chairs, a table (she cut down the legs), small cups, plates, table cloths, and some toys. The local Waldorf Kindergarten donated various articles, and Patsy uses some of

her youngest child's toys. As the group becomes established Patsy is looking toward funding applications, especially for toys and a library. She feels she has embarked on a path of self-development, and the whole endeavour is a continual process of observation and adjustment.

Norfolk Steiner Initiative, UK

This initiative was started in 1998 by a small group which held several coffee mornings 'for anyone interested in Steiner education'. A Parent and Child group was started almost immediately in two people's homes. After a year, a room was hired in a local hall. Beginning as a 'drop-in' group, after a year advance payment was introduced, and this enabled the leaders to be paid and encouraged more commitment.

The related Kindergarten Initiative co-emerged soon afterwards. A £2,000 grant from the Esmé Fairbairn Charitable Trust eased some of the early financial anxieties. The Norwich Steiner Kindergarten opened at Easter 2001, initially running part-time with both parents and children attending, pending registration; and it now runs full-time in new premises and at near full capacity. The first Class 1 of a new Steiner School is due to open in Norwich in September 2005. In just five years, then, the founding initiative group (which still meets regularly) had helped to spawn five full weekly Parent and Child groups attended by some 60 families, a Kindergarten, and separate groups for school steering and fund-raising, parental support, and craft-making.

Lancaster Educational Initiative, UK

The seed for this initiative, dating from 1991, was sown at a public talk on the importance of rhythm in childhood. Some 25 people attended, and after this talk a discussion group was formed to study child development and crafts from a Waldorf perspective. The parent-led Rainbow

Parent and Child group was formed four months later. One of the parents had experience of a Steiner Kindergarten; the rest of us were new and keen! The Parent and Child group, which began in families' homes, moved out into a local Community Centre and finally came to rest in the Friends' Meeting House in Lancaster. The Cherry Trees Kindergarten was started in 1993 and was first run as a child-minding business – with six children and two adults, it was like a family. It met four mornings a week from 9 to 12.30. In 1995, it moved to a local Methodist church where it could expand to take 15 children. In 1998 a small Steiner School was started in the area, and the Kindergarten and school now share premises in Lancaster.

The Acorn Parent and Child group, Clitheroe, UK

A public meeting was arranged in June 2000, and some 15 parents decided to start a group in a converted garage space in a private garden. Parents worked hard to renovate and decorate the room, and many of the toys and other items were donated. Tables and chairs came from a primary school. The sessions started in September 2000 with around seven families, meeting on a Monday, Wednesday, and Thursday morning. This has increased to around 10 families each session. In October 2001 a steering group was formed to work toward starting a Kindergarten.

There was another public talk, which generated a lot of interest. A Kindergarten teacher has recently been found and a Kindergarten will start in autumn 2004. For a while, a regular 'Saturday gathering' was created for the families with older children who had grown out of the Parent and Child group, to meet together for crafts, stories, and festivals. There are new families joining the group in September 2004, who will carry the initiative forward.

What situations suit the Waldorf approach?

Can the Waldorf approach be of help in areas of social and economic deprivation? Perhaps a few examples can show the ways in which individuals are taking this approach to working with parents and children deeply into mainstream situations.

Sophia House, West Oakland, San Francisco

Carole Cole and her husband have opened a centre for high-risk children and their mothers. Some are homeless, but most are struggling for stability after being homeless. These are families that face severe obstacles – enough food, clothing, heat, and electricity; the constant risk of drugs, alcoholism, and domestic violence. The task of the centre is to help build inner resources in the children and adults, with which they can then transform and rebuild their lives. Sophia House caters for 14 children of varying ages, who come each weekday. About 30 children come to the centre monthly, and families are involved for an average of two years. The children come to the Kindergarten, full day care, or after-school sessions, and they can also stay for weekends. Their mothers can come as well, and there is stability and support for them too. As the workers at the centre 'live in', the centre is like a family, with strong rhythm, meals around the table, special events, and the preparation and celebration of festivals.

Caldwell Early Childhood Program, Rudolf Steiner College, Sacramento, California

This multifaceted initiative includes an 'outreach' parenting programme in urban Sacramento. A government grant has funded the organizing and advertising of public talks in various different neighbourhood centres, to promote training in a Waldorf approach to family-style day care. From this, small groups of local parents are supported in training and then in the setting up of their own businesses in their local neighbourhoods.

Funding for Parent and Child groups in Brighton, UK

A government grant has been given to Brighton Steiner School to start a Parent and Child group for parents in a poor neighbourhood of Brighton. The grant will pay for the leader, assistant, and materials. The parents who attend the group over a year will be then be funded through the Steiner School. On appraisal of the scheme, the grant may be extended to three years. The Social Research Department at Brighton University is carrying out an ongoing evaluation of the enterprise.

Haus des Kindes and der Hof, Germany

This is a radically innovative enterprise in Frankfurt, based on the work of Rudolf Steiner and researchers into early childhood such as Hugo Kukelhaus, Emmi Pikler, and Jane Ayres. The centre has two arms: one is a pedagogical therapeutic centre which offers a wide range of services and advice to families with 'special needs' children. Referrals made by any doctor are funded by Social Services. The other, called 'der Hof', incorporates a wide range of Parent and Child classes, a Kindergarten, a school, and a day care centre, as well as artisans, a publisher, wholefood shop, and café and guest accommodation.

Parents Place, Sonoma County, California

Bonnie Romanow works for Parents Place, a comprehensive and very successful mainstream family resource service developed by the Jewish Family and Children's Services. It is very easy to include an anthroposophical perspective in her work, as so much of the recent research into early childhood validates Waldorf principles and can be framed in a way that parents readily understand.

Main points again

- Many successful Steiner educational initiatives and Steiner schools in the UK have started from the small beginnings of a Parent and Child group.

- There are various stages in the growth and development of an initiative. A big step is from a home-based Parent and Child group to one based in a public space. You need to be aware of the practical implications and responsibilities – these are comprehensively listed in the chapter.

- The Pre-school Learning Alliance and SPPA have leaflets and courses on the practical aspects of running a successful Parent and Child group in a public space.

- It is important to have a good support base, and parents with enthusiasm, energy, and commitment.

- If you wish to go the Waldorf way, do get in touch with the UK Steiner Schools Fellowship, who will advise you on local support.

- There are many ways in which the Waldorf approach to Parent and Child work can be brought into mainstream situations.

Useful information and organisations – UK

Steiner Schools Fellowship

Kidbrooke Park, Forest Row, Sussex RH18 5JB, UK; tel. 01342 822115; mail@swsf.org.uk Phone or email here to ask for the national Parent and Child group representative in the UK. www.steinerwaldorf.org.uk – this site lists all Steiner Educational Initiatives in UK and Ireland, and you can use this site to find your nearest one. www.anth.org.uk – this site has links to many anthroposophical websites.

Steiner Parent and Child Group UK website: www.steinerparentandchild.co.uk email: info@steinerparentandchild.co.uk

Pre-school Learning Alliance

69 Kings Cross Road, London WC1 9LL, UK; tel. 020 7833 0991; www.pre-school.org.uk; email: pla@pre-school.org.uk

Scottish Pre-school Play Association

45 Finnieston Street, Glasgow G3 8JU, UK; tel. 0141 221 4148; www.sppa.org.uk; email: info@sppa.org.uk

CHAPTER 12

If you had just one wish for your child…

'Whatever you can do or dream you can, begin it. Boldness has genius, power and magic in it, begin it now.'

Goethe

FOR PARENTS...

Part 12: If you had just one wish for your child...

If you had just one wish for your child, what would it be? I didn't know what mine was until I encountered the Waldorf way. I came to realise that my innermost wish for my son was that he was able to experience a childhood which was infused with a holistic perspective which understood and respected his journey into life as a spiritual being. I am more and more convinced that the wisdom of the Steiner perspective provides a real hope for the world. But it needs us as parents to 'wake up', and to love and understand ourselves and our children from the widest deepest context we can manage – and then find the courage to act.

When we become parents we have many wishes for our children – good health, happiness, creativity and purpose, friendships…We hope to give them the best of what we knew as children, and also the best of those things that we didn't know. But what if you had just one wish that could be granted by the child's fairy godmother or guardian angel… What would it be? For me, the wish – which I hadn't been consciously aware of but which must have been living deeply in me, barely a breath away from my questions and struggles as a parent – was granted when I found a little flyer about a talk on 'The importance of rhythm in childhood', organized by a visiting Steiner couple; and in total ignorance of the subject matter, I felt compelled to go.

As soon as I walked through the door of the hall, on that rather fateful evening, I knew I was on to something that was essential for my life. Perhaps it was the little line of felt gnomes marching across the front of the speaker's table, which immediately delighted and enchanted the 'little girl' inside me; or perhaps it was that, much to my surprise, I was signing up for a study group before the talk had even started! Or that there were faces in the room that I felt I already knew, but didn't… (yet!). Anyway, by the end of the evening I had seamlessly crossed over into a new wide country inhabited by those who had or wanted a spiritual understanding of childhood and parenthood... and I was deeply excited. I came away nourished to my bones, but also thirsting for more…

So started my own healing encounter with the work of Rudolf Steiner and an anthroposophical understanding of life and human existence; and so started, too, a wonderful adventure for my whole family, working alongside others to create a small community of parents – at the heart of which was a Steiner Parent and Child group and, subsequently, a Kindergarten for our children (…together with all the other things that have unfolded since then… like the journey of writing this book). There were the obvious tangible achievements of those early years, but there was so much, much more as well: the experience of shared purpose; the discovery of skills I never knew I had; a profound encounter with the inner journey through the cycle of the year; a new, huge, and enormously challenging context for my relatively unformed and fragmented personal cosmology – all this, and more, from a little flyer found in the corner of a counter in the local wholefood shop.

I came to realize that my deepest wish for my son was that he was able to experience a childhood which was infused with a holistic perspective which understood and respected his journey into life as a spiritual being. It was Teilhard de Chardin who wrote, 'We are not humans on a spiritual journey, but spiritual beings on a human journey!'. My slowly discovered heartfelt wish for my son, like a little package tied with a satin bow, unwrapped to reveal countless treasures, including the magic of story-telling and puppets, community lantern festivals on windy November evenings, the peace and beauty of the Advent Spiral, experiencing the glorious wisdom of imitation and natural creative play, the delicious common sense of rhythm and routine – and my own inner 'slowing down'… causing a gentle dawning of soul in the 'everyday'. And the beginning of a remembrance that I, too, underneath my awkwardness and conditioning, had come down, like all new babies into life, blazing from of an inner core of spirit.

I am not a 'natural' mother, and I feel I have made many mistakes. But I feel that my encounter with the Waldorf way ensured that I gave my son the best I was capable of, and it precipitated the beginning of my own inner healing in the process.

As I continue to learn and grow through my work with parents and very young children, I am more and more convinced that the wisdom of the Steiner perspective provides real hope for the world. As parents, we can help guide a new generation who have a love of the earth and simple timeless pleasures that do not pollute; who have experienced tolerance, acceptance, and authentic community; who haven't forgotten in their souls where they have come from before they were born; and who are incarnated enough in their bodies to embrace life fully, purposefully, and passionately. I feel this is the reality of what Steiner education offers. But it means that we need to 'wake up', to be conscious of what is appropriate to bring to our young children (and what is not) for their natural unfolding; to protect where necessary; to give freedom where necessary; and in order to do this we need to love and understand our children (and ourselves) from the widest, deepest context that we can manage.

My hope is that this book, inspired out of my own experiences and discoveries as a mother, will inspire you, dear mums and dads, to follow your own deepest wish for your children. And that if you feel stirred and excited by any of what you have read in these pages, you will find the courage (your spirit!) to take a new step toward fulfilling that wish…whatever it is!

Footnotes

Chapter 1

[1] Article reprinted in *Everyman*, Bath Anthroposophical Newsheet (UK), Spring/Summer, 2003.

[2] Martyn Rawson and Michael Rose, *Ready to Learn,* Hawthorn Press, Stroud, 2002, p.1.

[3] Sally Jenkinson, *The Genius of Play*, Hawthorn Press, Stroud, 2001, p. xiv.

[4] David Elkind, *The Hurried Child – Growing up Too Fast Too Soon*, 3rd edn, Perseus, Cambridge, Mass., 2001, p. xvi.

[5] Marie Winn, *Children without Childhood: Growing up Too Fast in the World of Sex and Drugs*, Penguin, Harmondsworth, 1984, p. 5.

[6] Sam Lister, *The Times* (London), 6 April 2004, quoting a report authored by Dr Dimitri Christakis, at the Children's Hospital and Regional Medical Centre in Seattle.

[7] See the end of this chapter for details.

[8] Pre-school Learning Alliance, 'Running a Parent and Toddler Pre-School', available from 69 Kings Cross Road London WC1X 9LL, tel. 020 7833 0991.

[9] The Steiner (Waldorf) education movement was founded by Rudolf Steiner, an Austrian scientist, philosopher, and spiritual adept. He lived in the last century and initiated a worldwide educational movement based on his spiritual insights into the nature and needs of children. This movement, which supports Parent and Child groups, Kindergartens, and Schools for 7-19 year olds, is thriving and expanding all over the world. Steiner's life legacy includes practical contributions in the spheres of agriculture, medicine, art, and architecture, as well as in education. Much of his genius is only now beginning to be understood and appreciated as we grapple with the complex consequences of technology and our present day life-styles. A list of useful introductory books on Steiner's work can be found at the end of this chapter.

The word 'Waldorf' refers to the first Steiner school. The school was founded as a result of Rudolf Steiner's responses to a question put to him by the owner of the Waldorf Astoria factory in Stuttgart, Germany, about how the spiritual understanding of the human being could be applied to the education of children. The school was opened for the factory workers' children at the end of the Great War in 1919. In some countries the term 'Waldorf' is used in preference to 'Steiner' to describe schools and other educational initiatives.

Anthroposophy, which means 'wisdom of humankind' or 'the consciousness of one's full humanity', is the term Rudolf Steiner gave to describe the spiritual perspective and knowledge which he researched and described, but which any – and everyone has the potential to access for themselves. The fruits of anthroposophy can be applied practically to many different spheres of life. There are Anthroposophical Societies in most countries, and many organisations are affiliated to the anthroposophical movement. The international organisational headquarters of the anthroposophical movement are in Dornach, Switzerland.

[10] Lynne Oldfield, *Free to Learn*, Hawthorn Press, Stroud, 2001, p. 191.

[11] Kim Billington, 'Creating a Steiner Playgroup: guidelines for working with parents and being with very young children', available as a download from www.steiner-australia.org

[12] Rudolf Steiner, *Awakening to Community*, Anthroposophic Press, New York, 1974 (quotation inside cover).

13 Lynne Oldfield, op. cit. (note 10), p. 192.

Chapter 2

[1] Rahima Baldwin, *You Are Your Child's First Teacher*, Celestial Arts, Berkeley, CA, 1989, p. 5.

[2] See David Marshak, *The Common Vision – Parenting and Educating for Wholeness*, Peter Lang, New York, 1997. The book describes a similar vision of child development given by three great spiritual leaders of the twentieth century – Rudolf Steiner, Aurobindo Ghose, and Inayat Khan.

[3] Mary Triulzi, private correspondence, April 2004.

[4] See for example Gilbert Childs' book *Steiner Education*, Floris Books, Edinburgh, 1991, pp. 33 and 68. Also, Rudolf Steiner, *The Roots of Education*, Rudolf Steiner Press, London, 1968, p. 42.

[5] Sally Goddard Blythe, from a paper entitled 'Early learning in the balance', 2000, available from the author – 4 Stanley Place, Chester CH1 2LU, UK; tel. 01244 311 414

[6] Ibid.

[7] Quoted in an article by Susan Weber in *Gateways: Journal of the Waldorf Early Childhood Association of North America*, Spring/Summer 2003.

[8] The address is given at the end of the book under 'Useful Organisations'. See also the book *Your Self Confident Baby* by Magda Gerber, Wilber Publishing, 1999.

[9] Private correspondence, April 2004.

[10] Rudolf Steiner, *The Education of the Child*, Anthroposophic Press, New York, 1996, p.20.

[11] Press article titled 'Seeing is believing', Robert Winston, the *Guardian* newspaper, 7 January 2004.

[12] LifeWays North America, Caldwell Early Life Center, Rudolf Steiner College, 9200 Fair Oaks Blvd, Fair Oaks, CA 405 447 2365, USA.

[13] Cynthia Aldinger, private correspondence, 2003.

[14] Rahima Baldwin, op. cit. (note 1), p. 118.

[15] Gilbert Childs, *Steiner Education in Theory and Practice*, Floris Books, Edinburgh 1991, p. 33.

[16] Freya Jaffke, *Work and Play in Early Childhood*, Floris Books, Edinburgh, 1996, p. 10.

[17] Barbara Patterson and Pamela Bradley, *Beyond the Rainbow Bridge*, Michaelmas Press, Amesbury, Mass., 2000, p. 74.

[18] May Gaskin, *Spiritual Midwifery*, 4th edn, Book Publishing Co, Ten., 2002, p. 251.

[19] Patterson and Bradley, op. cit. (note 18), p. 78.

[20] Mary Triulzi, op. cit. (note 4).

[21] Lynne Oldfield. in J. Thompson and others, *Natural Childhood*, Gaia Books, London, 1994, p. 224.

[22] Michaela Glöckler (ed.), *The Dignity of the Young Child*, International Waldorf Kindergarten Association, Medical School of the Goetheanum, School of Spiritual Science, 2000, p. 29.

Chapter 3

1 Christopher Alexander, *The Timeless Way of Building*, Oxford University Press, Oxford, 1979, *The Pattern Language*, Oxford University Press, Oxford, 1977; and Christopher Day, *Places of the Soul: Architecture and Environmental Design as a Healing Art*, Aquarian Press, Northamptonshire, 1990.

2 Freya Jaffke, *Work and Play in Early Childhood*, Floris Books, Edinburgh, 1996 p. 14.

3 Private correspondence, March 2004.

4 Kay Turner, *Beautiful Necessity: The Art and Meaning of Women's Altars*, Thames and Hudson, London, 1989.

5 Lynne Oldfield, 'Goethe's colour cycle in the seasonal garden', *Kindergarten Newsletter (UK)*, issue 4 (Autumn), 1984, pp. 7-8.

6 Letitia Costain, 'The Sistine Madonna', *The Anthroposophical Society in Great Britain Newsletter*, 79 (4), November 2002, p. 21.

7 Ibid.

8 Kim Billington, 'Creating a Steiner playgroup', at www.Steiner-australia.org

Chapter 4

1 Joan Almon, 'The vital role of play in childhood education', p. 1, adapted from the book by Sharna Olfman (ed.), *All Work and No Play*, Greenwood Press, Westport, Ct., 2003. The article was distributed at the Steiner World Teachers Conference, Dornach, Switzerland, Easter 2004.

2 Ibid., p. 10.

3 Magda Gerber, *Your Self Confident Baby*, John Wiley, Brighton, 1999, p. 16.

4 Michael Rose and Martyn Rawson, *Ready to Learn*, Hawthorn Press, Stroud, 2002, p. 71.

5 Susan Isaacs, *Intellectual Growth in Young Children*, Routledge, London, 1930, p. 104.

6 Donald Winnicott, *Playing and Reality*, Routledge, London, 1982.

7 Sally Jenkinson, *The Genius of Play*, Hawthorn Press, Stroud, 2001, p. 77.

8 Sally Jenkinson, 'Imagination: the Playground of the mind', *Juno* magazine, issue 1, Autumn/Winter 2003, pp. 6-8.

9 Almon, op. cit. (note 1), p. 7 (from Furlow Bryant, 'Play's the thing', *New Scientist*, no. 2294, 2001, p. 28.)

10 Almon, op. cit. (note 1), p. 1.

11 Freya Jaffke, *Toymaking with Children*, Floris Books, Edinburgh, 1988, p. 14.

12 Alexandra Frean, 'It's no fun being a toddler any more', *The Times*, 5 November 2003, p. 8.

13 Magda Gerber, op. cit. (note 3), p. 88.

14 Daniel Udo de Haes, *The Young Child: Creative Living with Two to Four Year Olds*, Floris Books, Edinburgh, 1986.

15 Jaffke, op. cit. (note 11), p. 14.

16 Carol Petrash, *Earthwise: Environmental Crafts and Activities for Young Children*, Floris Books, Edinburgh, 1993, p. 19.

17 Bonnie Romanow, Information leaflet, 'Parenting from the Heart', private correspondence, April 2004.

18 Jaffke, op. cit. (note 11), p. 22.

Chapter 5

1 Jane Winslow Eliot, *Let's Talk, Let's Play: Helping Children to Learn How to Learn from Life*, Association of Waldorf Schools of North America, Fair Oaks, Calif., 1997, p. 3.

2 Candy Verney, *The Singing Day*, Hawthorn Press, Stroud, 2003, p. xiv.

3 Winslow Eliot, op. cit. (note 1).

4 Kim Billington, 'Creating a Steiner Playgroup: guidelines for working with parents and being with very young children', available as a download from www.steiner-australia.org

5 Candy Verney, op. cit. (note 2), p. xv.

Chapter 6

1 Lourdes Callen, private correspondence, 2003.
2 Richard House, private correspondence, 2003.
3 Janni Nicol, private correspondence, 2003.
4 Richard House, op. cit.
5 Ibid.
6 Kim Billington, 'Creating a Steiner Playgroup: guidelines for working with parents and being with very young children', available as a download from www.steiner-australia.org
7 Lourdes Callen, op. cit.
8 Kathy McQuillen, private correspondence, 2003.
9 Janni Nicol, op. cit.
10 Ibid,
11 Kathy McQuillen, op. cit.
12 Richard House, op. cit.
13 Kim Billington, op. cit.
14 Janni Nichol, op. cit.
15 Kathy McQuillen, op. cit.
16 Kim Billington, op. cit.
17 Kath McQuillen, op. cit.
18 Letitia Costain, 'The importance of painting and colour for the young child' (article), private correspondence, March 2004.
19 Waldorf groups tend to use a brand of water-colour paint called *STOCKMAR* from Germany, which is available from Mercurius in England. These paints produce a very pure colour that mixes well and does not go muddy
20 Kathy McQuillen, op. cit.
21 Ibid.
22 Ibid.

Chapter 7

1 Estelle Bryer, 'The importance of mealtimes in the Kindergarten', *Kindling: Journal for Steiner Waldorf Early childhood Care and Education*, 2 (Autumn/Winter), 2002, p. 15.
2 Veronika van Duin, *Homemaking as a Social Art*, Sophia Books/Rudolf Steiner Press, London, 2000, p. 76.
3 Shea Darian, *Seven Times the Sun*, Gilead Press, Wisc. USA, 2001, p. 43.

Chapter 8

1 Wilma Ellersiek, *Giving Love – Bringing Joy: Hand Gesture Games and Lullabies in the Mood of the Fifth*, Waldorf Early Childhhod Association of North America, Spring Valley, NY, 2003, p. 40.
2 Rahima Baldwin, *You are Your Child's First Teacher*, Celestial Books, Calif., 1989, p. 211.
3 Rudolf Steiner, *The Kingdom of Childhood*, Rudolf Steiner Press, London, 1995, p. 110.
4 Joan Holbek, 'Music and the young child', *Waldorf Early Years Newsletter* (UK), issue 38 (Autumn/Winter), 2000, p. 9.
5 Rudolf Steiner, *The Education of the Child*, Anthroposophic Press, Va., 1996, p. 29.
6 Willi Aeppli, *The Care and Development of the Human Senses*, Steiner Schools Fellowship Publications, Forest Row, 1993.
7 Albert Soesman, *Our Twelve Senses*, Hawthorn Press, Stroud, 1998, p. 113.
8 Ellersiek, op. cit. (note 1), p. 78.
9 Ibid., p.11.
10 Ibid., p. 13.
11 Celia Barker Lotteridge, *Favourite Interactive Rhymes and How to Use Them in Your Parent-Child Mother Goose Program* (720 Bathurst Street, Suite 402, Toronto, Ontario), 1999.
12 Daniel Udo de Haes, *The Young Child: Creative Living with Two to Four Year Olds*, Floris Books, Edinburgh, 1986, p. 27.

13   Ibid., p. 29.
14   Nancy Mellon, *Storytelling with Children*, Hawthorn Press, Stroud, 2000, p. 162.
15   Bonnie Romanow, 'Parenting with heart' leaflet, private correspondence, April 2004.
16   Suzanne Down, 'Around the world with Finger Puppet Animals', Storyarts Publications, P.O. Box 17666, Boulder, CO, 1999.
17   Patricia Rubano, private correspondence, April 2004.
18   Romanow (note 15), op. cit.
19   Janet Parsons, private correspondence, April 2004.
20   Romanow (note 15), op. cit.
21   Ibid.
22   Parsons, op. cit. (note 19).

Chapter 9

1   Pamela Johnson Fenner and Karen Rivers, *Waldorf Education: A Family Guide*, Michaelmas Press, Mass., 1992, p. 144.
2   Ann Druitt , Christine Fynes-Clinton and Marije Rowling, *All Year Round*, Hawthorn Press, Stroud, 1995, p. 84.
3   These are made out of paper, the edges folded in such a way that they twirl round when pulled through the air. Instructions are given in *All Year Round*.
4   Druitt et al., op. cit. (note 2), p. 156.
5   Druitt et al., op. cit., p. 164.
6   Janet Parsons, private correspondence, April 2004.
7   Anne and Peter Thomas, *The Children's Party Book*, Floris Books, Edinburgh, 1998.
8   Janet Parsons, op. cit.

Chapter 10

1   Bonnie Romanow, 'Parenting from the Heart' Parent and Child programme, California; information leaflet, April 2004.
2   Steiner Early Years Third National Parent and Child Conference, held on Saturday 11 October 2003 at Temple Lodge, Hammersmith, London.
3   Richard House, 'Beyond "Paranoid Parenting": raising children in a fear-filled age', *The Mother* Magazine, 8 (Winter 2003-4), pp. 6-9.
4   Frank Furedi, *Paranoid Parenting: Abandon Your Anxieties and Be a Good Parent*, Allen Lane/Penguin, London.
5   Very simply defined 'the threshold' is a term used by Rudolf Steiner to describe the boundary between the sensory world and subtle spiritual realities. Our evolutionary journey as a human being eventually confronts us with experiences in life which may lead us to direct knowledge of these realms.
6   Donna Steele, Sophia's Hearth Speakers Series, *The Garden Gate: Journal of Sophia's Hearth Family Centre*, Vol. 3, No. 1 (Spring), 2002, p. 7.
7   Bonnie Romanow, private correspondence, April 2004.
8   Lourdes Callen, private correspondence, 2004.
9   Jill Hall, *The Reluctant Adult: An Exploration of Choice*, Prism Press, Bridport, UK, 1993.
10   Coenraad van Houten, *Awakening the Will: Principles and Processes in Adult Learning*, Temple Lodge, London, 1999.
11   Ibid., p 18.
12   Bonnie Romanow, op. cit. (note 7).
13   Lourdes Callen, op. cit. (note 8).
14   Richard House, private correspondence, 2003.
15   Lourdes Callen, Notes from the 'Working with Parents' Conference (note 2), mimeo, October 2003.
16   Lourdes Callen, op. cit. (note 8).
17   Bonnie Romanow, op. cit. (note 1).
18   Susan Weber, 'Magic happens on the floor', The Garden Gate: *Journal of Sophia's Hearth Family Center*, Vol. 2, no. 2 (Fall), 2001, p. 3.

Chapter 11

1 Sylvie Hétu, 'Consciously cultivating "Community": The example of the Waldorf Parent and child group', mimeo, April 2004.

2 Sylvie Hétu, *Working Together: Thoughts on Consensus*, Course Workbook (mimeo), Eye, Suffolk, March 2004.

3 Tom Stehlik, *Each Parent Carries a Flame: Waldorf Schools as Sites for Promoting Lifelong Learning, Creating Community and Educating for Social Renewal*, Post Pressed Flaxton, Queensland Australia 2002.

4 Christopher Schaefer and Tyno Voors, *Vision in Action: Working with Soul and Spirit in Small Organisations*, Hawthorn Press, Stroud, 1996, p. 23.

5 Hétu, op. cit. (note 2).

6 Ibid.

7 Robert Schiappacasse, 'Building a Waldorf community', in Pamela Johnson Fenner and Karen L. Rivers (eds), *Waldorf Education: A Family Guide*, Michaelmas Press, Mass., 1992, p. 86.

8 Schaefer and Voors, op. cit. (note 3), p. 205.

9 Ibid.

10 Hétu, op. cit. (note 2).

11 Rudolf Steiner, *Awakening to Community*, Anthroposophic Press, New York, 1974, p. 67.

12 Schaefer and Voors, op. cit. (note 3), p. 205.

13 Steiner, op. cit. (note 10), pp. 100 and 156.

14 Stehlik, op. cit. (note 2), p. 171.

Bibliography

Aeppli, Willi (1993) *The Care and Development of the Human Senses*, Steiner School Fellowship Publications, Forest Row

Alexander, Christopher (1979) *The Timeless Way of Building*, Oxford University Press, Oxford

Baldwin, Rahima (1989) *Your Are your Child's First Teacher*, Celestial Arts, Calif.

Barker Lotteridge, Celia (1999) *Favourite Interactive Rhymes and how to use them in your Parent-Child Mother Goose Program*, The Parent-Child Mother Goose Program, Toronto, Ontario

Berger, Thomas (1990) *The Christmas Craft Book*, Floris Books, Edinburgh

Berger, Thomas (1992) *Harvest Craft Book*, Floris Books, Edinburgh

Berger, Thomas and Petra (1993) *Easter Craft Book*, Floris Books, Edinburgh

Carey, Diana and Large, Judy (1982) *Festivals, Family and Food*, Hawthorn Press, Stroud

Childs, Gilbert (1991) *Steiner Education*, Floris Books, Edinburgh

Darian, Shea (2001) *Seven Times the Sun*, Gilead Press, Marshall, Michigan

Day, Christopher (1990) *Places of the Soul: Architecture and Environmental Design as a Healing Art*, Aquarian Press, Northamptonshire

Dhom, Christel (2001) *Making Magical Fairy-Tale Puppets*, Rudolf Steiner College Press, CA, USA

Druitt, Ann, Fynes-Clinton, Christine and Rowling, Marije (1995) *All Year Round*, Hawthorn Press, Stroud

Elkind, David (2001) *The Hurried Child: Growing up Too Fast Too Soon*, 3rd edn, Perseus Publishing, Cambridge, Mass.

Ellersiek, Wilma (2003) *Giving Love, Bringing Joy*, Waldorf Early Childhood Association of North America, New York

Furedi, Frank (2002) *Paranoid Parenting*, Allen Lane/Penguin, Harmondsworth

Gaskin, May (2002) *Spiritual Midwifery*, Book Publishing Co., Tenn.

Gerber, Magda and Johnson, Alison (1998) *Your Self Confident Baby*, John Wiley, Brighton

Glöckler, Michaela (ed.) (2000) *The Dignity of the Young Child: Care and Training for the First Three Years of Life*, Congress Proceedings, International Waldorf Kindergarten Association, Medical School of the Goetheanum, School of Spiritual Science, Dornach, Switzerland

Hall, Jill (1993) *The Reluctant Adult: An Exploration of Choice*, Prism Press, Bridport, UK

Isaacs, Susan (1930) *Intellectual Growth in Young Children*, Routledge, London

Jaffke, Freya (1996) *Work and Play in Early Childhood*, Floris Books, Edinburgh

Jenkinson, Sally (2001) *The Genius of Play*, Hawthorn Press, Stroud

Johnson Fenner, Pamela and Rivers, Karen (eds) (1992) *Waldorf Education: A Family Guide*, Michaelmas Press, Amesbury MA, USA

König, Karl (1984) *The First Three Years of the Child*, Anthroposophic Press, Hudson, NY (also Floris Books, Edinburgh)

Marshak, David (1997) *The Common Vision –*

Parenting and Educating for Wholeness, Peter Lang, New York

Mellon, Nancy (2000) *Storytelling with Children*, Hawthorn Press, Stroud

Oldfield, Lynne (2001) *Free to Learn*, Hawthorn Press, Stroud

Patterson, Barbara J. and Bradley, Pamela (2000) *Beyond the Rainbow Bridge*, Michaelmas Press, Amesbury, Mass.

Petrash, Carol (1993) *Earthwise: Environmental Crafts and Activities for Young Children*, Floris Books, Edinburgh

Rawson, Martyn and Rose, Michael (2002) *Ready to Learn*, Hawthorn Press, Stroud

Schaefer, Christopher and Voors, Tyno (1996) *Vision in Action*, Hawthorn Press, Stroud

Schmidt, Dagmar and Jaffke, Freya (1994) *Magic Wool: Creative Activities with Natural Sheep's Wool*, Floris Books, Edinburgh

Soesman, Albert (1998) *Our Twelve Senses*, Hawthorn Press, Stroud

Stehlik, Tom (2002) *Every Parent Carries a Flame*, Post Pressed Flaxton, Queensland

Steiner, Rudolf (1974) *Awakening to Community*, Anthroposophic Press, Hudson, NY

Steiner, Rudolf (1995) *The Kingdom of Childhood*, Rudolf Steiner Press, London

Steiner, Rudolf (1996) *Education of the Child*, Anthroposophic Press, Hudson, NY

Thomas, Ann and Peter (1998) *The Children's Party Book*, Floris Books, Edinburgh

Turner, Kay (1985) *Beautiful Necessity: The Art and Meaning of Women's Altars*, Thames and Hudson, London

Udo de Haes, Daniel (1986) *The Young Child: Creative Living with Two to Four Year Olds*, Floris Books, Edinburgh.

Van Duin, Veronica (2000) *Homemaking as a Social Art*, Sophia Books, Rudolf Steiner Press, London

Van Houten, Coenraad (1999) *Awakening the Will: Principles and Processes in Adult Learning*, Temple Lodge, London

Van Leeuwen, M. and Moeskops, J. (1990) *The Nature Corner*, Floris Books, Edinburgh

Verney, Candy (2003) *The Singing Day*, Hawthorn Press, Stroud

Winn, Marie (1984) *Children without Childhood*, Penguin Books, Harmondsworth,

Winnicott, Donald (1982) *Playing and Reality*, Routledge, London

Winslow, Eliot (1997) *Let's Talk, Let's Play*, ASWANA, Fair Oaks, CA.

Wolk-Gerche, Angelika (2000) *Making Fairy-Tale Wool Animals*, Rudolf Steiner College Press, CA

Resources

Useful early childhood and parenting organisations

Steiner organisations

Steiner Schools Fellowship
Kidbrooke Park, Forest Row, Sussex
RH18 5JB, UK; Tel: 01342 822115;
mail@swsf.org.uk
Phone or email here to ask for the national
Parent and Child group representative in the
UK.
www.steinerwaldorf.org.uk – this website lists
all Steiner Educational Initiatives in the UK
and Ireland, and you can use this site to find
your nearest group.
www.anth.org.uk – this website has links to
many anthroposophical sites.

Steiner Parent and Child Groups – UK website
Email: infor@steinerparentandchild.co.uk
www.steinerparentandchild.co.uk

**Waldorf Early Childhood Association of North
America**, 285 Hungry Hollow Road, Spring
Valley, New York 10977 Tel: (+1) 914 352
1690

**Australia Steiner Waldorf Early Childhood
Education**, Dr Renate Long-Breipohl, 44
Manor Road, Hornsby NSW 2077
Tel.: (+61) 02 9476 6222
Email: breipohl@smartchat.net.au

International Waldorf Kindergarten Association,
D-70188 Stuttgart, Heubergstrasse 18,
Germany Tel: (+49) 711 925 740
Email: Inter.Waldorf@t-online.de

New Zealand
Contact: Marjorie Theyer, c/o Kindergarten
Training Course, Taruna College, Havelock
North, Hawkes Bay, 33 Te Matu Peak Road ,
NZ
Tel.: (+64) 06 8777 174

South Africa
Contact: Peter von Alphen, c/o Centre for
Creative Education, PO Box 280, Plumstead
7801 Tel: (+27) 21 7976 802

**International Steiner Waldorf School,
Kindergarten and Nursery, Hong Kong**,
Highgage House School, 2/F Peak Road, The
Peak, Hong Kong Tel: (+00) 852 2849 6336
www.highgatehouse.ed.hk
info@highgatehouse.edu.hk

www.waldorfanswers.org

www.waldorflibrary.org

Toys, materials and crafts

Myriad Natural Toys, Ringwood, Hampshire,
    UK; tel. 01725 517085
    www.myriadonline.co.uk

Mercurius (UK), 6 Highfield, Kings Langley,
    Herts. WD4 9JT 01923 261646
    www.mercurius-international.com

Fibrecrafts, Old Portsmouth Road, Peasmarsh,
    Guildford, Surrey GU3 ILZ 01483 565800
    www.fibrecrafts.com

Waldorf toy websites

www.waldorf-toys.com

www.toyspectrum.com

Parents resources

Weleda (UK) Ltd, Heanor Road, Ilkeston,
    Derbyshire. DE7 8DR 0115 9448200
    www.weleda.co.uk

Smilechild – sustainable shopping.
    www.smilechild.co.uk

Auro – Water based paints – 01452 772020
    www.auro.co.uk

Birth and Baby 01323 722777
    www.birthandbaby.co.uk

Earthkind Babies 01202 722 024
    www.earthkindbabies.com

Greenfibres 0845 3303440 www.greenfibres.com

International Association of Infant Massage –
    promoting nurturing touch right from the
    beginning – www.iaim.net

General

Pre-school Learning Alliance, 69 Kings Cross
    Road, London WC1X 9LL, UK;
    Tel: 0207 833 0991 www.pre-school.org.uk
    Publications include:
    'Running a parent and toddler pre-school'
    'Parent and Toddler groups – self assessment
    for good practice'

Scottish Pre-school Play Association,
    45 Finnieston Street, Glasgow G3 8JU, UK;
    Tel: 0141 221 4148; www.sppa.org.uk
    Publications include:
    'Running a Toddler group – Code of Practice'
    'Learning through play for the under threes
    in Parent and Toddler groups'

The Alliance for Childhood (United Kingdom),
    Kidbrook Park, Forest Row, East Sussex
    RH18 5JA
    Email: alliance@waldorf.compulink.co.uk
    www.allianceforchildhood.org.uk

Parentline Plus
    Offers support, advice and information to
    anyone parenting a child. Runs Parent
    Network courses and freephone helpline.
    Tel: (+44) 030 7204 5500
    Email: centraloffice@parentlineplus.org.uk
    www.parentlineplus.org.uk
    Helpline 080 8800 2222

Children's furniture and play equipment

Community Playthings, Robertsbridge, East
    Sussex; Tel: 01580 880626
    www.communityplaythings.com

Puppetry, songs, and stories

Juniper Tree School of Story and Puppetry Arts
Seasonal collection of poems and stories for
early childhood teachers and parents. (Finger
puppets). Collected by Suzanne Down.
Available from
storyartpublications@juno.com
P.O. Box 17666, Boulder, Colorado 80308
(USA).
Includes:
* *Spring Tales*
* *Autumn Tales*
* *Around the World with Finger Puppet
  Animals*
www.junipertreepuppets.com

Parent-child Mother Goose Program Series
Available from mgoose@web.net
720 Bathurst Street, Suite 402, Toronto,
Ontario M5S 2R4 (Canada)

Kim Billington, **Stories and Songs Together,**
book and video
Available from P.O. Box 4034, Croydon
Hills, Victoria 3136, Australia

Some parenting-relevant Anthroposophical adult learning centres and courses

Rudolf Steiner House, 35 Park Road, London
W1 6XT, UK; tel. 020 7723 4400 Courses
and workshops

Hawkwood College, Painswick Old Road,
Stroud, Glos. GL6 7QW, UK;
info@hawkwoodcollege.co.uk; tel. 01453
759054. Adult education courses and
workshops.

'The First Three Years' early childhood course, for
Parent and Child group leaders, child care
providers and parents at York and London
tel. 01904 612683,
www.steinerparentandchild.co.uk
info@steinerparentandchild.co.uk

Education for a happy childhood, Parent
Development mornings (Bath, UK), Joy de
Berker, tel. 01225 891730

Parenting courses and workshops
Emma Tyer, Stroud, UK rtyer@freeul.com

'A time for childhood' courses and workshops –
Lourdes Callen. www.atimeforchildhood.com;
lcallen@atimeforchildhood.com

Trainings for early childhood carers

Faculty of Education, University of Plymouth,
Douglas Avenue, Exmouth, Devon EX8 2AT,
UK; tel. 01395 255325;
Abi.mccullough@plymouth.ac.uk (Steiner
Education degree and Foundation degree in
Early Years education).

*Part-time early years and kindergarten teacher
training diploma in London*, Woodbine
Cottage, Harescombe, Stroud, Glos GL4 0XD,
UK; lynneoldfield@lineone.net

Emerson College, Forest Row, East Sussex RH18
5JX, UK; info@emerson.org.uk;
www.emerson.org.uk; tel. 01342 822238.
Full and part time courses.

Sophia's Hearth Family Center, an Educational
Resource Center for families and educators
offering parent and professional courses and
seminars – 36 Carpenter Street, Keene, NH
03431 USA info@sophiashearth.net
www.sophiashearth.org

Lifeways North America, Caldwell Early Life Center, Rudolf Steiner College, 9200 Fair Oaks Blvd, CA 95628 USA. Seminars and training for those involved in the care of the young child; info@lifeways-center.org

Part-time early childhood teacher education program, Sunbridge College, 285 Hungry Hollow Road, Spring Valley, New York 10977; www.sunbridge.edu - info@sunbridge.edu

The Caldwell Early Life Center, Rudolf Steiner College, 9200 Fair Oaks Boulevard, Fair Oaks, CA 95628. USA Parenting courses and workshops www.steinercollege.edu

Seminare zur Leitung von Spiel Gruppen, Waldorfbildungswerk. E.V. Mergelteichstrasse 59, 44225 Dortmund, Germany; PSZD-Middelkamp@t-online.de

'The first three years' – courses and Parent and Child groups, Freie Bildungsstätte, Niederursel 51, 60439 Frankfurt, Germany; www.der-hof.de

Pikler Institute, Loczy Lajos u. 3. H-1022 Budapest – Ungarn Tel.: 00(36) 1-326-63-92 Email: pikler@matavnet.hu

Resources for Infant Educarers (RIE), 1550 Murray Circle, Los Angeles, CA 90026; Tel: (+1) 323 663 5330 Email: educarer@rie.org www.rie.org

Parenting magazines and information

Juno – A Natural Approach to Family Life, The Quarry House, Woodshill Lane, Ashurst Wood, West Sussex RH19 3RF, UK; Tel.: 01444 891 460 www.junomagazine.com Email:editor@junomagazine.com

Mothering Magazine – The Natural Family Living Magazine, P.O. Box 1690, Santa Fe, NM 87504, USA (Physical Address: 1611-A Paseo de Peralta, Santa Fe, NM 87501, USA); Tel: 1-800-984-8116, www.mothering.com

The Green Parent – positive parenting advice and information: editor@thegreenparent.co.uk

Practical Parenting, IPC Publishing.

Kindling – Journal for Steiner Waldorf Early Childhood Care and Education UK 3 Church Lane, Balsham, Cambridge; Tel: 01223 890988

Appendix 1 – Fund-raising

Right from the beginning, it is important to start thinking about setting the project on a solid financial footing. However, there are many ways a project can find funds, and there can also be a number of unexpected pitfalls and challenges. There is a very useful book called *Vision in Action: Working with Soul and Spirit in Small Organisations* (by Christopher Schaefer and Tyno Voors), which is a mine of information and advice to pioneer groups. There is a section which playfully addresses the 'childhood diseases of young initiatives'. Here is a summary of the authors' advice about the dangers of 'the silver spoon'.

Receiving a substantial grant or legacy at the beginning may get the group off to a flying start, but may also mask, for a while, the question of whether there is a real demand. There may be a shock when the funding ends or the money is used up. It is healthier for the group to have many small supporters who have an interest in the project – 'warm money' – rather than relying too much on large grants which are 'cold' and 'may not create the mantle of warmth so important for the small infant'. The authors suggest that it is very important for the project to be surrounded by a circle of well-wishers, whether these are grandparents, friends, or organisations. Being professional and appreciative, keeping contacts warm, always talking positively about the group, and offering a very good service will attract the support that will help the venture on its way.

Here is a list of fund-raising ideas from the Mayflower group in North Lincolnshire:

- Apply for grants and awards
- Set up a 'Friends' scheme for the project
- Use the Local Authority community funds
- Set up a 'grandparents' scheme
- Local donations from national companies
- Begging letters
- Donation box
- Participate in regional/national events to raise income, e.g. the Great Northern Run
- Organize your own sponsored event
- Organize seasonal suppers, with quality home cooking, live music/poetry/story-telling
- Organize a 'favours' auction
- Develop a craft group to make things for fairs and other events
- Raffles
- Organize your own calendar of events and repeat annually
- Organize adult/child craft workshops
- Produce own cook/nursery songs/poetry books to sell
- Car boot sales
- Print and sell Christmas cards/calendars
- Develop a puppet show/story-telling yurt/apron/singing/face-painting group or team to perform at children's parties
- Attend fund-raising courses

Finally – give something back! Once a year, raise

money for another local child-centred good cause.

Organizing fund-raising events is a wonderful way for parents and families to get to know each other, and a project is much strengthened over time by these activities.

Fund-raising activities and publicity all require a strong support group of families, and cannot be carried entirely by those souls who end up on the management committee. Every project needs people with drive, initiative, enthusiasm and commitment. In Chapter 11, the essential nature of conscious group work and community building will be discussed further. These projects are carried by 'parent power'.

Appendix 2 – The practical 'nitty-gritty' of running a Parent and Child group in a public space

From the spiritual to the earthly! Working out of a Waldorf perspective also requires that we have our feet firmly on the ground. General health and safety aspects, and all practical procedures involved in being 'public', need to be dealt with efficiently and professionally. Here are some reminders.

The register
This needs to include:

- Name, address, and phone number of each child and parent
- Date of birth
- Name and address of doctor and close friend
- Basic medical details

A record needs to be kept of who attends each session – this is particularly important in the case of an emergency, when you need to leave the building in a hurry.

Fire procedure
You need a procedure that you follow in the case of a fire, and to arrange fire drills twice a term so that everyone knows what to do – you'll need a register for this. Fire doors always need to be kept clear; and the outside of the building, through the fire exit, needs to be hazard free. Where can the buggies be kept? You need a no-smoking policy.

Accident record book and first aid kit
You need to have a First Aid kit and a book where you can keep a record of all accidents – the date and time, the nature of the accident, and how it was dealt with. It is very helpful if one group member is designated the health and safety person and has some training in First Aid. Local councils or the Red Cross usually run such courses.

Checking toys and equipment
This needs to be done regularly, removing broken toys and equipment and making sure everything is clean and in good order in the Parent and Child room, kitchen, and toilets. Again, it is helpful if one person takes responsibility for this aspect of group functioning.

An introductory leaflet
Many groups find it useful to have a printed leaflet, which can be given out to new parents attending the group. The leaflet can, for example, outline the approach to child development demonstrated in the session and the order of activities. It can gently explain what is and isn't expected of children and parents, suggest further reading material, and give a name and phone number for further discussion.

Appendix 3 – Marketing and publicity strategies

How we present ourselves and advertise our project to the wider community becomes increasingly important as the project progresses, and particularly important if you intend to make the leap from Parent and Child group to Kindergarten. The Mayflower group, North Lincolnshire, has been very successful in their publicity and marketing. I asked Vivienne Morpeth, to share with me some of her group's strategies. Here is a summary of her insights and experience.

Basics
- Have a name, house style and logo. Decide a font, colour and weight of paper and stick to it.
- Develop a resource file of photos, quotations, marketing statements, research statistics, press cuttings, local knowledge, national facts, and information from Preschool Learning Alliance, SPPA, local authorities and Steiner Waldorf Schools Fellowship.
- Keep an up to date address list of group members, organisations, interested partnerships etc
- Have a list of where information and material can be put
- Think about product associations – how you and other organisations can mutually support each other.
- Have a basic publicity plan and annual calendar of events planned in advance.
- Think about product associations – how you and other organisations can mutually support each other

Poster
- Use a strong image (your photos could come in useful!)
- Use concise accurate wording
- Provide a contact person
- Keep an up to date list of places which accept your posters

Information leaflet
- Look at examples from other groups
- Use warm friendly language
- Have facts and descriptive details
- Provide a contact person
- Give venue, price and times
- Find a relevant image

Newsletter
- Find outlets where these can be left, free of charge
- Include interesting articles, crafts, recipes, festival ideas
- Give details of up and coming talks, open days, festivals
- Give details of group venue, days and times
- Provide a contact person

A press release
- Find sympathetic media contacts
- Refer to relevant issues in the latest news
- Think about press releases in papers, free papers, town sheets, events listings and local radio
- Use a professional layout :
  * One side of A4
  * Double spacing

* House font and logo
* Four lines summary
* Six lines subtext
* Quotations
* Photo opportunity
* Contact person, role and title
* Telephone, email, date of release

Website and email address
* Consider setting up a website, particularly if planning a Kindergarten
* Have links with other associated websites
* Use email to get information out to individuals, organisations and groups
* From the beginning have a contact person with email and internet access

Events
* Attend local fairs and events with stalls, puppet performances, crafts
* Invite important national speakers, Waldorf or otherwise, to talk about 'hot' topics
* Run workshops on inspiring subjects – e.g. crafts, creative discipline, festivals

* Invite your local councillors, local authority Early Years person, health visitors, local college with child care courses, MP to visit your project.
* Engage in local educational debates with other Early Years providers

Norwich used a well designed leaflet to advertise the group all over the community – in libraries, with health visitors, in local GPs surgeries, the local Authority Early Years Partnership offices, and they put adverts in local papers and newsletters. The leaflet was also put in Local Veggie boxes. Door to door leafleting was done in the local area and distributed with 'holistic' mail outs. In Lancaster, a newsletter printed twice a year and left in shops and other public places generated a steady stream of interest.

Publicity, like fundraising, thrives on group brainstorming sessions involving all the group members, as each locality will have its own uniquely available opportunities.

Appendix 4 – Registering with the UK Steiner Waldorf Schools Fellowship

There is no registration required for Parent and Child groups where parents stay with the children – however, if parents leave their children with you for over two hours in any one day, you must register. In the UK, there is always help available from the Steiner Waldorf Schools Fellowship (SWSF) on these matters, or from the Parent and Child representative of the SWSF, or your SWSF regional representative. A list of these is available from the SWSF Membership Services Co-ordinator or Early Childhood Representative (see below).

Once you have done your research to show that there is a need in your area for a new provision, you can decide what type of registration you need to apply for. Please consult the SWSF regarding Fellowship registration in addition to what is needed by official bodies.

There are two types of registration: as an *Independent School* or as a *Sessional/daycare provider*.

If you need further information, the SWSF have a service which will help you. Please contact:

Kevin Avison, SWSF membership services coordinator Tel/Fax: 01384 393385
E-mail: kavison@yescomputers.co.uk

or

Janni Nicol, SWSF early childhood representative Tel/Fax: 01223 890988
E-Mail: JanniSteinerEY@aol.com

Sessional/childcare registration

If the school does not fall within the definition of an independent school because it caters solely for children under 5, it will be necessary to register the facility with Ofsted (Early Years Directorate, tel: 0845 601 4771).

Apply to your *local* Children's Information Service (CIS) of the Early Years Development and Care Partnership (EYDCP)/Opportunity Links/Childcare planning etc. (it is different in each district) to obtain the **application pack** and **registration guide**; or download it from the website: www.dfee.gov.uk/daycare

You can also get it from your *Local Education Authority* or *Early Years Development and Care Partnership (EYDCP)*. They will put you in touch with either a development worker or childcare advisor who will advise you about financial grants, availability of rooms in the area, policies and curriculum planning, etc.

You will also need insurance, registration with SWSF, charity status, and so on. Much of this information is available in the SWSF/SWEYG *Standards and Guidance*.

The application process can take up to 6 months.

Once you have applied, Ofsted will visit to see if the building is suitable, and will also do a 'fit persons' interview with the provider and manager (or member of the registered committee).

If you are a private provider you will register

as an individual; if you are a voluntary provider, it has to be a committee member and supervisor who register. Once Ofsted has visited (they will check that standards requirements are in place, e.g. policies, planning, safety, etc.), they will give an action plan stating what has to be done and by when. You need to do this via Ofsted as they will pay for the fire inspection, health and safety, and police checks. (Police checks are now being done through Ofsted, who will process them through the Criminal Records Bureau.) They will come again to check that everything has been done, and then you can register.

Ofsted registration helpline tel: 0845 6014771

At the same time, obtain:

1. The *National Standards* for your provision (probably 'Sessional Day Care') from the DfES (Department for Education and Skills), tel. 0845 6022260 (the Standards will tell you what you need to do to run your provision); and
2. *Guidance for National Standards* (again for your type of provision) from – tel. 0700 263 7833 (the guidance will tell you what you need to do to register and to meet the standards).

Alternatively, they can be accessed via: www.ofsted.gov.uk/publications

Independent schools registration

Establishments that cater primarily for children under the age of 5 are required to register as an independent school if they meet the definition of an independent school, i.e. *if they have at least 5 pupils of compulsory school age*. Starting from 1 September 2003, regulations require day care provision for under 8s in independent schools to be separately registered with the Ofsted Early Years Directorate, in line with requirements of Part XA of the Children Act 1989.

There is no need to register with OFSTED EY as a Sessional or Day Care provider if this is the case, unless you are also applying for funded places or out-of-school childcare.

Ring the *DfES Independent Schools Registration Team Helpline*: Tel. 01325 392160, Fax. 01325 392128;
or write to:
Independent Schools Registration Team, DfES, Mowden Hall, Staindrop Road, Darlington DL3 9BG. E-mail:
mailto:registration.enquiries@dfes.gsi.gov.uk

Childcare and out-of-school clubs

Children Act registration and inspection will apply to schools where the primary purpose of the childcare facility is 'looking after' children. As such, educational provision for under 8s, which takes place during the normal school day ('school day' is defined in regulations as a period of up to 6 hours between the hours of 08.00 and 16.00), will not require registration. Likewise, other activities such as supervision of homework after school, choir practice, and drama clubs will not generally require registration. It is envisaged that Ofsted will treat most facilities for under 3s as childcare, which will require registration.

It is always worth checking the latest information from Ofsted, as the registration process may change.

Appendix 5 – Foundation books for study groups and libraries

(* Denotes a book suitable for group study as well as library)

* Baldwin, Rahima (1989) *You Are your Child's First Teacher*, Celestial Arts, Calif.

* Gerber, Magda and Johnson, Alison (1998) *Your Self Confident Baby*, John Wiley, Brighton

* Jenkinson, Sally (2001) *The Genius of Play*, Hawthorn Press, Stroud

* Johnson Fenner, Pamela and Rivers, Karen (eds) (1992) *Waldorf Education: A Family Guide*, Michaelmas Press, Amesbury MA, USA

* Kenison, Katrina (2000), *Mitten Strings for God: Reflections for Mothers in a Hurry*, Warner Books, New York

* Large, Martin (2003) *Set Free Childhood*, Hawthorn Press, Stroud

* Patterson, Barbara J. and Bradley, Pamela (2000) *Beyond the Rainbow Bridge*, Michaelmas Press, Amesbury, Mass.

* Steiner, Rudolf (1996) *Education of the Child*, Anthroposophic Press, Hudson, NY

* Strauss, Michaela (1978) *Understanding Children's Drawings*, Rudolf Steiner Press, London

* Von Heydebrand, Caroline (1988) *Childhood: A Study of the Growing Child*, Rudolf Steiner Press, London

Carey, Diana and Large, Judy (1982) *Festivals, Family and Food*, Hawthorn Press, Stroud

Clouder, Christopher and Rawson, Martyn *Waldorf Education*, Floris Books, Edinburgh,

Druitt, Ann, Fynes-Clinton, Christine and Rowling, Marije (1995) *All Year Round*, Hawthorn Press, Stroud

Druitt, Ann, Fynes-Clinton, Christine and Rowling, Marije (2004) *The Birthday Book*, Hawthorn Press, Stroud

Glöckler, Michaela and Goebel, Wolfgang (1984) *A Guide to Child Health*, Floris Books, Edinburgh

Jaffke, Freya (1996) *Work and Play in Early Childhood*, Floris Books, Edinburgh

König, Karl (1984) *The First Three Years of the Child*, Anthroposophic Press, Hudson, NY (also Floris Books, Edinburgh)

Lievegoed, Bernard (1985) *Phases of Childhood*, Floris Books, Edinburgh, 1985

Marshak, David (1997) *The Common Vision – Parenting and Educating for Wholeness*, Peter Lang, New York

Mellon, Nancy (2000) *Storytelling with Children*, Hawthorn Press, Stroud

Oldfield, Lynne (2001) *Free to Learn*, Hawthorn Press, Stroud

Rawson, Martyn and Rose, Michael (2002) *Ready to Learn*, Hawthorn Press, Stroud

Soesman, Albert (1998) *Our Twelve Senses*, Hawthorn Press, Stroud

Steiner Rudolf (1988) *The Child's Changing Consciousness and Waldorf Education*, Rudolf Steiner Press, London

See also the craft books listed in Chapter 6, 'The Practical Activity'.

Appendix 6 – Working with the Twelve Senses

One way of supporting parents in their parenting path is to work consciously with the twelve senses, which were described in Chapter 2. Rudolf Steiner wrote at length about the importance of the right protection of the senses, particularly in the very early years of a child's life. However, we may ourselves find it hard to relate to and experience our full range of senses, and we therefore may not understand fully the need to protect young children. Exploring experientially how it feels to be a baby and young child, and concentrating on each sense individually for a while, can help us become more conscious of their importance.

An extraordinary sensory installation for adults called 'Red Axis' was created by directors of the 'Haus des Kindes' for an anthroposophical conference called 'The Dignity of the Young Child' held in Dornach, Switzerland, in 2001. The purpose of the project was to introduce a way for adults directly to re-experience the sense world of the small child. The installation comprises 19 sense experiments and experiences which lead adults, through immediate impact, astonishment, and feeling response, back into the sense reality of the young child. The installation has been very successful, and has since been shown in Berlin and other cities.

In the UK, Sasiki Hubberstey has developed workshops for adults as an introduction to the twelve senses, where each sense is explored in depth. Her approach is meditative and experiential: each sense is approached individually, and participants are encouraged to pay attention to how they wish to communicate their own experiences and to find ways of enriching each other's experiences through active listening. *'The Twelve Senses Workshops'* by *Sasiki Hubberstey* – contact sh_yumi@hotmail.com

The senses do not necessarily have to be worked with directly. Encouraging parents to observe their children, and to listen quietly and with love and respect, can allow a profound sense of their child's essential individuality to be experienced as well as their own. In the trusting sharing space which can be created between parents, a new subtle understanding of the body senses of life, movement, warmth, and balance can be experienced. In the creating of a beautiful environment, with food and all activities presented with care and attention, the middle or environmental senses of taste, smell, sight, and warmth are enlivened. This is a very huge and complex subject, and one which needs much exploration and research in its relevance and application to Parent and Child work.

Appendix 7 – 'Inner' and 'outer' qualities and abilities in a Parent and Child group leader

At the Steiner Parent and Child group leaders Conference held in London in 2003, entitled 'Working with Parents', Lourdes Callen addressed some of the 'inner' and 'outer' abilities that can be helpful in Parent and Child group work. The following lists are from notes taken at the conference.

'Outer' abilities

There are certain simple organisational, management, and artistry abilities which ensure that the Parent and Child group environment is welcoming and the session runs well. Many of these aspects of running a group have been mentioned many times already in this book, and include:

- Arranging the setting with care and beauty
- Ensuring the activities, songs, and stories are well presented
- Maintaining careful rhythm and transitions, beginnings, and endings
- Making sure that toys and equipment are clean and in good repair
- Welcoming parents and children in a way which makes each one feel 'seen'

'Inner' abilities for working with adults

In all Waldorf educational work, teachers are offered the opportunity and freedom to work on themselves, and to embark on their own inner journey of self-development and learning; and this is also the case for anyone who wishes to undertake Parent and Child work. It is work which requires many of the skills of a Kindergarten teacher with regard to the needs of the children, and also the skills of a counsellor and group facilitator for working with adults. The main 'inner' abilities that are helpful when working with adults are listed below.

Facilitating skills

- Holding the structure of the group
- Preparing a session but then facing it with openness
- The ability to listen to the 'group being'. What does the group need now?
- Being light and calm
- Trusting the situation
- Inviting parents to be an active part of the group
- Listening with empathy
- Remembering what parents tell you
- Making a connection with the parent and the child
- Respecting differences – everyone's opinion is fine

Inner awareness

- Being calm and centred in one's own being, but being aware of the periphery at the same time
- Having a presence of heart and mind – this can dissolve anxieties in others

- Making arrangements, and sticking to them
- Being aware of our own moods
- Being aware of, and working with, our own temperaments
- Keeping an inner connection to all the adults and children
- Noting and remembering who is not there
- Valuing parenthood
- Standing in one's own principles but listening at the same time
- Being willing to learn from each other
- Working through one's own difficulties with another person

One-to-one Relating
- 'Meeting' the other
- Respect
- Receiving each other with love, tolerance, and empathy
- Attentive listening without judgement
- Trusting in parents on their own journey
- Trusting the children
- Avoiding taking a 'position' – not reacting
- Respecting differences
- Being honest
- Sharing feelings

In addition to the abilities raised by Lourdes at the 'Working with Parents' conference, there is also the need for a grounding of young children's needs within a spiritual perspective. These are the various aspects of the Waldorf approach which have been introduced in this book, and which include:

- An understanding of child development from a spiritual perspective
- The vital importance of play
- Free movement
- Rhythm, reverence, and repetition
- Imitation
- The twelve senses
- Festivals
- Songs, rhymes, puppetry, and story-telling

It is important, finally, to realise that the qualities that are helpful to develop if you are working with Parent and Child groups are those very same qualities that parents today are wishing to find in themselves, to help them in the parenting of their children. These are abilities that we can experiment with as parents in the home as well as in the Parent and Child group session. In the striving and inner work of a leader, the parents find a reflection. It matters not, in the end, whether a Parent and Child group is parent- or facilitator-led. For as long as the individuals involved in a group are aware of the possibilities of creating a supportive learning community, and understand the inner and outer abilities that encourage this to happen, then the right conditions can be fostered.

Many Parent and Child group leaders will 'unconsciously' bring these inner and outer qualities to their work. However, by beginning to name and define them, we help to facilitate both our own learning journeys and those of others.

Appendix 8 – Towards a holistic refoundation for early childhood: The Hawthorn Press 'Early Years' series *by Richard House series editor*

'The traditional Parent and Child group… is often the first and most important place where parents with very young children go to be with others and to share experiences of parenting. This place of meeting… needs to be wholly rooted in an understanding of what is truly healthy for the child and the family. As parents, we need Parent and Child groups that we can trust to show us what is appropriate for our young children and families.'

Dot Male, The Parent & Child Handbook

Introduction: The dismembering of childhood

Hawthorn Press's highly successful 'Early Years' series – to which the present book is the latest addition – is providing much-needed nourishment and inspiration in the face of modern culture's 'managerial' ethos of over-active, prematurely intellectual intrusion into *the very being* of young children. Since the mid-1990s, a formal-schooling ideology has been colonizing England's early years policy-making and practice – with the relentless bureaucratization of early learning environments stemming from, for example, mechanistic developmental assessments, centrally dictated 'Early Learning Goals', and the imposition of a 'curriculum' on to children as young as 3. Although Wales's and Scotland's degree of

political independence has enabled those countries to pursue significantly more progressive early childhood policies than the worst excesses of the English system, these trends are widely observable in the educational systems of the Western world.

In England, for example, we read in the *Times Educational Supplement* of 17th January 2003 that reception teachers are now having to work their way through no less than *3,510 boxes* to tick, as they are forced to assess every child against a staggering *117* criteria. This story broke again, when in the *Daily Telegraph* of the 21st June 2004, we read of teachers having 'to write reports the size of novels' alongside test scores for five-year-olds. David Hart, the general secretary of the National Association of Head Teachers, was quoted as saying that 'I cannot think of another Government intervention which has caused so much anger among teachers of the early years, and it must be addressed urgently'. And Ted Wragg, emeritus professor of education at Exeter University, said the 117 judgments were 'ludicrous' and 'brainlessly vague'. Teachers were being diverted from their work with children by the need to make more than 3,500 assessments every term, he said. A spokesman for the British Department for Education retorted that 'it was important to measure children's progress at an early age'…

All this should be seen in the context of the take-over of responsibility for early-childhood settings by OFSTED (the Office for Standards *in Education*), with a 'surveillance culture' ideology cascading down the education system, right to the earliest of ages. Not without reason did the prominent sociologist, Professor Nikolas Rose, write some years ago that 'Childhood is the most intensively governed sector of personal existence'. As a whole range of factors continues to reinforce the cognitive 'hot-housing' atmosphere pervading modern mainstream education, the Hawthorn Press Early Years series is just one cultural manifestation of a deep and widespread disquiet with the manic politicization of early-years learning which has occurred with breathtaking rapidity – and with virtually no informed public or political debate –over recent years.

While there seems to be an endless stream of narrowly conceived 'positivistic' research on our utilitarian education system's narrow obsession with 'driving up' standards and educational 'targets', there is little if any empirical research being carried out on the medium- and long-term effects on children's overall social and emotional development of the soullessly mechanistic educational 'regimes' and one-sidedly materialistic values and practices to which young children are being unremittingly subjected. This is nothing short of a national scandal, at which future, more enlightened generations will surely look back aghast at our crass immaturity and almost wilful neglect of what really matters in living a healthy life.

In the face of the mounting malaise and anomie experienced by young people in modern culture, the mechanistic, 'modernizing' juggernaut simply ploughs on, apparently quite impervious to the insight that *its own* policies and practices are substantially contributing to this cultural chaos, and are storing up an anti-social disaster whose dimensions and ubiquity can scarcely be dreamt of.

One common effect of these disturbing trends – and this is a recurring theme throughout the series, not least in Dot Male's new book – is what we might call *the dismembering of childhood*. Yet as the books in the Early Years series compellingly demonstrate, there are tried and tested, viable alternatives to the aforementioned developments, grounded in a potent combination of perennial wisdom and cutting-edge research and understanding about child development, care, and learning. Certainly, there is a growing 'counter-cultural' public mood which is clamouring for a humane and demonstrably effective alternative to the deeply unsatisfactory fare currently on offer in 'mainstream society' – which fact no doubt throws much light on just why this series has been so well received since its first book appeared in the year 2000.

The books in this series have an overriding focus which is ***holistic, informed, and practical*** – offering readers state-of-the-art information for those who are involved in early-childhood settings (i.e. from birth to about 6 years), be they familial or professional. The books offer practical, theoretically informed insights into a whole range of early-years-related questions and issues –thereby making a major contribution to the global cultural movement of concerned parents that educationalist Neil Postman was referring to when he wrote: 'There are parents… who are defying the directives of their culture. Such parents are not only helping their children to have a childhood… Those parents… will help to keep alive a human tradition. [Our culture] is halfway toward forgetting that children need childhood. *Those who insist on remembering shall perform a noble service*'. Indeed, Postman's inspiring championing of childhood could hardly provide a more fitting epigraph for the Early Years series.

Childhood under siege

The distorting effects of anxiety on healthy development and learning constitute a theme which recurs throughout the series. As Stephen Spitalny has so emphatically pointed out, under conditions of anxiety, play activity is markedly compromised and distorted. Certainly, the crucial role of free creative play is repeatedly emphasized by a number of Early Years series authors – Evans, Goddard Blyth, Jenkinson, Oldfield, Rawson and Rose, Large: for, as Professor Tina Bruce said to the Anna Freud Centenary Conference in November 1995, 'Play cannot be pinned down and turned into a product of measurable learning. This is because play is a process [which] enables a holistic kind of learning, rather than fragmented learning'; and Dot Male agrees: 'Free, imitative, and imaginative play is vital for healthy child development. Allowing free uninterrupted movement in a safe space encourages self-confident, independent children'.

The young child, then, needs an *unintruded-upon space* in which to play with, elaborate, and work through her deepest wishes, anxieties, and unconscious fantasies; and in turn, the child will thereby gain competence in healthily managing – with her own freely developed will – her curiosities and anxieties about human relationship. Sally Jenkinson's seminal Early Years book, *The Genius of Play*, develops these arguments at much greater length.

Another consistent theme in the Early Years series is the pernicious deforming effects on young children of *premature cognitive-intellectual development* – a theme which Dot Male emphatically carries forward in *The Parent and Child Handbook*. Indeed, the damaging effects of such one-sided learning become all the greater, the younger the child in question: as Dot Male puts it,

'[In the first three years] the physical foundations of the bodily constitution for life are being laid down, and the child's spiritual individuality, albeit unconsciously, is gradually moving into this growing, forming body. During this time the child is very open and impressionable on every level, and learns everything through imitation. Early intellectual learning, over-stimulation, and the unnatural forcing of any skills disturbs this delicate process. The first three years are critical in this respect, as during this time the child is learning to walk, talk, and think with memory.'

There are now convincing *neurological* as well as social rationales which argue against the one-sidedness of over-intellectually 'left-brain', *unbalanced learning*, particularly at young ages. As Professor Patrick Bateson and Paul Martin have written, 'Children who are pushed too hard academically, and who consequently advance temporarily beyond their peers, may ultimately pay a price in terms of lost opportunities for development'. Certainly, at least some Western governments are narrowly preoccupied with a control-obsessed mentality – leading to a child 'hot-housing' ideology which may well be harming a whole generation of children, as even the British Parliament's Education Select Committee has cautioned. Certainly, the inappropriate and highly damaging pressures on young children do seem to be relentless and ever-increasing – at cultural as well as at purely educational levels.

We are already witnessing signs of the harm being done by a one-sidedly materialistic culture in general, and by the current early years educational regime in particular. A study by the National Health Foundation reports record levels of stress-related mental health problems in children. And one press report writes of the frightening scale of medically diagnosed child 'behavioural disorders', with 'tens of thousands of schoolchildren with mild behaviour problems [now] being drugged with Ritalin… simply in order to control them'. It is by no means far-fetched to propose some kind of causal relationship between the burgeoning and comparatively recent epidemic in child 'behavioural disturbances', and recent early years policy 'innovations' which demand a relentless and intrusive surveillance, measurement, assessment, and testing of children's developmental process – not to mention the forced imposition of adult-centric, anxiety-driven cognitive-intellectual learning at ever-earlier ages. It comes as no surprise, then, when we increasingly find press reports under headlines like 'Mental health problems rise in all children', 'Hyper-parents beware: hot-housing "is making children ill"', 'Today's child has no time for unfettered fun', 'It's not fair, say stressed-out children', 'Children's learning suffers if they start school too soon', 'The young are "over-examined and overloaded"', 'Early learning may put boys off school'… Dot Male's comprehensive rationale for balanced early development certainly provides a compelling antidote to these pernicious and misguided cultural trends.

On this view, then, symptoms of so-called 'attention deficit disorder' and the like are surely far better understood as children's understandable response to, and unwitting commentary on, technological culture's ever-escalating manic overstimulation (cf. see Martin Large's book, *Set Free Childhood*) – and not least, its cognitively-biased distortions of early child development. Until our policy-makers develop the insight (and humility) to recognize and then respond to this malaise at a cultural and political level rather than at an individualized medical level, the prevalence of children's 'behavioural difficulties' will inevitably continue to escalate – Ritalin or no Ritalin.

The Nobel Prize-winning physicist Murray Gell-Mannis is quite specific about the harm caused by *unbalanced* educational experience:

an elementary school program narrowly restricted to reading, writing, and arithmetic will educate mainly one hemisphere [of the

brain], leaving half of an individual's high-level potential unschooled. Has our society tended to overemphasize the values of an analytical attitude, or even of logical reasoning? Perhaps in our educational system we lay too little emphasis on natural history.

The very latest scientific brain research by F. Ostrosky-Solis and colleagues at the National Autonomous University in Mexico is corroborating these concerns, with their recent finding that learning to read and write does indeed demand interhemispheric specialization, with preliterate subjects showing patterns of brain activation that are significantly different from those of literate subjects. A clear implication of these findings is that *the forced, 'adult-centric' imposition of early literacy (and numeracy) learning on to the developing brains of young children is something that should only be pursued with extreme caution*: indeed, that at the very least, a strict 'precautionary principle' should be followed in this field, such that the onus of proof is on those who would press early formal learning to demonstrate that it is not harmful to the neurological development of young children, rather than the burden of proof lying with those who argue against the 'too much too soon' educational ideology. In short, there might, at last, be sound scientific-experimental evidence beginning to emerge for the view, long held in Steiner Waldorf educational circles, that *premature intellectual (left-brain) development is acutely harmful to young children's development.*

Re-membering Childhood: The Early Years Series

The principal focus of the Early Years series, then, is the promotion of healthy child development in its physical, emotional, and spiritual dimensions. Each book arises from parents' own pressing questions and concerns about their children, such as: 'Why is creative play important?'; 'How can I tell when my child is ready to start formal schooling?'; 'How can I help sick children?'; 'How can I learn to be a family story-teller?'; 'What is distinctive about Steiner (Waldorf) early childhood education?'; 'How can I most effectively nourish my young child's experience of music in the early years?'; 'What effective "holistic", balanced approaches are available for special needs children?' – and so on. The series is therefore very much driven by the experience of *parents themselves*, rather than being primarily professionally or 'expert'-driven, as is much of the early-years literature.

The distinctive approach represented in these books is strongly, but not exclusively, informed by the flourishing world-wide network of some 1,500 Steiner (Waldorf) Kindergartens, with the 80 years of accumulated wisdom on child development that this global movement has built up – founded on the original indications of the educationalist and philosopher Rudolf Steiner. The series freely draws upon the wisdom and insight of other prominent holistic approaches, including Froebel, Montessori, and other respected holistic early-years specialists – thus embracing the emerging 'company of like-minded friends' working together in their distinct yet complementary ways for healthy child development.

A defining feature of each book is its focus on a specific topic or question for which parents, teachers, or other early years workers commonly require sound information and effective practical input. Books are based on up-to-date research and practice, and are written by an authority in the field in question. Hawthorn Press is working in close consultation with a range of parent educational organisations in developing the series – for example, Parent Network and Winston's Wish, the Steiner (Waldorf) Kindergarten movement, and the British Steiner Schools Fellowship, the Alliance for Childhood, and Human Scale Education. In this way, the issues that the series is covering are emerging organically from the

concerns of parents and educators themselves in today's demanding and complex world.

Each book contains 'Resources' and Further Reading sections so that interested readers can follow up their interest in the field in question. Future books are envisaged on such prescient issues as: child development from a holistic perspective; music in the early years; Special Needs questions; holistic baby care; and creativity and the imagination in early childhood – to name just a few. Titles published to date are already proving to be ideal study-texts for reading, study, and support groups, as well as authoritative sources for holistic perspectives on early-years training courses of all kinds. Many books in the Early Years series promise to become *the* definitive works in their particular fields for many years to come, and have already received very favourable reviews and widespread acclaim from a range of sources right across the globe.

From *Helping Children Overcome Fear...*

This latter, the first book in the Early Years series, by Russell and Jean Evans, emphasizes the crucial importance of expression through free play; and explicitly recognizes the importance of the emotional and spiritual dimensions in early life. A consideration of fear and grief in early childhood is a particularly apt focus for the first book in the series, and for a number of reasons. First, the book highlights the way in which it is crucial that parents and professionals are aware of the *developmentally appropriate* needs of the child – and to relate with the child accordingly. As Professor David Elkind among many others has pointed out, children are not 'mini-adults', and are positively harmed through having to cope with *age-inappropriate demands*. This was also one of the many crucial developmental insights that Rudolf Steiner emphasized, and on which his original pedagogical indications for Steiner (Waldorf) education are based – and it also recurs throughout Sally Goddard Blythe's *The Well Balanced Child*.

Second, as is demonstrated by both psychoanalytic theory and the important work of Daniel Goleman in his celebrated book *Emotional Intelligence*, the feeling life plays a crucial yet often neglected role in the young child's world. As a leading academic in this field, Dr Judy Dunn, has put it,

> Emotions are at the center of children's relationships, well-being, sense of self, and moral sensitivity and are centrally linked to their increasing understanding of the world in which they grow up. Yet we have only recently begun to pay serious attention to the significance of children's emotions.

Fear and anxiety are certainly 'core' emotions which all children must learn to cope with and healthily manage in a balanced and socially enabling way; and Jean Evans' book provides us with an exemplary holistic approach to the child's emotional world in what can often be an exceptionally demanding and alien environment – that of professional medical care.

Third, grief and loss are central to human experience; and the way in which young children are helped to integrate these primary human experiences can set up life-long 'templates' which in turn significantly influence both children's and adults' capacity for 'emotionally competent' and relatively non-neurotic relating in later life. Jean Evans' work again provides us with a wealth of insight into how these challenging emotions can be successfully worked with and integrated.

...via *The Genius of Play; Storytelling with Children; Free to Learn; Ready to Learn; Set Free Childhood; Kindergarten Education; The Well Balanced Child...*

Play and 'story' have traditionally been recognized as absolutely central accompaniments of a healthy well-rounded education – and the Early Years books by Sally Jenkinson (*The Genius*

of Play) and Nancy Mellon (*Storytelling with Children*) offer wonderfully inspiring testimonies to the importance of play and story in healthy child development. Recent research suggests that children who are deprived of stories in early life are statistically far more likely to grow up to possess anti-social criminological tendencies; and there is compelling reason to think that a similar fate might well await children who are deprived of creative, unintruded-upon play in early childhood (the celebrated High-Scope project in the USA certainly presents some suggestive corroborative evidence on this). Parents and educators wanting a comprehensive and heartening rationale for the importance of play and story could certainly do no better than to read, respectively, *The Genius of Play* and *Storytelling with Children*.

Steiner (Waldorf) education is one educational pedagogy which embodies both play and story in a comprehensive holistic framework which is developmentally attuned to the growing child in an explicit and fully theorized way. Lynne Oldfield's book *Free to Learn* represents the most comprehensive outline of Steiner (Waldorf) early-childhood education currently available in the English language, and in the comparatively short time since its publication it has already become *the* seminal text in this field – indispensable reading for all those seeking a sensitive and *sensible* alternative to the assessment-driven hot-housing mentality which currently saturates mainstream early-years learning environments.

The most up-to-date research on learning and the brain is beginning to confirm the insights bequeathed to us by Rudolf Steiner, and upon which Martyn Rawson and Michael Rose substantially draw in their Early Years book *Ready to Learn* (again, Goddard Blythe's book is essential reading in this regard). To take just one example, Steiner's indication to teach 'from the whole to the part' (rather than 'atomistically' from the part to the whole) is amply confirmed by neuro-psychologist Robert Ornstein when he recently wrote that, in education, 'We should emphasize more of a top-down approach – …first teaching the overall framework… We don't need a special right-brain learning program, but simply to put the large picture first in front of the student'. Rawson and Rose draw upon insights such as these to develop a systematic description of the main developmental processes involved in early learning and development, which in turn lay the essential foundation for later, more formal learning – or *school readiness*.

As do most of the books in this series, these authors draw heavily on Steiner's educational insights, implicitly adopting a *Goethean approach* which favours knowledge gained through personal experience, insight, and accumulated wisdom about child development, rather than through so-called 'objective' research and positivistically derived data (cf. Henri Bortoft's book *The Wholeness of Nature: Goethe's Way of Science*, Floris, 1996). It is in this context that holistically inclined, *genuinely balanced* learning, along the lines outlined in Oldfield's *Free to Learn*, Rawson and Rose's *Ready to Learn*, and Goddard Blythe's *The Well Balanced Child*, clearly becomes an absolute necessity for the future well-being of our modern world.

Recent press stories are at last beginning to report accumulating research which is confirming the grave concerns about the harmful effects of televisual culture that the Steiner movement has been warning us about for decades. To take just one example, in *The Times* of the 2nd February 2004, we read a report headlined 'TV "hampering children's speech development"':

Television viewing is affecting the verbal and communications skills of a growing number of pre-school age children, with some confused by simple questions such as 'what would you like to play with?', a charity [I CAN] says.

I CAN's survey of nursery staff found one in five workers saying that children often had difficulty explaining what they were doing, and almost *90 per cent* of nursery workers said that they thought the occurrence of speech, language, and communication difficulties was a growing problem amongst pre-school children, with one in three believing the problem to be growing significantly. The rise in the problem was attributed to a number of factors: the passive use of television was cited as a factor by 82 per cent of respondents; and additional comments predominantly criticised the use of videos and computers.

In 2003, the British Chief Inspector of Schools, David Bell, also said that the verbal and behavioural skills of five-year-olds appeared to be suffering; and the British Education Minister, Charles Clarke, has recently (January 2004) spoken out on the mal-effects of an unremitting diet of TV violence on the anti-social behaviour of young people. There are signs, indeed, that, notwithstanding the manifold vested interests militating against it, the message about the harm done by televisual culture is beginning to reach the highest political offices. In this context, Martin Large's well-received book *Set Free Childhood* explains in great detail the causal mechanisms involved, in the process performing a great service to those seeking a solid, convincing rationale for reducing or even eliminating the influence of the toxic 'screen culture' from their children's young lives.

Large's argument against the screen culture is especially germane to the concerns outlined earlier in this article – not least the burgeoning incidence of behavioural and 'deficit disorders' in young children. Yet what also becomes clear in Large's book is that we should not underestimate the vested material(istic) interests which wish to maintain and extend the status quo: for what we needs must address in all this – and urgently – *is political, institutional, and centralized economic power*. Moreover, as Large makes clear, Information Technology constitutes another highly contested terrain within early-years learning. The British Government's latest early-childhood policy guidance, *Curriculum Guidance for the Foundation Stage*, approvingly advocates – *and makes compulsory* – computer use and a strong ITC presence in all state-funded early years settings. Yet the findings of recent British Department for Education-funded research on the alleged educational benefits of (for example) computer games have been strongly challenged by Dr Aric Sigman, among others – challenges which are taken much further in Large's new book. Such narrowly circumscribed research, preoccupied as it is with cognitive-intellectual capacities at the expense of wholesome, rounded development, is indeed quite incapable of the kind of holistic, well balanced perspective that is absolutely essential in a field concerned with the effects upon the vulnerable child's mind-brain of these relentless technological intrusions. We can only hope that the policy-makers might ultimately fund some telling psycho-sociological research on the possible link between this arid techno-world and the ever-mounting existential malaise, mental ill-health, and criminality manifesting in the lives of young people in Western culture.

Certainly, we should be deeply concerned when we find relatively conventional neuroscientists like Professor Susan Greenfield of Oxford University beginning to suggest that an increasingly ubiquitous Information Technology may entail profound long-term risks, including, as she writes, 'the potential loss of imagination, the inability to maintain a long attention span, the tendency to confuse fact with knowledge, and a homogenisation of an entire generation of minds'. 'These risks', she continues, 'could even actually change the physical workings of the brain'. Little surprise, perhaps, when the average child will now have watched a staggering 15,000 hours of television by the time they leave school. For anyone even remotely concerned about these possible effects, Large's new book is indispensable reading.

At its best, the Kindergarten educational experience serves as at least some kind of antidote to the pernicious forces highlighted in this appendix; and in her recent book *Kindergarten Education*, the inspirational Californian Kindergarten teacher Betty Peck has given us an invaluable insight into her unique Kindergarten, distilling decades of experience of her work with young children. Many in the broad 'holistic' education movement passionately believe that *inspiration* is one of the most important qualities that teachers can bring to their relationships with children; and there is certainly no substitute for the kind of rich life experience and perennial wisdom which permeate Peck's wonderful book.

In *Kindergarten Education* you will find, in abundance, heart, soul, love, tenderness, wisdom, creativity and imagination, aliveness, wholeness, reverence, and wonder. What we find in these pages is a passionate refoundation of what I call the *art of being* with young children, in a way that intuitively understands the subtleties of a child's learning, and the importance of adults' *sensitively attuned* enabling role in it; that respectfully nourishes their unfolding individual developmental paths; and which above all acknowledges and nurtures reverence, wonder, co-operation, and social and emotional intelligence.

In entering Betty Peck's Kindergarten we find a refreshing alternative to the instrumental learning which has recently swamped early-childhood education in the developed world. *Kindergarten Education* beautifully describes just what it is possible to create in the Kindergarten, and we should be deeply grateful to Betty Peck for championing what is rapidly becoming a dying art by creating a book which communicates the very 'soul' of Kindergarten teaching in the midst of this bleak utilitarian age. As Betty Peck herself so aptly writes, 'The teacher is responsible for keeping alive the magic [of learning], in whatever form she can manage'.

The reader who has reached this far in this editorial appendix may well be aware of Sally Goddard Blythe's excellent book *The Well Balanced Child*, so I shall not dwell on it at length here – except to say that this is a book that falls squarely and impressively in the tradition of Rudolf Steiner's educational philosophy. That is to say, it places equal emphasis and value upon both science and perennial wisdom, and it demonstrates a mature understanding of the holistic nature of learning, and the subtle interrelationships entailed in healthy early learning that by far transcends the crassly mechanistic approaches that dominate modern mainstream thinking and practice. As Goddard Blythe puts it:

> Whilst science – the testing of observations and ideas – constitutes an essential part of civilization and progress, intuition is the spark that lights the fire of scientific investigation. In looking at child development, I wanted to marry the processes of science and intuition, to find an explanation as to why certain social traditions and child-rearing practices have been consistently successful, despite a vastly changing world and a diversity of cultural ideals.

The Well Balanced Child is a book that demonstrates all that is best in the emerging 'New Science' that will surely soon replace the tired and increasingly irrelevant world-view of 'modernity' and all its worst features – arid soullessness, technocratic 'control-freakery', over-intellectualization, and an abject inability to see the whole for the parts.

...to *The Parent and Child Handbook*

As parents, we can help guide a new generation who have a love of the earth and simple timeless pleasures that do not pollute; who have experienced tolerance, acceptance, and authentic community... We need to 'wake up', to be conscious of what is appropriate to bring to our young children (and what is not) for their natural unfolding; to protect where necessary; to give freedom where necessary; and in order to do this we need to love and understand our children (and ourselves) from the widest, deepest context that we can manage.

Dot Male, The Parent and Child Handbook

The books published to date in the Early Years series are fully described in an earlier version of this essay in Sally Goddard Blythe's book *The Well Balanced Child* (Hawthorn Press, 2003, pp. 201-6), and the reader is referred to that discussion for further information. The current book, Dot Male's *Parent and Child Handbook*, has a particular prescience because of the policy context in which it is being published. Thus, early in 2004 the British press was reporting how Prime Minister Tony Blair is now committed to substantially increased investment in the early years sector. According to an article in *The Times* newspaper (9 January 2004), 'more childcare and toddler groups were... mentioned by the Prime Minister as crucial to giving children the best start in life'; and 'These services have to be expanded', he is quoted as saying. According to the reporting journalist, 'The Prime Minister said that it was clear from the feedback [he had received] that *education* needed to start not at five, when children begin school, but from birth or even before' (emphasis added). Not least, this is because government research has found that many parents feel abandoned shortly after the birth of their child, when health visitors stop coming.

Now in the context of recent policy developments in British early childhood education, many educationalists will no doubt be visibly wincing at the prospect of the central state's involvement in bringing '*education*' to very young children!... However, when no less than the British Prime Minister himself is quite explicitly referring to the importance of 'toddler groups' (or 'Parent and Child' groups, to use Dot Male's and Steiner Waldorf parlance) in early childhood, then clearly the theme of Dot Male's new book could hardly be more pressingly relevant. Not least, and as Dot Male points out, the relative importance of *reverence, love and warmth*, and an unashamedly *spiritual perspective* increases at ever younger ages. Notwithstanding strong denials from Prime Minister Blair himself that this is the intention, a major and understandable concern with this government-led drive to support toddler groups is that an over-regulating, over-prescriptive and overly mechanistic ideology will be imposed on groups which receive state funding or support, as is observable with the 'curriculum' which the UK government has recently imposed on all state-funded pre-school early years settings in Britain.

In this early years policy context, then, Dot Male's book is an enormously important and timely intervention – and it deserves to have a profound influence upon the trajectory of developments in this field as they unfold in the coming years. Indeed, it should be indispensable reading for all those involved either professionally or voluntarily in this important Parent and Child work.

Love and early learning – or cultivating the 'pedagogy of love'

'Pleasure and delight are the forces that most properly enliven and call forth the organs' physical forms… The joy of children in and with their environment, must therefore be counted among the forces that build and shape the physical organs. They need teachers that look and act with happiness and, *most of all, with honest, unaffected love.* Such a love that streams, as it were, with warmth through the physical environment of the children may be said to *literally 'hatch' the forms of the physical organs.'*

Rudolf Steiner (emphases added)

The unambiguous conclusion to which working with young children surely leads the sensitive practitioner is this: that *non-possessive love and warmth are crucial and perhaps even decisive factors in whether or not young children develop healthily and fully.* One need only look at the burgeoning clinical literature in psychology, child psychotherapy, and infant massage to witness the manifold negative influences that the *absence* of love or nurturing touch can have on child development. It is surely testimony to the mechanistic utilitarianism that is now informing early years policy-making and praxis that it can almost feel *revolutionary* to speak of *love* in this way. It seems to take courage even to dare to mention the crucial developmental role of love in 'professional' discussions of 'scientific' pedagogy; yet, as illustrated in the above epigraph, Rudolf Steiner (and others) have clearly recognized the quite literal way in which love can decisively influence healthy development – physically as well as emotionally and spiritually.

That love is indeed a central factor in successful early learning is also consistent with recent findings of the British Effective Provision of Pre-school Education longitudinal research project, led by Professor Kathy Sylva of Oxford University. In their study of 141 randomly selected pre-school settings, the researchers found that the best settings actually combine care [for which read 'love'] and education – or in other words, that love is a necessary condition of early (and perhaps all?) healthy learning. In addition, a recent welcome book by psychoanalytic therapist Sue Gerhardt – *Why Love Matters* – shows how the young child's earliest relationships actually shape the child's nervous system – yet another example, then, of the way in which modern science is only now beginning to catch up with and confirm the indications laid down by Rudolf Steiner almost a century ago.

Dot Male is all too aware of this in her *Parent and Child Handbook* – as she writes, 'It needs us as parents to 'wake up', and to love and understand ourselves and our children from the widest, deepest context we can manage – and then find the courage to act'. Of course, there is a crucial question in all this about what, precisely, we mean by 'love'; and holistic commentators like Rudolf Steiner and Dot Male would surely avoid any mechanistic, formulaic definition which would inevitably miss perhaps the most crucial aspects of love's intangibilities. In closing this discussion, I would contend that each and every early-years training should have at its heart *the cultivation of love* both internally (that is, growing healthily to love oneself on a personal-developmental path) and externally, in terms of finding the capacity to cultivate and deepen developmentally appropriate, non-possessive, freedom-bestowing love in one's relationships with children. Rudolf Steiner himself emphasized that all true education is an intrinsically healing experience, and non-possessive love is of course an essential aspect of each and every healing educational encounter.

Dot Male's marvellous book illustrates with great clarity, and sometimes moving honesty, the manifold dimensions of what we might call the 'pedagogy of love' in all its complexity, clarity, beauty, and truth. For this reason alone, the book deserves to become seminal, indispensable reading in its field.

The jury is still very much 'out', then, on just how the early years debate is going to play out in future – with profound implications for the kind of settings for early child development that will be culturally 'normal' and widely accepted across modern culture. On the one hand, we see the very recent research evidence from the UK which strongly suggests that, all other things being equal, very young children do best when raised in the home rather than being placed in childcare. Hence, for example, the *Daily Mail* headline of Monday 3rd October 2005 – 'CHILDREN DO BEST IF MOTHER IS THERE: Experts' seven-year study of

hundreds of families fuels debate over childcare' (referring to an Oxford University research project led by Professor Kathy Sylva, Dr Penelope Leach, and Alan Stein). The press report began, 'Young children... looked after by their mothers at home... are more socially and emotionally advanced than youngsters cared for by nannies, childminders or grandparents. Babies and toddlers fared even worse when they were given group nursery care...'. Welcome research such as this is, of course, entirely consistent with the Steiner Waldorf way as set out in this book; but the cultural and political forces reigned against taking any notice of findings such as this are indeed formidable. For example, and moving in entirely the opposite direction, we find the British Government's recent Childcare Bill (8th November 2005), in which a *compulsory* 'curriculum for babies and toddlers' is proposed for all childcare settings. The almost universal hostile public outcry that this Bill and its proposals received gives those in the Steiner and holistic education movements at least some encouragement that a cultural sea-change is beginning to occur in the field of early childhood – and the Hawthorn Press 'Early Years' series has certainly made a significant contribution to any such trend towards sanity in the early years.

Dot Male's seminal book certainly champions an approach to our very youngest children that is holistic, non-formal, informed by warmth, beauty and love, and recognising the spiritual aspect of our youngest children. It deserves to have the widest critical and practical success, and to take its rightful place as a key text in challenging the 'madness of modernity' that has threatened to engulf early-childhood learning in recent years.

Conclusion: Finding a better way

There is now a growing, discernible sense that the tide is beginning to turn against those pernicious cultural forces that have been systematically dismembering childhood – and towards a *re-membering* of a holistic vision of childhood which recognizes the damage that is being wrought by modern culture, and which offers practical and effective alternatives. At the political level, for example, both Wales and Northern Ireland have long since scrapped school League Performance Tables; Wales have recently abolished SATS tests for 7 year-olds; and Welsh Assembly Education Minister Jane Davidson has shown a refreshing open-mindedness in relaxing the over-academic pressures in Welsh early-years education. In 2003 the Secretary of State for Education, Charles Clarke, surprised many by relaxing (albeit in a minor way) some of the worst excesses of the SATS testing regime for 7 year olds; and ministers may even be starting to consider the incontestable benefits deriving from a later start to formal schooling. To the extent that the Hawthorn Early Years series can buttress and reinforce this mounting sea-change in attitudes to childhood, it will have more than served its purpose.

In sum, the key to building a better world surely lies in just how successfully we can facilitate our children's healthy development. Hawthorn Press's Early Years series is making available a rich range of books which will 'help parents defy the directives of modern culture' (Neil Postman), and *find a better way* to raise their children and help them realize their full potential. These books are helping parents and professionals alike to *reinvigorate* the rapidly disappearing art of *understanding children and their developmental needs*, which modern materialist culture has done so much to undermine; and both of these countervailing trends are illuminatingly illustrated in Dot Male's new book.

Above all, the authors in the Hawthorn Early Years series would all agree that education should nourish and facilitate, rather than subvert, children's innate *love of learning*. By way of closing, we invite you, the reader, to support this important series – and in so doing, to join the rapidly growing body of parents and educators who are determined to reinstate 'the pedagogy of love' at the heart of the learning environments we create for this and future generations of children.

Richard House
Norwich, England
November 2005

Holistic perspectives on child learning: Resource bibliography

Note: 'Early Years' Series books are set in bold type.

Alliance for Childhood (2000) *Fool's Gold: A Critical Look at Computers in Childhood*, College Park, Md

Anon (2000) 'Nursery lessons "damage" learning', *Times Educational Supplement*, 28th January, p. 6

Anon (2004) 'Parenting: are you a hyper-parent?', *Sunday Times* (Review), 11thApril

Anon (2004) '117 ways to assess a child – and none of them useful', *Daily Telegraph*, 21st June

Anon (2004) 'Mothering may prevent aggression', BBC News Online, 19 July

Baldwin Dancy, R. (2000) *You Are Your Child's First Teacher*, 2nd edn, Celestial Arts, Berkeley, Calif.

Begley, C. (2003) 'Pupil behaviour at all-time low, says Ofsted', *Independent on Sunday*, 31st August

Bennett, R. (2004) 'Labour promises more money for childcare', *The Times*, 9 January

Brown, T., Foot, M., and Holt, P. (2001) *Let Our Children Learn: Allowing Ownership, Providing Support, Celebrating Achievement*, Education Now Books, Nottingham (from 113 Arundel Drive, Bramcote Hills, Nottingham NG9 3FQ)

Browne, A. (2000) 'Mind-control drug threat for children', *The Observer* newspaper, 27th February, pp.1, 2

Carlton, M. P., and Winsler, A., (1998) 'Fostering intrinsic motivation in early childhood classrooms', *Early Childhood Education Journal*, 25 (3), pp. 159-65

Cassidy,, S. (2003) 'Forget the bedtime story: one in three children under four "has a television"', *The Independent*, 3rd September

Charter, D. (1998) 'Early learning may put boys off school', *The Times* newspaper, 24th March, p. 8

Coles, J. (2000) 'Hyper-parenting: are we pushing our children too hard?' *The Times* newspaper, 'Times 2' Supplement, 13th April, pp. 3-4

Coyle, D. (1999) 'What our children really need is a regime of benign neglect', *The Independent* newspaper (Review), 3rd August, p. 3

DeGrandpre, R. (2000) *Ritalin Nation: Rapid-Fire Culture and the Transformation of Human Consciousness*, W. W. Norton, New York

Donahue Jennings, K. and Abrew, A.J. (2004) 'Self-efficacy in 18-month-old toddlers of depressed and nondepressed mothers', *Journal of Applied Developmental Psychology*, 25 (2), pp. 133-47

Elkind, D. (1981) *The Hurried Child: Growing Up Too Fast Too Soon*, Addison-Wesley, Reading, Mass.

Elkind, D. (1987) *Mis-education: Pre-schoolers at Risk*, A. A. Knopf, New York

Elkind, D. (1990) 'Academic pressures – too much, too soon: the demise of play', in E. Klugman and S. Smilansky (eds), *Children's Play and Learning: Perspectives and Policy Implications*, Teachers College Press, Columbia University, New York, 1990, pp. 3-17

Evans, R. (2000) *Helping Children to Overcome Fear*, Hawthorn Press, Stroud

Farenga, P. (2000) 'The importance of computers in education does not compute', in R. Miller (ed.), *Creating Learning Communities*, Foundation for Educational Renewal/ Solomon Press, Brandon, VT, pp. 192-4

Fisher, A. L. (2000) 'Computer caution', in R. Miller (ed.), *Creating Learning Communities*, Foundation for Educational Renewal/ Solomon Press, Brandon, VT, pp. 195-8

Fisher, R. (2000) 'Developmentally appropriate practice and a national literacy strategy', *British Journal of Educational Studies*, 48 (1), pp. 58-69

Frean, A. (2003) 'Today's child has no time for unfettered fun', *The Times*, 3rd September

Frean, A. (2004a) 'The young are "over-examined and overloaded"', *The Times*, 27th February

Fræn, A. (2004b) 'It's not fair, say stressed-out children', *The Times*, 27 February

Garner, R. (2004) 'Free nursery scheme for two-year-olds', *The Independent*, 13th July

Gerhardt, S. (2004) *Why Love Matters: How Affection Shapes a Baby's Brain*, Brunner-Routledge, London

Goddard Blythe, S. (2004) *The Well Balanced Child*, Hawthorn Press, Stroud

Haller, I. (1991) *How Children Play*, Floris Books, Edinburgh

Halpin, T. (2001a) 'Why four is just too young to start lessons at school', *Daily Mail*, 12th January, p. 45

Harris, S. (2001) 'Hyper-parents beware: hot-housing "is making children ill"', *Daily Mail* newspaper, 22nd February, p. 17

Hartley-Brewer, E. (2001) *Learning to Trust and Trusting to Learn*, Institute for Public Policy Research, London (www.ippr.org.uk)

Healy, J. M. (1990) *Endangered Minds: Why Children Don't Think and What We Can Do about It*, Touchstone/Simon & Schuster, New York

Healy, J. M. (1998) *Failure to Connect: How Computers Affect Our Children's Minds – for Better and Worse*, Simon & Schuster, New York

Hirsh-Pasek, K., and Golinkoff, R.M. (2003) *Einstein Never Used Flash Cards: How Our Children Really Learn – and Why They Need to Play More and Memorize Less*, Rodale

House, R. (2000) 'Psychology and early years

learning: affirming the wisdom of Waldorf', *Steiner Education*, 34 (2), 10-16

House, R. (2001) 'Whatever happened to holism?: *Curriculum Guidance for the Foundation Stage* – a critique', *Education Now: News and Review*, 33, p. 3

House, R. (2002a) 'Loving to learn: protecting a natural impulse in a technocratic world', *Paths of Learning*, 12 (Spring), pp. 32-6

House, R. (2002b) 'The central place of play in early learning and development', *The Mother* magazine, 2 (Summer) 2002, pp. 44-6

House, R. (2002-3) 'Beyond the Medicalisation of "Challenging Behaviour"; or Protecting our children from "Pervasive Labelling Disorder"', *The Mother* magazine, issues 4-7 (in four parts)

House, R. (2004a) 'Putting the heart back into education – before it's too late', *The Mother* magazine, 9 (Spring), 2004, pp. 6-10

House, R. (2004b) 'Television and the growing child: a balanced view?', *New View*, 32 (Summer), 2004, pp. 21-5

House, R. (2004c) 'How to put children and teacher off school' (Letter to the Editor), *Daily Telegraph*, 22nd June, p. 19

House, R. (forthcoming) *The Trouble with Education: Stress, Surveillance and Modernity*, Ur Publications, Toronto

Institute for Public Policy Research (2001) 'Exam mania could scar children's emotional health', press release, 24th August (www.ippr.org.uk)

Jaffke, F. (2000) *Work and Play in Early Childhood*, Floris Books, Edinburgh

Jenkinson, S. (2001) *The Genius of Play*, **Hawthorn Press, Stroud**

Judd, J. (1998) 'Children's learning suffers if they start school too soon', *The Independent* newspaper, 25th January

Kay,, W. K. (2003) 'Book review article: Spirituality and education: two millennia of thought and practice', *International Journal of Children's Spirituality*, 8 (3), pp. 291-5

Large, M. (1992) *Who's Bringing Them Up?*, 2nd edn, Hawthorn Press, Stroud

Large, M. (2003) *Set Free Childhood*, **Hawthorn Press, Stroud**

Laurance, J. (1999) '"Holistic" children can fight allergies', *The Independent* newspaper, 30th April

Leonard, T. (2003) 'The 5-year-olds hooked on telly: it's turning our kids into dunces', *Daily Star* newspaper, 3rd September, p. 6

Lightfoot, L. (2004a) 'Children "start school lessons too soon"', *Daily Telegraph*, 19th May

Lightfoot, L. (2004b) 'Teachers' reports now the length of novels', *Daily Telegraph*, 21st June

McVeigh, T. and Walsh, N. P. (2000) 'Computers kill pupils' creativity', *The Observer* newspaper, 24th September, p. 14

Maude, P. (2001) *Physical Children, Active Teaching: Investigating Physical Literacy*, Open University Press, Buckingham

Medved, M. & Medved, D. (1998) *Saving Childhood: Protecting Our Children from the National Assault on Innocence*, HarperCollins, Zondervan

Mellon, N. (2000) *Storytelling with Children*, **Hawthorn Press, Stroud**

Mills, D. and Mills, C. (1997) 'Britain's Early Years Disaster: Part 1 – The Findings', mimeograph

Moore, R. S. & Moore, D. N. (1975) *Better Late than Early: A New Approach to Your Child's Education*, Reader's Digest Press (Dutton), New York

Oldfield, L. (2001a) *Free to Learn*, **Hawthorn Press, Stroud**

Oldfield, S. (2001b) 'A holistic approach to early years', *Early Years Educator*, 2 (12), pp. 24-6

Ornstein, R. (1997) *The Right Mind: Making Sense of the Hemispheres*, Harcourt Brace, New York

Ostrosky-Solis, F., Garcia, M. A., and Pérez, M. (2004) 'Can learning to read and write change the brain organization? An electrophysiological study', *International Journal of Psychology*, 39 (1), pp. 27-35

Paths of Learning (USA), 12 (Spring), 2002 – special issue of education and spirituality

Patterson, B.J. and Bradley, P. (2000) *Beyond the Rainbow Bridge: Nurturing Our Children from Birth to Seven*, Michaelmas Press, Amesbury, Mass.

Peck, B. (2004) *Kindergarten Education*, Hawthorn Press, Stroud

Pierce, S. (2004) 'Why toys aren't us: it's time to ditch the plastic and encourage imaginative play', *Daily Telegraph*, 7th February

Postman, N. (1994) *The Disappearance of Childhood*, Vintage Books, New York

Prickett, S. (2002) 'Managerial ethics and the corruption of the future', in S. Prickett and P. Erskine-Hill (eds), *Education! Education! Education!: Managerial Ethics and the Law of Unintended Consequences*, Imprint Academic, Thorverton, Britain, pp. 181-204

Professional Association of Teachers (2000) *Tested to Destruction? A Survey of Examination Stress in Teenagers*, PAT, London

Pyke, N. (2003) 'Do tests fail children?', *The Independent* (Education suppl.), 6th November, pp. 4-5

Rawson, M. and Rose, M. (2002) *Ready to Learn*, Hawthorn Press, Stroud

Reynolds, D. (2003) 'Mindful parenting: a group approach to enhancing reflective capacity in parents and infants', *Journal of Child Psychotherapy*, 29 (3), pp. 357-74

Riddell, M. (2002) 'This exams madness', *The Observer* newspaper, 9th June

Salter, J. (1987) *The Incarnating Child*, Hawthorn Press, Stroud

Sanders, B. (1995) *A is for Ox: The Collapse of Literacy and the Rise of Violence in an Electronic Age*, Vintage Books, New York

Schweinhart, L.J. and Weikart, D. P. (1997) *Lasting Differences: The High/Scope Preschool Curriculum Comparison Study through Age 23*, High/Scope Press, Ypsilanti, MI; Monographs of the High/Scope Educational Research Foundation No. 12

Sharp,, C. (1998) 'Age of starting school and the early years curriculum', paper presented at the National Foundation for Educational Research Annual Conference, London, October (available at www.nfer.ac.uk/conferences/early.htm)

Shlain, L. (1998) *The Alphabet and the Goddess: The Conflict between Word and Image*, Viking Penguin, New York

Smithers, R. (2000) 'Exams regime "harms pupils"', *The Guardian* newspaper, 4th August, p. 1

Spitalny, S. (2003) 'Finding joy', *Kindling: Journal for Steiner Waldorf Early Childhood Care and Education*, 4 (Autumn/Winter), pp. 5-7

Steiner, R. (1995) *The Kingdom of Childhood*, Anthroposophic Press, Hudson, New York

Steiner Education, (2000) Special Issue: 'Caring for Childhood: Waldorf and the Early Years Debate', Vol. 34, No. 2

Thompson, J. B. & others (1994) *Natural Childhood: A Practical Guide to the First Seven Years*, Gaia Books, London

Tweed, J. (2000) 'Mental health problems rise in all children', Nursery World, 6th April, pp. 8-9

Index of names

Subject index

Other books from Hawthorn Press

Free to Learn
Introducing Steiner Waldorf early childhood education

LYNNE OLDFIELD

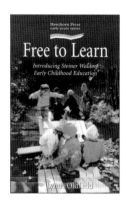

Free to Learn is a comprehensive introduction to Steiner Waldorf kindergartens for parents, educators and early years' students. Lynne Oldfield illustrates the theory and practice of kindergarten education with stories, helpful insights and lively observations.

'Children are allowed freedom to be active within acceptable boundaries; who are in touch with their senses and the environment; who are self-assured but not over-confident; who are developing their readiness to receive a formal education – in short, children who are free to be children and "free to learn".'
Kate Adams, *International Journal of Children's Spirituality*

256pp; 216 x 138mm; 1 903458 06 4; pb

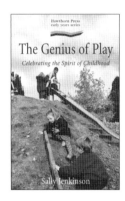

The Genius of Play
Celebrating the spirit of childhood

SALLY JENKINSON

The Genius of Play addresses what play is, why it matters, and how modern life endangers children's play. Sally Jenkinson's amusing, vivid observations will delight parents and teachers wanting to explore the never-ending secrets of children's play.

'Enchanting photos and vignettes of young children at play … do enjoy the account of the 'wedding dress den' and the old Suffolk recipes for 'preserving children.'
Marian Whitehead, *Nursery World*

224pp; 216 x 138mm; 1 903458 04 8; pb

Set Free Childhood
Parents' survival guide to coping with computers and TV

MARTIN LARGE

Children watch TV and use computers for five hours daily on average. The result? Record levels of learning difficulties, obesity, eating disorders, sleep problems, language delay, aggressive behaviour, anxiety – and children on fast forward. However, *Set Free Childhood* shows you how to counter screen culture and create a calmer, more enjoyable family life.

'A comprehensive, practical and readable guide… the skilful interplay between academic research and anecdotal evidence engages the reader.'
Jane Morris-Brown, *Steiner Education*

240pp; 216 x 138mm; 1 903458 43 9; pb

Storytelling with Children

NANCY MELLON

Telling stories awakens wonder and creates special occasions with children, whether it is bedtime, around the fire or on rainy days. Nancy Mellon shows how you can become a confident storyteller.

'Nancy Mellon continues to be an inspiration for storytellers old and new. Her experience, advice and suggestions work wonders. They are potent seeds that give you the creative confidence to find your own style of storytelling.'

Ashley Ramsden, Director of the School
of Storytelling, Emerson College

192pp; 216 x 138mm; 1 903458 08 0; pb

Kindergarten Education

Freeing children's creative potential

BETTY PECK

Educator Betty Peck celebrates the power of Kindergarten to help children find their creativity and imagination – opening the door to a passionate relationship with learning. The result is an essential resource for teachers and parents who want to give their children a meaningful education.

'This is an astonishing, impressive and magnificent work. ... this is must reading for every parent, would-be parent and teacher world-wide.'

Joseph Chilton Pearce, author 'Magical Child'

224pp; 216 x 138mm; 1 903458 33 1; pb

The Well Balanced Child

Movement and early learning

SALLY GODDARD BLYTHE

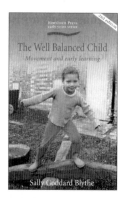

'Learning is not just about reading, writing and maths,' says Sally Goddard Blythe. 'A child's experience of movement will help play a pivotal role in shaping his personality, his feelings and achievements.' Her book makes the case for a 'whole body' approach to learning which integrates the brain, senses, movement, music and play. It examines why movement matters; how music helps brain development; the role of nutrition, the brain and child growth; and offers practical tips for parents and educators to help children with learning and behavioural problems.

'A thought provoking and helpful book which makes a vital contribution to understanding child development. I would strongly recommend it to all parents, teachers and child health-care professionals.'

Ewout Van-Manen, Waldorf Educator, Michael Hall School

304pp; 216 x 138mm; 1 903458 63 3; pb

Ready to Learn

From birth to school readiness

MARTYN RAWSON AND MICHAEL ROSE

Ready to Learn will help you to decide when your child is ready to take the step from kindergarten to school proper. The key is an imaginative grasp of how children aged 0-6 years learn to play, speak, think and relate between birth and six years of age.

'Sound points about the risks of making developmentally inappropriate demands, including the headlong rush to get children to read and write ever earlier.'

Jennie Lindon, *Nursery World*

192pp; 216 x 138mm; 1 903458 15 3; pb

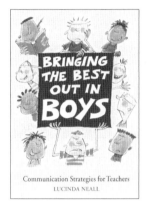

Bringing the Best out in Boys

Communication Strategies for Teachers

LUCINDA NEALL

These time tested communication strategies help get the best out of boys. The tips for tackling difficult behaviour will result in more classroom co-operation and learning – so that everyone benefits.

'Strongly recommended.'   Times Education Supplement

'This book makes a notable contribution because it tries to tackle the issues in a positive way, without reducing opportunities for girls. It emphasises positive steps that teachers can take.'

Ted Wragg, Professor of Education at Exeter University

'A godsend to harassed classroom teachers.'

Mike Shankland, Liverpool Hope University

288pp; 210 x 148mm; 1 903458 29 3; pb

Bringing The Best Out In Boys (video)

Communication Strategies for Teachers

Using real-life classroom scenes and lively interviews, this video and facilitator's guide explores what boys think about school, what motivates and de-motivates them, and suggests communication strategies to engage them in learning. Topics featured include: channelling boys' energy; structure, boundaries and discipline; praise and admiration; and teaching styles. The video can be used by individual teachers, small groups or as the basis for an in-service training session for larger groups. The facilitator's guide gives a summary of the video, highlighting the key points and commenting on the examples of classroom practice.

50 minute PAL (UK) format video with 48pp facilitator's guide
198 x 114mm; 1 903458 41 2

Pull the Other One!

String Games and Stories Book 1

MICHAEL TAYLOR

This well-travelled and entertaining series of tales is accompanied by clear instructions and explanatory diagrams – guaranteed not to tie you in knots and will teach you tricks with which to dazzle your friends!

'A practical and entertaining guide, which pulls together a wealth of ideas from different cultures and revives a forgotten art....

Sheila Munro, parenting author

128pp; 216 x 148mm; drawings; paperback; 1 869 890 49 3

Now You See It...

String Games and Stories Book 2

MICHAEL TAYLOR

String Games are fun, inviting children to exercise skill, imagination and team-work. They give hands and fingers something clever and artistic to do! Following the success of *Pull the Other One!*, here are more of Michael Taylor's favourite string games, ideal for family travel, for creative play and for party tricks.

136pp; 216 x 148mm; paperback; 1 903458 21 8

Ordering books

If you have difficulties ordering Hawthorn Press books from a bookshop, you can order direct from: **Booksource,** 32 Finlas Street, Glasgow G22 5DU
Tel: (08702) 402182 Fax: (0141) 557 0189 E-mail: orders@booksource.net

or you can order online at **www.hawthornpress.com**

For further information or a book catalogue, please contact:

Hawthorn Press, 1 Lansdown Lane, Stroud, Gloucestershire GL5 1BJ
Tel: (01453) 757040 Fax: (01453) 751138 E-mail: info@hawthornpress.com
Website: www.hawthornpress.com

Dear Reader

If you wish to follow up your reading of this book, please tick the boxes below as appropriate, fill in your name and address and return to Hawthorn Press:

☐   Please send me a catalogue of other Hawthorn Press books.

☐   Please send me details of Early Years events and courses.

Questions I have about Early Years are:

Name

Address

Postcode   Tel. no.

Please return to:

Hawthorn Press, 1 Lansdown Lane, Stroud, Gloucestershire. GL5 1BJ, UK
or Fax (01453) 751138